SCIENCE WITHOUT MYTH

SUNY Series in Science, Technology, and Society
Sal Restivo and Jennifer Croissant, editors

SCIENCE WITHOUT MYTH

On Constructions, Reality, and Social Knowledge

Sergio Sismondo

STATE UNIVERSITY OF NEW YORK PRESS

Published by
State University of New York Press, Albany

©1996 State University of New York

All rights reserved

Printed in the United States of America

No part of this book may be used or reproduced in any manner
whatsoever without written permission. No part of this book may be stored
in a retrieval system or transmitted in any form or by any means including
electronic, electrostatic, magnetic tape, mechanical, photocopying,
recording, or otherwise without the prior permission in writing of the publisher.

For information, address State University of New York Press,
State University Plaza, Albany, NY 12246

Production by Dana Foote
Marketing by Bernadette LaManna

Library of Congress Cataloging-in-Publication Data

Sismondo, Sergio.
    Science without myth : on constructions, reality, and social
knowledge / Sergio Sismondo.
        p. cm. — (SUNY series in science, technology, and society)
    Includes bibliographical references and index.
    ISBN 0–7914–2733–1 (hc : acid-free). — ISBN 0–7914–2734–X (pbk.
: acid-free paper)
    1. Science—Social aspects. 2. Science—Political aspects.
3. Science—Philosophy. 4. Constructivism (Philosophy). 5. Realism.
I. Title. II. Series.
Q175.5.S56 1995
306.4'5—dc20   94-40526
                                                                                CIP

10 9 8 7 6 5 4 3 2 1

CONTENTS

Preface and Acknowledgments — ix

1. Introduction — 1
   The primary goal of this book is to combine the best insights of constructivist and realist studies of science, showing that science is a social and political process while maintaining that it produces some knowledge about the material world.

2. The Grounds for Truth in Science:
   An Empiricist/Realist Dialogue — 13
   Some of science's successes are best explained as resulting from knowledge about the material world: we should believe the knowledge implicated in reliable methodology. The argument for this unites entity realism and theory realism. The position that results makes some important concessions—it is thus a deflationary realism: first, although we can make inferences to the approximate truth of some statements about unobservables, the realm for which we can do this is limited and its boundaries are not clear; and second, that truth is not the only, and might not even be the central, goal of science.

3. Epistemology by Other Means — 27
   If knowledge cannot be grounded with absolute certainty then rationalist explanations for the production of knowledge can be partial at best. Epistemology should become more empirical, and pay attention to the social and other processes by which what is taken to be knowledge is produced. Recent work in science and technology studies provides novel accounts of scientific practice and rationality and, through these accounts provides a counterbalance to the ideology of science often accepted by epistemologists. But while "science as social knowledge" conflicts with traditional rationalist ideas on the production of knowledge, looking at the social structures of natural science communities we can see how "science as social knowledge" contributes to an evolutionary picture of science.

4. Exploring Metaphors of "Social Construction" — 49

In science and technology studies the "social construction" metaphor has a number of distinct senses, many of which contribute to valuable insights on science. They provide the resources to see science as a set of institutions and social activities with multiple goals. Only one type of social constructivism, the neo-Kantian claim that representations construct their objects, is inconsistent with a deflationary realism. This neo-Kantianism has only weak arguments supporting it and is the least important of the different senses to the practice of science and technology studies.

5. Neo-Kantian Constructions — 79

In neo-Kantian constructivism, the posited connection from representation to represented violates our best understandings of causes and does not account for failures of knowledge. In addition, this constructivism hides important social processes behind a taken-for-granted production of the represented by the representation. These hidden processes, connecting knowledge and power, representation and represented, are well worth study from the perspectives of the sociologist, the philosopher, or the critic of science. Furthermore, and most obviously, neo-Kantianism presents enormous problems for the feminist critic of science, who cannot be willing to simply accept that science produces its objects, but needs room to argue that specific representations of women are wrong and not merely interested.

6. The *Structure* Thirty Years Later — 89

Thomas Kuhn's *The Structure of Scientific Revolutions* can be interpreted as offering a pluralistic scientific realism that emphasizes the complexity of nature and hence the contingency and partiality of our descriptions of nature. This is one valuable reading of the "construction" metaphor because it shows that theoretical frameworks, methods, and tools "construct" views of the material world by defining the entities and causal structures that disciplines investigate.

7. Creeping Realism:
Bruno Latour's Heterogeneous Constructivism — 113

Bruno Latour's recent work solves some of the problems faced by the earlier strong program in the sociology of science, the problems of providing closure to sociological and anthropological accounts of science, and of providing plausible accounts of technological success. The solution to these involves important changes to science and technology studies. In particular, Latour brings the material world into his descriptions and in so doing provides a novel way of seeing some of the relationships between knowledge and power in science—knowledge and power are parasitic on each other because scientists use the material and social worlds as resources in order to increase their control over both of those worlds.

8. Metaphors and Representation   127

The ubiquity of metaphor in science is sometimes taken to argue against realism. But metaphors can easily be seen as tools for representation and, because of this, are valuable resources for science. Metaphors are constructive in the sense that they shape our knowledge, yet this need not take away from their representing function. Because of their constructiveness, metaphors can be a site for the location of ideology: the directions in which metaphors abstract and the language in which they are couched reflect interests and ideologies.

9. Power and Knowledge   145

There are many relations between power and scientific knowledge. These relations show that paying attention to issues of power in science does not entail a rejection of truth, because power can be productive of knowledge (and vice versa). As a result it turns out that realism does not require any overarching scientific rationality beyond means-end rationality and the norms of different disciplines. The overall philosophical position that has been built up through earlier chapters can be seen to recognize the social character of scientific knowledge, to allow space for contingency and plurality in science and complexity in nature, to recognize the constructed nature of some phenomena and of social objects, and to recognize that science is part of a field of discourses, sharing metaphors and results, and participating in the same ideological struggles as other social enterprises.

Notes	163
Works Cited	175
Index	195

PREFACE AND ACKNOWLEDGMENTS

Science is near the center of Western cultures today, but relatively few people know much about how it works. Those who have spent some time studying how science works are divided by discipline—they are scientists, historians, sociologists, and philosophers—and are deeply divided on important issues. One strain of the study of science is the emerging interdisciplinary field of Science and Technology Studies, or S&TS, which approaches science with a serious but also irreverent perspective. It is serious in its recognition of the importance, and usually value, of science, yet it is irreverent about common myths and perceptions. This book is about the pictures of science developed by S&TS, pictures of science as importantly social in its constitution and importantly shaped by its environments. The book takes a philosopher's view—though one informed by perspectives and debates that range across disciplines—and addresses a particular set of problems around the status of scientific knowledge: *Science without Myth* enters a debate about scientific representation, and in particular the "re" part of *re*presentation. Does scientific knowledge really depict nature? Does it depict characteristics of nature that exist before the knowledge does? How, and in what circumstances? And how does what we might have to say on these issues connect with the picture of science as social knowledge?

Since this book was written, there have been several books highly critical of S&TS. In particular, Paul R. Gross and Norman Levitt's *Higher Superstition: The Academic Left and Its Quarrels with Science* (1994) is highly critical of some of the authors I discuss here, though it takes a somewhat wider view, being a critique of a broad range of humanistic and sociological writing about science. Although I find a number of things to agree with in *Higher Superstition*, I hope that *Science without Myth* will provide something of an antidote to their quick dismissals. One of the things I offer here is careful and sympathetic, though certainly not wholly sympathetic, readings of some literature on the sociopolitics and culture of science. Though Gross and Levitt present some powerful arguments against their opponents' claims, their apparent revulsion at what they read sometimes leads them to miss the point, or at least some of the more valuable points, of recent Science and Technology Studies. Gross and Levitt, and many others, seem to see S&TS as an attack on science and scientists. I hope that readers of this book will not come away with such an impression, however odd some of the things I have to say about science may be.

This book began as a dissertation. As such, the members of my advising committee at Cornell University have contributed to my thinking in and about it. Specifically, thanks go to Peter Taylor for his comments on drafts of many of the chapters and also for providing stimulating insights on science and politics. I will not forget Will Provine's energetic and enthusiastic encouragement. Richard Boyd's hand is implicated in all parts of what follows, even those parts in which I criticize positions he has taken. I have appreciated and benefited from his clear and incisive comments on the various stages of this project, and have enjoyed our discussions.

There are many others whom I thank for reading and commenting on portions: David Bakhurst, Trevor Pinch, Ron Kline, Rachel Laudan, Bill Lynch, Carl Matheson, James Wong, Alison Wylie, and Alex Zieba. Karin Knorr-Cetina's response to a journal article forced me to think harder about a number of things here. Steve Fuller and an anonymous reviewer for SUNY Press read through the entire manuscript and made a number of provocative comments.

Peter Dear, Tom Gieryn, Ian Hacking, Jim Brown, Kavita Philip, and David Takacs were, in different ways, all wonderful teachers who shaped my interests and ideas, probably more than they know. But most of all, on that score I have to thank Laura Murray. Her strategic advice has been invaluable, as have been our ongoing discussions of the grand and small issues of the humanities today.

Chapter 4 is modified from an article that appears in *Social Studies of Science*, 23, 3 (1993): 515–53, and appears by permission of Sage Publications of London. A much earlier version of chapter 6 was published in D. Hull, M. Forbes, and K. Okruhlik (eds.), *PSA 1992*; that chapter appears by permission of the Philosophy of Science Association. The long quotes from Thomas Kuhn in chapter 6 appear by permission of The University of Chicago Press; the long quote from Stefan Hirschauer in chapter 4 appears by permission of Sage Publications of London; and the quotes from Paul Feyerabend in chapter 6 appear by permission of the Journal of Philosophy. Stephan Fuchs's chart of cognitive styles, reproduced in chapter 3, appears by permission of the State University of New York Press. My work as a graduate student was supported in part by a grant from the Social Sciences and Humanities Research Council of Canada, for which I am grateful. A William Webster Postdoctoral Fellowship in the Humanities at Queen's University allowed me to transform the dissertation into a very different and much better book.

It is customary to give credit to others for the merits in one's work and to take the blame upon oneself for its faults. But it is unreasonable not to distribute at least some blame among my many teachers for a few of the faults of this book. Since they all know that knowledge is a social product, I am sure that they will not mind.

One

INTRODUCTION

A GROWING NUMBER OF HISTORIANS, sociologists, and philosophers of science start their work from a recognition that science is in important ways a social and political activity. It is social in that scientists are always members of communities, trained into those communities and necessarily working within them. Communities, among other things, set standards for inquiry and evaluate knowledge claims. The politics comes in at many levels: science is an arena for rhetoric and alliances, ideology and values of many different types are important components of ongoing research, and scientists are engaged in struggles to gain resources and to promote their views. Importantly, scientists have investments in skills, prestige, knowledge, and specific theories and practices. And conflicts in a wider society may be mirrored by and connected to conflicts within science; splits along gender, race, class, and national lines occur both within science and in the relations between scientists and nonscientists. In short, scientific knowledge is always connected to power.

This book is a philosophical discussion of recent social and political studies of science. It is thus a discussion of the *social construction* of scientific knowledge, of that knowledge as a product of communities and societies, and marked by the circumstances of its production. It shows that there are a number of ways and a number of senses in which scientific knowledges are social constructions; this book is therefore an essay on mediation, on the mediatory roles of scientists between nature and knowledge.

Social constructivism about science and technology is often seen not as a thesis about mediation but as the thesis that scientists and engineers construct the world with their ideas or representations: what they study is not independent of them. I argue that as a universal metaphysical thesis *that* constructivist thesis is untenable, though it is right about some types of cases. It is also not particularly valuable or representative within the constructivist program of science and technology studies. Almost never does actual work called "constructivist," or discussion of constructive processes in science, rest on the thesis that representations literally and simply construct reality; that is rarely at issue in today's science and technology studies. What *is* at issue is more complicated: the flexibility of scientific data, the indeterminacy of debates, the methods that are used to end or avoid debates and create knowledge, science as a set of practices, and so forth.

In addition to the obvious myths they dispute, social constructivist studies are often taken as indicating that scientific theories and beliefs cannot represent reality, that scientific *realism* is wrong. The claim is that realism cannot be sustained because the epistemological picture on which it rests is flawed; that is, talk of truth in the sciences is taken to be attached to a questionable picture of science's methods and rationalities. One of my goals here is to argue that, while we should reject most versions of the realist position we should not reject its commonsense core: there are grounds for believing that some scientific knowledge represents a pre-existing material world. What is right about realism can be disconnected from realists' idealized views of science, and the issue of truth can be disconnected from the discredited mythology. Thus I will be arguing for realism as well as for constructivism. The book shows how scientists can often produce accurate knowledge of nature, yet it insists that that knowledge is a human and social product.

My overarching aim, then, is to reconcile the possibility of scientific representation with an understanding of science as a social and political institution. Such an understanding does not just mean being able to point to this or that piece of science as poor, infected by ideology, and so on: traditional pictures of science have enabled us to do this handily, showing ways in which some particular piece of science has diverged from the truth. We have learned from work in science and technology studies (S&TS) and feminist critiques that good science, science as usual, has important political components. This is what appears to cause epistemological problems for realism.

A small aside on terminology is needed: I use the terms *science and technology studies* or *S&TS* to refer to the emerging interdisciplinary field studying science and technology as institutions, or as social enterprises—thus I treat it as a singular term. Because it is an *emerging* field, its boundaries are not entirely clear, which makes for some ambiguity in the term. In addition, although I keep the "and technology" part of the label, my focus in this book is almost exclusively on science.

The difference between finding ideological inputs in this or that piece of science and finding politics in all of science is part of, for example, the difference between feminist empiricism and feminist standpoint epistemologies. A central premise in feminist empiricism is that scientific methodology, when properly applied, is sufficient to correct for gender biases. But feminist standpoint theorists, impressed by the wealth of examples of gender bias in science, say that scientific methodology is clearly *not* in general capable of producing nonsexist science and that inputs from feminist thinking—"thinking from women's lives," in Sandra Harding's (1991) phrase—will produce preferable science. So science as usual is seen as routinely incorporating sexist assumptions prevalent in our society. Thus this book can be seen to respond to the problem Helen Longino and Evelynn Hammonds pose when they say that "above all, we have yet to demonstrate how the scientific method can provide successful representations of the physical world while at the same time inscribing social structures of domination and control in its institutional conceptual, and methodological core" (Longino and Hammonds 1990, 181). The flip side of that task is to understand the constructed nature of scientific knowledge.

A strong constructivist theme—the claim that representations routinely shape the material world—appears over and over again in S&TS (e.g., Haraway 1989; Latour and Woolgar 1986; Collins 1992; Foucault 1980). For the political critic of science—for example for the feminist historian, sociologist, or philosopher of science—one problem with the strongest versions of constructivism, and antirealism in general, is obvious. While a thoroughgoing skepticism about scientific knowledge can potentially provide tools for delegitimating all of science, it does not allow for certain specific, more local, criticisms; it does not allow, or at least makes difficult, the task of showing that a particular piece of scientific knowledge is poor. But this is an important part of—in fact a strong motivation for—feminist science and technology studies. Feminist critiques of science are often aimed at showing that specific accounts of women, their psychologies, their sexualities, and so forth, are simply wrong as well as ideologically motivated. *Truth* and *falsity*, and hence the qualities of the material and social world, are valuable resources for feminism. Attempts to undermine truth cut against falsity, removing a key foundation of feminist critiques of science and, more generally, political critiques of science. This provides another motivation for the investigation of social constructivism and realism with respect to these critiques, a motivation present in the background throughout the book.

MULTIPLE MEANINGS AND INSIGHTS: AN EXAMPLE

Ruth Bleier's short article "Lab Coat: Robe of Innocence or Klansman's Sheet" (Bleier 1986a) is one of many programmatic articles for feminist S&TS. It lists some accomplishments—the demonstration of sexism in all parts of science, the demonstration that science is a part of culture, one set of social practices among others—and presents some goals—to force scientists to be reflective about the values that influence their work and to articulate a feminist epistemology that avoids some flaws of traditional science. Feminist work on the natural and social sciences has far to go to achieve these goals, Bleier says, because it has not begun to make much of a dent on the sexism and sexist ideology found in so much of scientific discourse.

To show us some sexism in high places she quotes Nobel Prize winner James Watson complaining, in 1985, about U.S. Government science policy: "The person in charge of biology is either a woman or unimportant. They had to put a woman some place. They only had three or four opportunities, so they got someone in here. It's lunacy" (Watson, quoted in Bleier 1986a, 55–56). To show us how sexist ideology makes its way into some everyday good science, she introduces us to one of her areas of expertise, brain lateralization research, and summarily dismantles an article purporting to link brain lateralization with abilities that supposedly differ with sex.

Bleier's brain lateralization target is a study by Norman Geschwind, the results of which were published in the *Proceedings of the National Academy of Sciences* and reported in the journal *Science*. She argues that the sources drawn upon by Geschwind were used selectively, that he put forward implausible hypotheses on brain development, that he assumed without evidence that there is "greater spatial orientation" in male rats than in female rats, and so on. In short, Geschwind's argument fails on a number of counts, and his claim to be able to link sex and certain skills is unjustified.

Brain lateralization research, part of intelligence research generally, is a clear site of controversy, a site where feminists and nonfeminists—not to mention racists and antiracists, conservatives and radicals—might argue about the naturalness of current social stratification or apparent stratification. The cultural meaning of the results were easily picked up:

> In news reports of his work in *Science*, Geschwind suggested that testosterone effects on the fetal brain can produce "superior right hemisphere talents, such as artistic, musical, or mathematical talents." The *Science* news article was titled "Math Genius May Have Hormonal Basis." (Bleier, 61)

But the translation from lateralization to 'superior talents' still has to be made in order for the cultural meanings of such a study to become understood. That translation is made, Bleier argues, through the subtle substitution of the word *specialized* for *lateralized*. *Specialized*, in turn, can easily be translated into *superiority*. Feminist S&TS has to pay attention not only to discrimination, overt sexism, and to the ideological basis of scientific claims but also to the language in which claims are made. Feminist critics must become literary-textual critics. They have to correct some blindnesses of scientists, who do not acknowledge the "multiplicity of meanings of their texts" and "do not recognize or acknowledge the degree to which their scientific writing itself participates in *producing* the reality they wish to present" (61).

Like the scientific texts about which Bleier is talking, her own has multiple meanings. In particular, this last claim that scientific writing produces reality can be interpreted along different lines. In important ways the claim sits alone in the text, unsupported by and relatively unconnected to anything else in the article, which increases its ambiguity. The "reality they [scientists] wish to present" might be brain lateralization, or the biological justification for stratification of society along gender lines, or it might be gender differences themselves. The distinctions are important. If Bleier means that scientists produce lateralization, her text is part of a constructivism that assumes that the characteristics of the natural world are invented, rather than discovered, by science; the characteristics of brains do not have definition until scientists describe them. If Bleier means that science produces justifications, she is pointing to the connections between science and social issues and the weight of scientists' words in the political arena; the *Science* article implies that many skills are linked to sex and, therefore, that a sex-stratified society is a natural one. If she means that science produces gender differences, then Bleier is probably pointing to the effects of oppression, that presuppositions of inferiority of skills (in music, art, and mathematics) can lead to real inferiority; gender is the result of training, and science contributes to decisions about that training.

I do not want to defend any one of these options over the others with respect to this particular text. All three, and others of the "multiplicity of meanings" of such a phrase, are themes that run through feminist criticism of the sciences, and S&TS more generally. All three are interesting and worth exploring; all three produce insights on science as a social process.

VARIETIES OF CONSTRUCTIVISM AND REALISM

For the purposes of sketching the disagreement between realists and constructivists, we can imagine scientific knowledge as a map, corresponding in its contours to features of the material world. Of course relatively few realists and constructivists believe that much knowledge is like maps, and they should not believe that maps are much like my caricatures below: language, even cartographic language, doesn't have such neat correspondences with the world.

Realists tend to emphasize the impact of the material world on the resulting representation, and minimize the effects of human agency; for realists, scientists and their work are essentially transparent. While mapping may not be easy, once one develops the right tools the presence of the explorers (experimenters) and cartographers (theoreticians) is essentially irrelevant to the resulting picture.

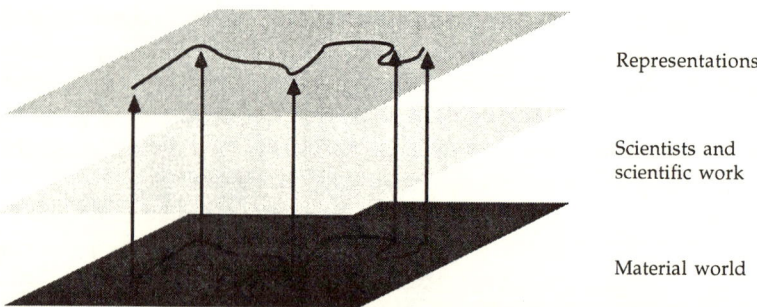

Figure 1.1 Realist mapping

Constructivists, on the other hand, emphasize the middle plane—the scientists and their work—and minimize the importance of the material world; for them the material world is essentially featureless, at least before there is some consensus on those features. Constructivists look to empirical studies of scientific practice, and draw our attention to efforts to produce stability and agreement.

There is a very different position, which has some affinities to constructivism but which I will put in a separate camp. "Empiricism" emphasizes the central plane, but not to the point of saying that theories or representations affect the material world. Instead, the material world is simply an unknown, though one which affects scientists' depictions of it. Empiricists see theories as systematically accounting for data, telling a good story but not one about the real makeup of the world. Empiricists take seriously the idea that science is not mapmaking.

Of course these pictures are too simple because, as with most philosophical doctrines, there is no real consensus on what "scientific realism,"

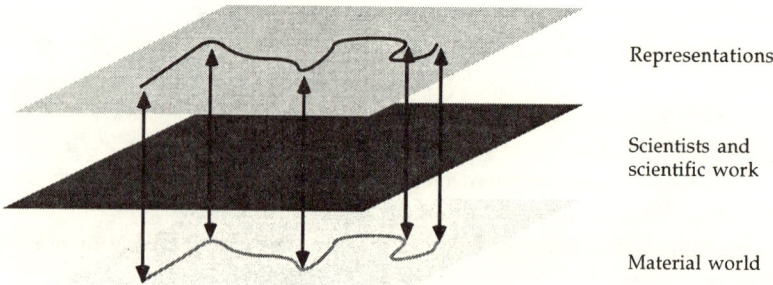

Figure 1.2 Constructivist mapping

Introduction

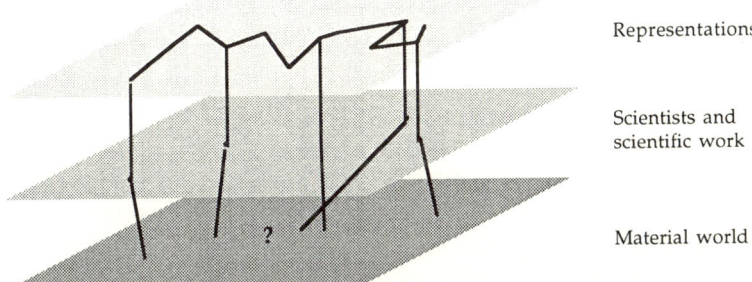

Figure 1.3 Empiricist science

"social constructivism," and "empiricism" mean and how each should be defended. One result of these multiple meanings is miscommunication in the discussions that take place—people routinely attack straw positions without being able to see how their targets differ from real positions taken. Later chapters sort out some of the multiple meanings.

My goal with respect to realism is to create and justify a position compatible with insights from science and technology studies. To do this I will be taking realism in its most deflationary form, a minimal and piecemeal realism. My minimal realism claims that the entities experimenters appear to fruitfully manipulate usually exist, and that researchers have knowledge about some of the properties of these entities.[1] It also claims that obtaining true theories is one of scientists' aims, but not that this need be an overriding aim.[2] The "piecemeal" part of my realism comes from the fact that I argue that cases can be made for the approximate truth of certain specific scientific statements about unobservables; that is, there is good justification for being realists about those theories, though not all theories. Such a position, in its refusal to adopt a picture of science as a unitary activity, makes no commitment about science's general aims or results.[3]

Any realism must also maintain that the objects scientists study and know about usually exist independently of those scientists. That is, features of the material world are independent of human inquiry and the processes involved in that inquiry. This "mind-independence" tenet rules out the constructivist claim that the characteristics science attributes to the world are more accurately described as parts of conceptual schemes. I will not argue for the mind-independence tenet exactly as it stands, but will instead try to elaborate on it so that it is right, taking account of insights from the different forms of constructivism. I will limit the independence of objects of knowledge by spelling out some plausible forms of constructedness.

Realists, good rhetoricians that they are, tend to slide from something like the deflationary position to much stronger ones (Fuller 1988). For that reason, realism is sometimes thought to entail the strong metaphysical position that "the world consists of some fixed totality of mind-independent objects. There is exactly one true and complete description of 'the way the world is'" (Putnam 1981, 49). Although it is a tendency toward which realists move, few philosophers would *assent* to one-true-theory realism; it is almost always a characterization of realism provided by its opponents rather than its defenders.

Similarly, realism is sometimes thought to entail the position that I will call "rationalism," which claims that to understand science is to understand a rational method used by individual scientists. Rationalists see a unitary method at the core of scientific work, and that method is exemplified in scientists' decisions about the collection of data and the arguments that they make on the basis of that data. From the rationalist position, the study of the core of science is the domain of logic and traditional epistemology, and any type of social analysis is irrelevant. Although few realists would endorse this position, it is nonetheless a significant part of work in the philosophy of science today.[4]

The minimal and deflationary realism above is what I will mean when I use the term in a general way, when I claim that something is compatible or incompatible with realism. The deflationist stance captures what I see as right in scientific realism. I do not want to include any version of either the "one-true-theory" thesis or the rationalist thesis as part of a deflationary realism; those positions, or attitudes, are the part of the baggage of realism I most want to jettison.

My goals with respect to constructivism are more complicated. For most readers the idea that scientists in some sense make or remake the world as they go along is immediately implausible. By articulating a number of separate constructivist claims, I will try to make some versions of the position more plausible at the same time that I make others even less so. For example, I use "neo-Kantian" as a label for the family of positions asserting that there is some special causal or semantic connection from what scientists say (or do) to the structure of the material world. Neo-Kantian constructivists assert that scientific consensus has some direct material import, that representations create their own objects.

In contrast, "heterogeneous" contructivism pays particular attention to the ways in which scientists attempt to construct stable structures and networks of power (Taylor 1995a, 1995b; Latour 1987). It attempts to draw together into one account the variety of resources available to scientists and shows how these are used. And the position can be made more social: theories and other scientific products may be *socially* constructed in the sense that they are the products of many people interacting, possibly with different motivations and different background beliefs. They are genuinely social products, rather than the direct consequence of people's interactions with the material world.

There are many other constructivist positions, but I will add only one more to the ring for the moment: something may be socially constructed in the sense that its reality depends on social interactions. When a large number of people act as though something is the case, they may be making it the case (Berger and Luckmann 1966; Barnes 1988; Harré 1986). Self-validating statements and social norms are often examples of this type of interaction—a presumption by a sufficient number of people that it is improper for middle- and upper-class women to work is all that is needed for it to *be* improper for these women to work. This is at least a large part of the constructivism of constructivism/essentialism debates about the causes of such things as sexual orientation and gender and racial characteristics.

In this book I argue against strong versions of neo-Kantian constructivism. Other varieties represent important insights on science and culture that need to be *more* fully recognized in science and technology studies. Like the realism I argue for, the constructivisms I argue for are deflationary ones, not the overarching neo-Kantian metaphysical position; that latter position tends to obscure the more mundane, though often more interesting, constructivisms that concretely display effects of the social world on scientific knowledge.

STRATEGIES

There has been relatively little realist/constructivist discussion; this is true even though both realism and constructivism are dominant in different parts of the science and technology studies community. There has been contact, of course—some scholars on both sides have taken the other side seriously enough to argue about it (e.g., Brown 1989; Giere 1988; Bloor 1991) and even to get tired of arguing (Shapin 1982). But the contact has not matured into a discussion that affects both sides the way that empiricism and realism have influenced each other.

There are a number of reasons why realist/constructivist debates have not been as common or close as realist/empiricist ones. One of these has to do with the history of Anglo-American philosophy of science, a history that shows roughly the middle third of this century dominated by logical positivist conceptions of science, which were for the most part in the empiricist camp.[5] Although logical positivism as a force within philosophy of science is pretty much dead, current work occurs in the context of a strong tradition of empiricist arguments and presuppositions. Even after the death of positivism, within philosophy empiricism remains to some extent the dragon to be slain.

A second reason for the lack of realist/constructivist debate lies in the fact that each side usually views the other position as obviously untenable. Philosophers of science, even antirealist philosophers of science (e.g., Laudan 1991), often dismiss the philosophical arguments for strong forms of constructivism as badly flawed. On their part, constructivist historians and sociologists often believe that realism is necessarily attached to a too-rational, progressive, and monistic picture of science, a picture that is implausible given recent empirical studies. Related to this is a divide in style: because constructivists are often working from historical and sociological studies, their and philosophical realists' arguments do not often meet each other head on. The constructivist historian or sociologist and the realist philosopher disagree as to whether constructivism or realism provides the better interpretative framework, but the considerations to be interpreted are different: the nature of language and of causality on the one hand and scientific practice on the other.

This book attempts to bridge some of these divides. With the realist philosopher I maintain that philosophical considerations weigh against neo-Kantian constructivism. And with the constructivist historian or sociologist I maintain that the practice of science does not cohere with the rationalist picture. But I don't want to leave matters there, for that would be merely to repeat the existing sides in the nondiscussion. Other strategies make up the bulk of the book, and together they form what I think of as a gently therapeutic approach. I reconcile realism and constructivism by showing that realism need not be attached to an overly rationalist picture of science or to the idea that there can be unmediated knowledge of nature. At the same time I remove, piece by piece, the reasons for adopting the neo-Kantian position, arguing that that position does little or no intellectual work and, thus, is not worth its price. My argument has the following components:

1. There is a strong case to be made for the premise that science sometimes represents pieces of the material world. The best explanation of scientists' successes in providing empirically adequate accounts of phenomena is that some of their assumptions are approximately right. Yet, while this argument shows that some of scientists' work adequately represents nature, it does not show that scientists are always so successful or even that representation is an overarching goal.

2. S&TS introduces a number of different senses in which scientific knowledge is constructed, and we should take these senses on their own terms. In particular, historical and sociological studies considered constructivist by their authors do not typically employ any assumptions that are constructivist in strong, neo-Kantian senses. This removes the ground for saying

either that S&TS depends on neo-Kantian social constructivism for its foundations or that the successes of S&TS in providing explanations or accounts of scientific activity indirectly support its supposed neo-Kantian foundations. Rather than showing the impossibility of representation and truth in the sciences, S&TS is engaged in the empirical study of scientists' use of available tools and resources to achieve their goals, goals which include accurate representation.

3. There are strong philosophical arguments against neo-Kantian constructivism. Possibly more importantly for the sociologist and political critic, there are also some methodological considerations against this neo-Kantianism. I argue that nonrealist forms of constructivism don't cohere well with our notions of causation, since they seem forced to posit nonmaterial causal links from representations to that which they represent. These constructivisms also don't cohere with our understanding of the distinction between epistemology and ontology, since they deny that the order of being is distinct from the order of knowing. In positing a nonmaterial link from representation to represented, neo-Kantian constructivisms hide *material* links that I argue can often be found. And finally, as I have already mentioned, constructivisms and other antirealisms disarm the strongest arguments and rhetoric of the political critic by denying the validity of the discourse of truth.

4. Some paradigmatic S&TS texts—Thomas Kuhn's *The Structure of Scientific Revolutions* (1970a) and Bruno Latour's *Science in Action* (1987)— are read for their insights on the effects of scientific work. My readings make these texts arguments for distinctive and innovative positions within a framework of deflationary realism, positions that challenge versions of mind independence—thus showing senses in which scientists *do* construct worlds—and rationalist assumptions.

5. Yet the ways in which scientific knowledge is dependent on actions and the social world are relatively mundane. For example, the observation that metaphors are ubiquitous in science shows a form of social shaping of knowledge, but it does not speak against realism, given the representative power of metaphors. And the insight that scientific knowledge is social knowledge—a community product—can contribute to an evolutionary picture of science, whereby the creation of knowledge is possible through variation and selection.

6. Collecting some of the other strategies together, it is possible to articulate a version of scientific realism that incorporates and celebrates (rather than is merely consistent with) important constructivist insights; conversely, it is possible to articulate a version of constructivism that is fully consistent with scientific realism.

There are important affinities between the realism/constructivism discussion in S&TS and the modernism/postmodernism discussion in the other humanities and social sciences. When real positions are examined, as opposed to the caricatures so often trotted out, both are debates about the right ways in which to respond to the apparent failure of foundationalist positions—attempts to ground knowledge absolutely. Postmodernism and sophisticated modernist positions agree in their rejection of foundationalism. What they disagree about is what we can learn from foundationalism's failure; they disagree about the possibility of knowledge, given this failure. This situation is mirrored in the debates between scientific realists and their constructivist counterparts; they agree that science is not rational in a foundational way but disagree about the resultant status of knowledge. This book, especially in its attempt to find a via media, is thus an attempt to contribute to the ongoing discussion on the status of modernity.

Two

THE GROUNDS FOR TRUTH IN SCIENCE: AN EMPIRICIST/REALIST DIALOGUE

My main goal for this chapter is to set aside the realism/empiricism debate, by arguing that realism is right at least some of the time; empiricism is thus not a viable global philosophical position on science. This is an important conclusion for the larger argument of the book because some versions of constructivism are versions of empiricism. In addition, my argument here removes one possible motivation for adopting a neo-Kantian constructivist position by showing that there are grounds for accepting that some of our beliefs about the world are approximately true, in a traditional sense of "true"—true beliefs represent an antecedently existing world. If there were no such grounds, if the realist framework were not viable, then it would seem that the world of beliefs is relatively autonomous and that "representations" are relatively independent of the properties of the material world.

My discussion is a development of the "abductive" argument for realism, or the argument for truth as the best explanation of success. Hilary Putnam's (1975) formulation of this is well known and an important part of these debates. The more sophisticated version that I build on later in this chapter is mostly due to the work of Richard Boyd (e.g., 1985). The argument of this chapter, which serves as a foundation for later discussions, is the most technical part of the book.

The central empiricist claim is that there is no warrant to believe that science ever arrives at the truth, or the approximate truth, about unobservables. Statements "about" electrons, viruses, or evolutionary pressures are thought of as accounting devices, unifying and organizing data. The abductive argument for realism is an attempt to show that it is difficult or impossible to understand the success of scientific theories without believing that what they say is true. For example, if an epidemiological theory can be used to correctly predict patterns of disease in a population, how can the mechanisms it postulates, say the transfer of bacteria through certain media or along certain vectors, be merely fictions? If they were fictions, would not the predictions quickly break down, failing as soon as the situation became the least bit complicated? Truth is thus the best explanation for the success of the theory, and successful theories are likely to be true ones. (The realist of this argument as I am presenting it is a realist about theories, taking the position that some scientific theories, including ones that invoke unobservable entities, are literally true of the world. As I refine it, a different version of realism will become justified, less committed to the truth, or even approximate truth, of theories.)

That argument does not get us very far. I will mention two of the ways in which it fails. First, for every set of predictions about observables there are an infinite number of different theories that can account for those predictions. The one held to be true is thus one of an infinite set of empirically equivalent theories. Even if it *is* successful, there are so many other theories that would be equally successful that thinking the favorite one to be true is simply wishful thinking. Second, the argument pins too much on success. That a theory is a good predictive device shouldn't be surprising, since it probably was, after all, designed that way. In the epidemiological example above, the theory would be used for exactly what it was intended, predicting the courses of a disease. Since being able to do that effectively was almost certainly an aim of the researchers who developed the theory, such success should no more surprise us than the success of any enterprise into which resources have been put. So the most simple abductive argument for truth fails; this has been pointed out by many participants in this debate (see, for example, van Fraassen 1980; Rouse 1987).

THE ABDUCTIVE ARGUMENT ON METHODOLOGY

Another version of the abductive argument for realism has more potential for success, a version that has been developed by Richard Boyd (1985 and elsewhere). Its central claim is that we should be realists about "what is implicated in instrumentally reliable methodology" (Boyd 1990, 186): the truth of background theories is the best explanation of the success of scientific methods. The strategy here is to focus not on the instrumental success of theories but on the instrumental success of methodologies—"methodology" is used here in its modern, colloquial sense, to mean "methods" or "a collection of methods," rather than in its original sense of "the study of method."

Boyd's argument is basically captured by the following schema: the empiricist's main point is that theories are massively underdetermined by data. David Hume, for one, took that to its logical conclusion and claimed that not only theories but also *predictions* are underdetermined and, hence, so are *empirically adequate* theories; a set of data never uniquely determine the next data point. Yet it is clear that scientists routinely draw inferences and make good predictions. What allows them to do this is a set of background or metaphysical beliefs that partition the set of theories compatible with the data into the plausible and the implausible. Good background beliefs are more likely to lead to theories that continue to be at least partially empirically adequate.

To turn more explicitly to science: methods are dependent on theory. For example, accepted theoretical perspectives suggest important experiments. Theories can provide a range of hypotheses that might apply to a given area of inquiry, so the hypotheses that researchers consider are theory-dependent. Then, if all of the alternative hypotheses agree on one part of the domain—call it A—but disagree on another part—B—experiments concerning B will be much more sensitive in discriminating among hypotheses than those concerning A. To discriminate between Newtonian and relativistic physics, experiments and observation using massive or fast-moving objects are more helpful than observations on everyday objects. The theory dependence of method doesn't end there: importantly, theories also suggest controls. Theoretical knowledge suggests what other occurrences, besides the ones in which the investigators are interested, might result in positive or negative results relative to their hypothesis. These other occurrences will have to be controlled for.

The claim is not merely that theories are valuable heuristically, a point accepted by van Fraassen (1980), who I will take as a representative empiricist. Methods are theory dependent to such an extent that experimentation cannot be divorced from theory. The scientist cannot decide which experiments to do without some ideas about what to test. She won't know how to design them without some ideas about what might happen. And once she's done the experiments she needs ideas about how to interpret them. So some theoretical knowledge is needed.

A real, if simple, example might help to clarify things. I will briefly describe one of the well-known spontaneous generation experiments that Louis Pasteur performed.[1] The episode was part of a long-standing discussion about the origins of living creatures; more specifically, Pasteur was engaged in a debate with Felix Pouchet over the spontaneous generation of microbes.

In the swan-necked flask experiment Pasteur placed a liquid—sugared yeast water—inside a number of flasks, the necks of which were then drawn out to become extremely thin tubes which dipped toward the ground at some point. Then he boiled the liquid so as to allow vapor to escape for a few minutes. The liquid remained sterile indefinitely, though if he cut the neck of the flask at a wide point—A—the liquid would quickly become clouded and full of life. A small amount of liquid, condensation, would collect in the

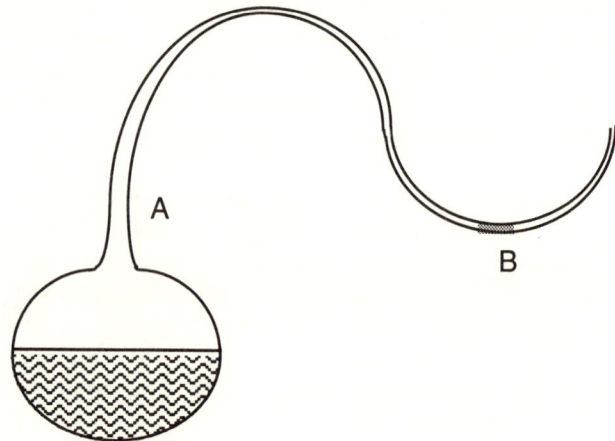

Figure 2.1 Pasteur's Swan-necked Flask (after Duclaux 1920, 99)

dip of the neck—B. When Pasteur tipped the flask gently so as to allow some of this liquid to enter the main body of the flask, the sugared yeast water would once again become clouded. The dip in the neck, with its condensed liquid, was effectively acting as a filter for microbes. When some of that was allowed to enter the flask, it carried those microbes along with it.

For the purposes of the abductive argument for realism it is important to think about the things that Pasteur was trying to achieve. Some of the spontaneous generation dispute concerned air, since air was thought necessary for the creation of life. It had been argued, for example, that heating changed the quality of the air somehow, preventing spontaneous generation. With this elegant and simple experiment Pasteur showed that if the quality of the air changed, that change was reversible with the introduction of a little bit of liquid from the neck; he did not allow new air to enter the flask.[2]

It could be argued that the liquid from the neck transferred from the atmosphere a nonliving ingredient, crucial to spontaneous generation, into the gases in the flask. This would have to have been an ingredient which needed a certain amount of surface area to be transferred to those gases, and hence was not transferred when the liquid sat in the neck. But that is not and was not a plausible theoretical hypothesis, and Pasteur knew it. Nothing that he knew about behaved in that manner. On the other hand, it was perfectly conceivable that spores could travel through the air and rest in the liquid. So there was a certain amount of theoretical knowledge or "theory" that was crucial to the design of the experiment and to its interpretation.

Methodologies in many areas of current science help to produce instrumentally reliable theories. The empiricist, usually a fan of science, will likely agree to this, especially since empiricists accept that scientific theories are often extremely successful. Instrumental reliability, the ability of theories to make good predictions and account for the data, is what empiricists hold up as the chief virtue of scientific theories, and hence they must accept that current methodologies produce reliable theoretical knowledge. For convenience, we can apply the label to methodologies as well as theories. Boyd provides the following definition: "Call a methodology instrumentally reliable if it is a reliable guide to the acceptance of theories which are themselves instrumentally reliable." That is, a methodology is instrumentally reliable if its employment often results in instrumentally reliable theories.

To pull the argument together: reliable methods are theory-dependent; without background theories scientists can't begin to design an experiment or know how to interpret its results; but how can we explain instrumentally reliable methodologies without accepting that their metaphysical commitments, the theories that are implicated in their production of reliable knowledge, are approximately true? We should agree, then, to accept realism about those background theories, if not necessarily the ones that are produced as a result of them.

Essentially the same point can be made in another way. Let us imagine that a group of researchers have a domain in which there is an instrumentally reliable methodology and an instrumentally reliable set of theories. Because of some mathematical messiness, they might want to replace all of their theories in this domain with substantially different but empirically equivalent ones, ones that will be easier to calculate with but which run strongly counter to their best beliefs about the unobservable part of this domain. The empiricist would think this change a useful exercise, similar in kind to buying a better computer and hiring a good programmer, but doing nothing terribly original with the new resources.[3] Empirically it will leave this research community with the same situation it had before. But because these new theories embody different conceptions of the set of alternative hypotheses and will make different statements about the unobservable, methodology will also change. The experiments that had been designed before may be useless in discriminating between new hypotheses that come up and may be useless in helping to confirm or disconfirm hypotheses. The realist's intuitions would have it that a change of this sort, an almost random change in the type of experiments performed, is extremely unlikely to help in the production of good theoretical knowledge; the chance that the process will result in a new instrumentally reliable methodology is vanishingly small. So, instead of taking the empiricist's advice, the researchers should buy the new computer and go on in an unoriginal way, believing in the approximate truth of their background theories.

OBJECTION 1: THE STATUS OF ABDUCTION

The largest challenge to this argument is to the pattern as a whole: to the pattern of abduction, or, Inference to the Best Explanation (IBE). Without IBE we would have no reason to *believe* the hypothesis that offers the best explanation, above and beyond thinking it the most likely of the hypotheses available. Yet we have little reason to believe that a collection of historically given hypotheses includes the true one, and hence little reason to believe that the best among these is true. That is, we have no warrant to believe that the best explanation, among the explanations we've thought of, is true or even approximately true. The true one is more likely to be among the ones that haven't been thought of. So inference to the best explanation, or abduction, appears to be a principle that takes us away from the truth (van Fraassen 1989; Fine 1986b).

While this objection is very effective against the simple version of the abductive argument for realism, it has much less force in the more complex version just given. It comes as no surprise to the realist that IBE isn't a deductively valid principle. Instead it is merely the best resource available: nobody would seriously suggest trying IFBE, "Inference to the Fourth-Best Explanation." The argument I gave for realism does not depend on IBE as a principle that nets truth but, instead, in a deflationary spirit, demands that we should accept the best explanation for what it is: the best explanation. If it is the best that scientists have, they should accept it as a working hypothesis.

The empiricist's challenge to abduction or IBE comes because IBE is used as an argument for truth in science: truth is the best explanation for the success of scientific theories or the success of methodologies. But even if we should not *believe* the results of abduction, we should accept them for their heuristic value. Thus, we should accept realism, the truth in theories, for its heuristic value. The main effect of the challenge to abduction, then, is to point out that realism or truth might in the long run turn out not to be the best available explanation for success in science. In the meantime, though, empiricism fails on pragmatic and heuristic grounds, precisely the grounds empiricists find most important.

My reply might not be convincing to everybody. A rephrasing of the conclusions of my argument for realism might be as follows: method M_1 is successful because theories T_1, U_1, V_1 are approximately true, and method M_2 is successful because T_2, U_2, V_2 are approximately true, and so on. Each of these clauses is shorthand for "M_i is successful because T_i, U_i, V_i."[4] It might be claimed, then, that realism is shorthand for a very long conjunction of theories that the realist believes or has the appropriate evidence for. Under this interpretation it is not the philosophical doctrine, realism, that should be accepted on pragmatic grounds, but only the theories in question.

That an empiricist might be willing to do. But the rephrasing has some problems. If I had been only making the argument about a specific methodology and a specific set of background theories, then the new version would certainly capture my point. But my argument is about a wide variety of methodologies and theories, and I do not claim to use and believe all of them; in fact there isn't anybody who believes all of them, and they haven't even all been formulated. Therefore "true" is doing plenty of work, allowing me to talk about theories I've never encountered. Furthermore, one interpretation of the main point of the abductive argument is that belief in the heuristic power of theories, including their power to generate successful methodology, is unfounded without a belief in their approximate truth. Accepting theories on pragmatic grounds without believing that they're true leaves one unable to explain some of their pragmatic virtues, in particular their virtue of being useful in the generation of other empirically adequate theories. But this takes us back to a philosophical rather than a scientific position: it has become a philosophical task to explain the successes of science. If we conclude that the best explanation for instrumentally reliable methodology is the truth of some background theories, then to achieve our philosophical goals we cannot merely agree that the theories have pragmatic virtues but must agree that they are approximately true.

OBJECTION 2: PLAUSIBILITY

The empiricist's arguments often come back to the fact that, in principle, for every theory there are an infinite number of empirically equivalent theories. This fact tells us something about the form of abductive arguments like the one I put forward. If success is a sign of truth, then, since all theories equivalent to a successful theory will also be successful, they will all be true. But that is absurd, so success is not a sign of truth. Similarly, for any given set of successful (or instrumentally reliable) experimental practices, there are presumably infinitely many sets of theories that would yield the same practices. Hence if success is an indication of the truth of the background theories that yield a certain methodology, it is also an indication of the truth of equivalent background theories, which is absurd. If this is right, then the abductive argument fails.

One way to rescue the argument—and the principle of abduction—is through the notion of plausibility: we shouldn't think that any old empirically successful theory is approximately true, only that ones the scientific community finds *plausible* are good candidates for near truth. Plausibility has to be considered a criterion on which to judge success, in addition to empirical criteria such as prediction and control. A theory that isn't plausible isn't successful. So although there are an infinity of theories empirically equivalent to any given theory, most of them won't be candidates for success or truth, on grounds of implausibility. It is usually difficult to come up with many plausible theories that make the same predictions and sometimes difficult to come up with *even one* empirically adequate theory for a set of data. Alison Wylie (1989) claims that this is often the case in archaeology; and K. Amann and Karin Knorr-Cetina (1990) report that in the laboratory they studied, it was usually difficult to come up with a consistent interpretation of even a quite limited set of data. Therefore, there simply aren't an infinity of successful theories.

Plausibility, however, is difficult to define. Worse, the notion of plausibility might be seen as begging the question against the strict empiricist, who should deny that plausibility judgments serve real functions in science. To see this, we simply have to note that plausibility judgments are conditioned by the past; the beliefs that were accepted in the past were not accepted because people carefully sifted through an infinity of equivalent beliefs but because they decided to accept the first empirically adequate one they found. Past judgments of truth can be no better founded than present ones.

When plausibility judgments are relatively free from history, the situation is no better. A radical new hypothesis doesn't become plausible until people have worked with it, explored it a little, invested some time in it.[5] And if they have invested time in it they are going to have an interest in maintaining its plausibilty, since that is how the new hypothesis will be taken up and used. Andrew Pickering's study of the high-energy physics community (1984) shows this principle in action, not merely in terms of favorite hypotheses but also in terms of skills. Experiments and even research programs are developed that utilize the skills of particular people. Hence we should suspect judgments of plausibility.

Yet there is still something very attractive about the idea of plausibility. The abductive argument for realism that I put forward shows that it would be a remarkable coincidence if theories that were designed solely to be empirically adequate turned out to be good bases for plausibility judgments and, hence, good at producing instrumentally reliable methodology. But it would be no coincidence at all if theories that were true turned out to be good at producing instrumentally reliable methodology. Thus an attempt to explain the instrumental reliability of methodology without some idea like plausibility would involve betting on something with very low odds.

By introducing plausibility we start to make sense of the idea that scientists don't choose from an infinite set of theories, that they only choose from among those theories that stand some decent chance of being accepted as true. It should then become part of the realist's research project to understand how ideas of plausibility are built up, along with strategies for obtaining better approximations and methods for discrimination among hypotheses, such that they can contribute to the attainment of approximately true theories. This leaves plenty of work to do; but giving up on notions of plausibility means giving up on understanding large chunks of methodology.

SOME REFINEMENTS AND DELIMITATIONS

Often the realist assumes that science is basically a story of success. But it is possible, even likely, that the successes we normally attribute to science and scientific knowledge, in particular the technological successes that are prominent in such discussions, owe more to technology and efficient bureaucracies. A number of historians of technology have argued that technologists are not applied scientists and that many technological problems are not scientific ones. The basic position is summed up by the slogan "science owes more to the steam engine than the steam engine owes to science" (Laudan 1984, 1; see also Hughes 1989).[6]

And perhaps, as Arthur Fine suggests, scientific successes have been relatively few in comparison to the failures, which have been forgotten (Fine 1986b, 1991). Scientists' conceptions of the history of their disciplines always emphasize the successful work and tend to forget the unsuccessful. History of science, by tending to focus on the "important" figures, both the recognized innovators and the forerunners, also leaves an impression of more success than there may actually be—though a number of historians have recognized this point and tried to correct it. And history gets rewritten through a number of interesting strategic moves. Boundaries are created around disciplines (see Gieryn 1983; also Fuller 1988, chap. 9) which exclude the unsuccessful, leaving the successful within science and the unsuccessful outside.

I raise these questions about success not because they are, strictly speaking, a part of the realist/empiricist debate—*both* realists and empiricists tend to be impressed by science's successes.[7] Rather, these questions help to delimit the sphere of the abductive argument. The argument assumes that there are enough successes to deserve an explanation and it offers one: successes will often—though not always—be explained by the truth of the background theories. But the argument does not make more substantial claims about the relative proportion of failures and successes. Although the abductive argument does not validate all of science, the realist position, incautiously stated, might appear to. It is important to keep in mind that the argument only applies to the achievements. That is, the deflationary realism that I'm advocating is a limited one, applicable to some but not all aspects of science. Its application in each case has to be argued. My approach results in a partial and retrospective position; I am not making a claim about all of science but only selected bits of it.

Thus it seems as though the abductive argument works as an answer against empiricist positions, but its positive conclusion is less clear. Its conclusion is that we should believe the theory that is implicated in instrumentally reliable methodology, but how do we learn to recognize instrumentally reliable methodology? What level of theory is implicated? And how do we know which theory is implicated in reliable methodology? What about cases in which ideology affects judgments about the instrumental reliability of methodology?—for example, in the nineteenth century almost all social scientists would have agreed that the assumption of a hierarchy of races was an extremely productive one in terms of data, including numerical data, produced (Gould 1981; Stepan 1986).

As long as the argument for realism is an appropriately qualified retrospective, or post hoc one—that certain results of inquiry justify an inference that some of the premises are approximately true—then the issue of the impact of ideology is not directly related. Of course we will have to worry that our post hoc argument for realism in any particular case is not so ideologically conditioned as to be itself suspect, that our judgments of the empirical success of some piece of scientific knowledge are not biased by our ideological or other presuppositions: if we were to take as more than expected and contrived numerical achievements the correlations produced by nineteenth-century racist science, then we would probably be ignoring some important lessons of statistics—and helped to do so by ideology. This shows that we might have to do social, political, and evaluative work to sort successes from failures. But although this type of worry is important and often justified, it is a second-order concern for which we should demand justification in most cases; these worries should not be sufficient to initiate a generalized skepticism.

What is implicated in reliable methodology is not, in most cases, a full theory but certain very limited conceptions of causal mechanisms at work. When somebody performs a routine experiment designed to tell them something about the hypothesis that substance X causes cancer in laboratory rats, most of the controls aren't attempting to distinguish alternative hypotheses of the same sort but only to control against other aspects of the experimental set-up causing cancer. In complex experiments generally, one tries to control for all manner of aspects of the set-up that could throw the results out of whack. The "theory" that is involved here is relatively minimal and built up more from experience in labs than from work by theoreticians. In Pasteur's swan-necked flask experiment, one piece of knowledge I mentioned as necessary was knowledge that a certain model of how gases might become enriched is implausible, or at least blatantly ad hoc. That is not theoreticians' knowledge as much as practical experience.

Therefore, the abductive argument for realism, while it tells us lots of interesting things, does not tell us that we should be realists about theories but only about entities and low-level causal properties. We might be led to a position more like Ian Hacking's entity realism than Richard Boyd's theory realism. Hacking says about electrons, "If you can spray them, then they are real," and then denies that theories about electrons are likely to be right (1983, 22). In general, Hacking asserts the existence of entities that experimenters know how to use but denies that theories need to be realistically interpreted.

This statement of entity realism creates some immediate problems. For example, in the paradigm case of electrons, the fact that they are "them" (that is particulate, or individuals, as opposed to stuff) is given by theory, even if for reasons established by experiment.[8] Reference cannot be wholly divorced from description. Therefore in affirming the existence of electrons Hacking seems to be affirming at least some low-level theory, and thus it might seem one cannot have entity realism without theory realism. But one interpretation of Hacking's point is that he simply doesn't want to grace the knowledge involved with the label "theory." On this view, entity realism denies that we can move from accepting this low-level knowledge, mostly of causal properties, to accepting that any of the particular current theories of electrons are true (Hacking 1984).

Obviously this is in part a debate about how to use the word *theory*. In general, scientists use *theory* fairly loosely, maintaining no firm criteria that distinguish theories from hypotheses, models, or from single pieces of knowledge. With some exceptions, philosophers have taken more notice of this lack of criteria than have scientists and, consequently, try to draw some firm line. For philosophers, "theory" is usually contrasted with "observation." "Genes are composed of DNA" can be a theory for philosophers, even though it lacks the complexity to make it a theory for scientists. I am not sure what to call that sentence, besides a sentence, statement, or claim, but I would like to insist on using "theory" more as scientists do, even if we lack clear demarcations between theories and related objects.[9] Scientists do not usually contrast theories with observations but, instead, see theories as reasonably well-developed structures. Even when they contrast theories with facts or hypotheses, the theory side usually has a certain degree of complexity. Under this conception of theories, it makes sense to be an entity realist without being a theory realist.

It turns out that the abductive argument on methodology supports entity realism. It tells us to believe what is implicated in instrumentally reliable methodology: what is implicated in instrumentally reliable methodology is the existence of the entities experimenters seem to manipulate and the correctness of their basic knowledge about them, especially the knowledge needed for experimental manipulation. This point has not been recognized in discussions of theory- and entity realism. Though many people find the position compelling, Hacking's presentation of entity realism is typically criticized for lacking an argument (e.g., Shapere 1993). Yet, as I have developed it here, the abductive argument for realism provides strong support for Hacking's position.

Entity realism becomes more attractive when we see that there are well-established theories that are unlikely to be true. A simple example is Mendelian genetics, a well-established biological theory if there is one. Mendel's genes are rigid, self-contained units that, at least in the paradigm case, map one-to-one onto traits. The results that can be derived are about these idealized units, not *about* anything real. When Mendel's framework is applied, particular instantiations of it become comparable to observations of real organisms. Yet it is not in itself true of empirical data but, rather, a tool. The theory can be used, it can be applied, but it is not true.[10]

This is not to deny that there are many approximate correspondences between the assumptions of classical genetics and what happens in biological systems; there are numerous respects in which classical genetics makes approximations and idealizations of the truth. The theory claims that genes sort themselves independently of each other, which is approximately true, especially for pieces of DNA on different chromosomes. Classical genetics usually assumes that genes are inherited intact and not affected by meiosis or mitosis, although pieces of DNA can split, recombine, mutate, and so forth. These assumptions are idealizations of the findings of molecular genetics, yet we still teach classical genetics. High-level theories abstract *away* from the truth rather than toward it: the assumptions are idealizations *away* from what is known to be roughly true. Even if theories do rest on some approximately true assumptions, it is important to recognize the theory for what it is: it is often a tool, not simply an attempt to get a more accurate picture of the world. The accurate picture is what it is based on and what it is escaping.

True theories are often too unwieldy and cumbersome to be successful. Thus, there are different types of theories, some of which are intended to tell the truth about a situation and some of which are intended to be convenient abstractions (Cartwright 1983). True theories that encompass a lot are unlikely to be very useful and, hence, very successful, because the world is too complicated for the use of true theories. Hence the highest level theories, explaining the most, are abstractions away from, not toward, the truth. Certain theories shouldn't be interpreted realistically; they abstract from messy reality to describe certain tendencies or "capacities" (Cartwright 1989a, 1989b).[11]

Seeing theories and models primarily in true-or-false terms misses their pragmatic aspects. Yet this need not translate into a blanket skepticism; skepticism about theories should be focused on particular aspects of them which look to be approximations away from the truth. Some, perhaps most, theories and statements about unobservables *do* aim for truth, and many statements about unobservables are approximately true.

CONCLUSIONS

The knowledge implicated in instrumentally reliable methodology is at least partly approximately true. Evidence for this comes from the fact that scientists have to have methodologies that tell them where to look for a hypothesis's potential failures: they have to test their hypotheses against other plausible ones. The background knowledge that is assumed in defining these other hypotheses or points of failure has to be approximately true for them to frequently arrive at empirically adequate accounts.

Yet theories are often deliberate approximations away from the truth. Theories idealize messy realities; this makes theories more attractive, more general, and, perhaps oddly, more useful. Thus we should not assume that the knowledge implicated in instrumentally reliable methodology is the best-developed theory supposedly behind that methodology. Instead, the implicated knowledge might be low-level causal generalizations, well-established facts about the subject matter, or even tacitly held beliefs. Although my argument tells us that successful methodology is a sign of the truth of some background assumptions, it leaves us with much work to do to decide which of the background assumptions are approximately true. I have not provided a neat formula to identify what we should take as true because what is "implicated in instrumentally reliable methodology" is not necessarily obvious; in particular it is not necessarily grand theory that is responsible for a string of successes.

The realism that results from my argument need not be an overarching legitimation of science. Positivists tried to preserve and enhance the cultural authority of science by describing it in rationalistic terms. By and large realist critics of positivism have attempted to do the same, bending somewhat on rationalism but arguing that science nevertheless aimed at the truth. But my discussion in this chapter *limits* realism to certain classes of statements, which are unfortunately left unspecified. And I have made no claims about the rationality of science. So the deflationary realism we are left with is as compatible with critical views of science as it is with laudatory views.

Three

EPISTEMOLOGY BY OTHER MEANS

THE PREVIOUS CHAPTER ARGUED that there is evidence for the approximate truth of at least some scientific statements about unobservables; it argued for a deflationary scientific realism. But even if the argument is right, it does not provide us with an understanding of *how* scientists can arrive at such approximate truths. This issue is particularly important in the context of social and political analyses of science, which often seem to emphasize the irrationality and interestedness of scientific researchers. In this chapter I provide an answer, in its outlines at least, to the question of how science can arrive at truths.

My strategy here is to give an evolutionary argument, an argument that truths and epistemic virtues can be *selected for* in science. The social structure of science creates—at least often—settings which make possible the systematic production of knowledge. I start by showing that scientific knowledge is importantly social in its production and definition. That science is social knowledge usually poses a problem for scientific realism, because realism is generally tied to individualistic pictures of knowledge production. This is, in part, because realism has been associated with a rationalistic picture of science; dominant models of rationality are individualistic and those of irrationality are social—Bacon's idols still play an important role in our conception of objective inquiry. Despite the apparent conflict, a picture of science as social knowledge can actually contribute to the justification of a deflationary realism.

Scientists use available resources in the production of their own results and give credit to others for some of the most useful resources: pieces of knowledge. This sets up a dynamic in which the continued construction of knowledge is likely. And it is by attending to that dynamic that we can create an evolutionary picture of the development of scientific knowledge—a picture in which the ideas that are most useful remain central and prominent. Those ideas that are not useful are either forgotten or disputed. If truth is sometimes useful, then truths will be among the ideas retained. Therefore a deflationary realism can be maintained even when the rationalist picture of science has been discarded.

Stephan Fuchs (1992) provides one way of seeing the evolution of facts, in his use of grid/group theory to describe differences between some scientific and other knowledge-producing communities. The basic tools that Fuchs brings to play in his analysis of cognitive styles are two concepts: "task uncertainty" is the "extent to which scientific production is routinized and predictable" (Fuchs 1992, 82); and "mutual dependence" is the dependence of scientists on their colleagues for resources and rewards (81). In addition to these variables is a problematic definition, which does much of the work of the theory: he adopts a strongly antirealist position in which facts are *defined as the things that the relevant communities decide to call "facts."* I find this definition unsatisfactory—I follow the standard convention in using "facts" to refer to states of affairs—but it is nonetheless worthwhile to see where it leads.

The following table shows how Fuchs's variables are expected to correlate to cognitive styles:

		Mutual Dependence	
		low	high
Task Uncertainty	low	*Area Dogmas* — Low overall, but high specialty integration; Anti-metaphysical; Moderate future orientation.	*Facts* — Paradigmatically unified; Tacit metaphysics; Strong future orientation.
	high	*Conversation* — Several coexisting paradigms; Debates on metaphysical foundations; Strong historical orientation.	*Science-in-the-Making* — Constant innovation and cumulation; Changing paradigmatic structure; Very strong future orientation.

Figure 3.1 A Model of Cognitive Styles (from Fuchs 1992, 92)

The combination usually taken as paradigmatically scientific is what Fuchs describes as high mutual dependence and low task uncertainty, or the box labelled "Facts." Workers in the natural sciences are often more mutually dependent than workers in the humanities and social sciences, because access to tools (such as laboratory equipment) and research subjects is relatively more expensive in the natural sciences. In such cases there is considerable pressure to produce facts, as opposed to interpretations; scientists will be interested in using, and potentially able to use, each other's results, and create pressure to clarify, verify, and solidify those results. Thus the "hard" sciences participate in the fact-producing cognitive style, resulting in their authoritarian style.

By definition, however, new and innovative research areas are less routinized and, hence, have high task uncertainty, which dampens the authoritative style at least temporarily, until facts have solidified ("Science-in-the-Making").[1] In disciplines with relatively well-distributed resources, that is, disciplines in which there is low mutual dependence, there is less social pressure to solidify results into accepted facts and researchers make fewer attempts to use others' resources. Authority can be fragmented, and built on relatively local grounds, since there is less need to share resources ("Area Dogmas"). When, in addition, problems and procedures are less routinized—that is, high task uncertainty—there is less possibility of stability and more likelihood of continuing disagreement ("Conversation").[2]

Distribution of resources and structure of problems can (at least partly) define a cognitive style, and one potential cognitive style is the fact-producing one, when there is high mutual dependence and low task uncertainty. These conditions are the ones we see most often in the natural sciences, and a priori they should produce a strong pressure toward stabilization of facts. Scientific communities are organized in such a way as to provide incentives for knowledge-productive uses of power.

The social nature and particular social structuring of science creates pressure toward the stabilization of facts, but that pressure is by itself not sufficient to ensure that science arrives at facts. In addition, science must have tools and resources that are capable of mapping the world and identifying facts. My argument for realism shows that this is a relatively unproblematic assumption: science's predictive successes indicate the power of scientific resources in this respect. In addition, the cognitive style of the natural sciences, as analyzed by Fuchs, should be expected to encourage the development of such powerful tools. To understand in a more concrete way the reasons for that power requires looking more closely at actual practices, at the opportunistic use of resources to solve problems and achieve ends. To that end, in the second half of this chapter, I provide a reading of some recent work in science and technology studies (S&TS), a reading that goes against the normal grain. S&TS dismantles the ideology of science as a purely rationalist, objective enterprise, but rather than suggesting that science can never reach truths, these studies of science examine the development and deployment of scientific rationality; that is, S&TS shows us how scientists use available resources to attempt to achieve their immediate goals. S&TS is integral to the epistemological study of science.

SOCIAL KNOWLEDGE

Helen Longino's *Science as Social Knowledge* (1990) is an attempt to understand how social ideology and the larger social context can play an important role in scientific inquiry, without giving up the idea that there can be some objectivity and room for specific criticism in science. Longino wants to be able to discuss the role of values in science, without saying that the value-ladenness of science gives us no foothold to criticize specific claims and their justifications. She does not want to follow some sociologists of science who, on the grounds of the relativity of reason and knowledge, try to rule out normative evaluations of knowledge claims. And equally, she is not content with a particularist project that criticizes sexist aspects of science yet makes no attempt to understand in general the ways in which social values play a part in scientific inquiry. Attention to this difficulty might be seen as one of the contributions of feminist S&TS. The political critic who wants to think systematically about science usually wants to hang onto both horns of the dilemma, wanting to assert simultaneously that certain scientific accounts and theories are poor ones and that science is systematically value laden.

For Longino the solution to the difficulty involves two steps. To a fairly conventional view of how reasoning does and should work she adds an analysis of the way in which background assumptions affect evidential reasoning: what a fact is evidence for depends on what background assumptions are held. This dependency of evidence relations on background assumptions allows people to agree on facts and yet disagree about the conclusions to be drawn from them. At the same time Longino insists that background assumptions are articulable and may be criticized. Thus she maintains a nonfoundationalist picture of knowledge in which there can be an indefinitely long process of questioning and criticizing background assumptions. Which background assumptions we choose and which ones we choose to question will have a lot to do with social values. For example, feminist scientists of the past twenty years, with experience of sexism and antisexist movements, approached their subject matter with some different and novel presuppositions, creating a wealth of feminist work in the sciences.[3] It is at the level of background assumptions, then, that Longino thinks values enter the process of inquiry.

Seeing science as social knowledge allows for objectivity in a fairly direct way: it shrinks the room for individual subjectivity and idiosyncrasy. Scientists are heavily interdependent, and they are well socialized; and science necessarily borrows values, norms, and metaphors from the larger society of which it is a part. These values, norms, and metaphors are always implicit in theory choice, given the underdetermination of theory by data. Scientific communities enforce certain shared standards, which cannot be left behind at the drop of a hat. But Longino would not want to leave matters there, because communities can share undesirable standards, ones she would hardly think of as warranted. So she needs, and provides, a processual and normative notion of objectivity of communities and their methods: "A method of inquiry is objective to the degree that it permits transformative criticism. Its objectivity consists not just in the inclusion of intersubjective criticism but in the degree to which both its procedures and its results are responsive to . . . criticism" (76).

Because background assumptions are linked to social values, an important prerequisite for greater objectivity in scientific communities is representation of differing social groups, with different experiences, in science itself. Otherwise the community may not have a wide enough experience to enable it to criticize illegitimate background assumptions. More objective communities will tend to be those that are diverse and representative of the societies in which they are embedded; Longino's normative stance amounts to a recommendation of democracy and affirmative action.

So we end up with the balance Longino wants. On the one hand we can have specific criticisms of scientific views, because feminist empiricists can question reasoning and background assumptions. On the other hand we can have criticisms of the objectivity of scientific communities, if those communities are not responsive to challenges to background assumptions. In the bargain we get a general picture of the effects of social values on science. Somewhat simplified, it is an empiricist picture of the interplay of background assumptions and data to produce theory sitting on top of a picture of the production of values and, from them, background assumptions, on the basis of social experience.

While Longino achieves her goals, her model is unsatisfying in its limits. She wants to examine science as practice, but in the end, because of her attention to background beliefs, she ignores many parts of the practice that may be relevant to a feminist understanding of science and parts that may be relevant to understanding how feminist researchers can change it. Looking to other social studies of science, one of the things that recent research teaches us is that background beliefs aren't the only important backgrounds in sci-

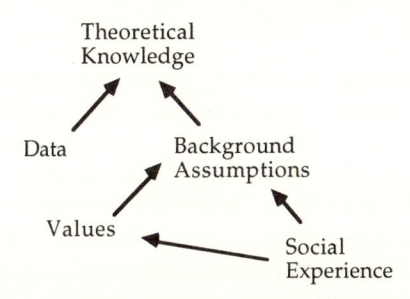

Figure 3.2 Longino's Picture of Knowledge Production

ence. S&TS shows us the importance of skills (Collins 1992), tools (Pickering 1984), material settings (Latour 1983, 1987), and linguistic resources (Shapin and Schaffer 1985; Pickering 1992a). These are among the things that communities use to produce knowledge and that individuals use to gain authority within a community. There is something that feminist work can take from this: changing scientific outputs is not simply a matter of challenging and changing background beliefs. While beliefs are important, obtaining them is only a small portion of scientific work and, therefore, "perspectives" and differing "experiences" don't engage all aspects of science.[4]

The claim that science is social knowledge is, as we have seen, an important one, providing reason to think that science has some measure of objectivity. Because it is important, I am going to amplify and strengthen it by appealing to other work by sociologists and philosophers of science. I want to add to and expand upon Longino's reasons why knowledge is social; in particular I point out some of the ways in which scientists are mutually dependent, and I argue that community standards work to produce even such mundane things as observation reports.

(i) *Experiment and observation is done by groups rather than individuals.* Some forms of scientific interdependence are well known: Karin Knorr-Cetina (1981), Greg Myers (1990), and others have drawn attention to multiauthored papers and the negotiation involved in their writing; Bruno Latour (e.g., 1987), Michel Callon (1986), and others have described the extensive networks of alliances and resources that have to be built up to create knowledge. But probably the most important sense in which scientists are mutually dependent is the straightforward one in which scientists use each others' results, methods, tools, ideas, and even equipment and skills, in their own work. In the natural sciences these resources are relatively expensive to create anew, and thus they are exchanged, shared, or held in common. Because of this, there is a well-developed system of credit, in which use of certain types of resources produced by others is acknowledged through citation, and sometimes even co-authorship. Credit becomes itself an important commodity (Latour and Woolgar 1986; Hull 1988b).

(ii) *The importance and status of experiment and observation is decided by communities.* Philosophers of science have long claimed that observation is theory laden, but "theory laden" doesn't capture all of the ladenness that goes into experimental observation reports. An observation report doesn't just presuppose all of the theory that goes into an experiment, but also the labor and the nontheoretical materials and methods that form the context of the experiment. Trevor Pinch, writing about a well-known solar-neutrino experiment, contrasts possible observation reports such as "splodges on the graph were observed" with "solar neutrinos were observed" (Pinch 1985, 9).

Clearly the latter presupposes more *theory* than the former, but it also presupposes more experimental material, skill, and labor than the former. Were the instruments properly cleaned? Were they of sufficiently high quality? Where were they placed?

This (exaggerated) contrast points to the sociality of the production of knowledge, not just because experimental skill and labor is typically dispersed, but because the experimenter and the community have choices about the *evidential context* of the published reports—what the results can be taken as evidence about. We can think of evidential contexts as having different possible levels of importance. What the level turns out to be is the result of a social process, a process of negotiation, not just after articles are published, but before. Reviewers routinely problematize aspects of the experiment and demand more mundane conclusions, and critics attack aspects of the experimental set-up and the experimenters' skills, often forcing conclusions about a more narrow evidential context.

The controls on an experiment are designed such that the results help us to choose between competing hypotheses. But they don't help us to choose between *any* competing hypotheses, only the ones that the community is willing to take seriously, the "projectable" ones (Boyd 1984). Thus, the scientist designs her experiment so as to meet the standards of the community. Whether this is successful or not, the community as a whole decides on evidential context: the community, in negotiation with the experimenter, decides what knowledge obtains from the data and the experimental set-up. To stick with Pinch's example, the data may tell us something about solar neutrinos, or it may tell us something about the limits of the equipment and the theory employed, or even about the limits of the experimenter—in the actual case, all three of these have been seriously proposed, and each has had a following. Evidential context is not fixed once and for all. Thus, what an experiment serves to justify is socially regulated.

(iii) *Scientific knowledge is externalized.* Not only is scientific knowledge not produced by independent individuals, it is not even contained in them. Individual instances of belief, passing as commonly accepted knowledge, are interpretations of the more standardized versions contained in textbooks and journals. Scientific knowledge is what can be abstracted from its embodiment in machines, in everyday practice and everyday beliefs. Karl Popper (1979), as a result of his attempt to divorce subjective from objective knowledge, reaches the conclusion that the latter is not primarily in people's heads. Objective knowledge, which is produced only by communities, he places in a separate world, "World Three," inhabited by art, the contents of books, and other products of civilization. Popper arrives at that conclusion not by looking at the details of the social production of knowledge but by privileging contexts of justification and searching for necessary conditions for the production of objective knowledge. He would disagree with many of the other positions I am putting forward, but he would agree that scientific knowledge is not the type of thing that can be created by individuals.[5]

(iv) *Scientists are necessarily socialized into various communities.* None of what I have said means to deny a basic sociality of knowledge rooted in the socialization of scientific researchers—and people more generally—a sociality present not just in scientific knowledge but in everyday knowledge as well. Language, problems, patterns of reasoning, and conceptual resources are all community resources, reproduced in the individual. In this sense, that scientific knowledge is social knowledge is an old claim. For example, Karl Marx makes a number of the above points when he claims that science is a social activity:

> But again when I am active scientifically, etc.,—when I am engaged in activity which I can seldom perform in direct community with others—then I am social, because I am active as a man. Not only is the material of my activity given to me as a social product (as is even the language in which the thinker is active): my own existence is social activity, and therefore that which I make of myself, I make of myself for society and with the consciousness of myself as a social being. (Marx 1964, 137)

(v) *Socialization is necessary for the application of concepts, for understanding what remains "the same" across contexts.* One place analysts have found particularly striking examples of necessary socialization is in the delocalization of technology, the movement of a working technology from its initial site to others. Technological knowledge, skills, and artifacts are surprisingly difficult to move from one setting to another, as is suggested by the problems of technology transfer from industrialized to nonindustrialized parts of the world. But technologies can even be difficult to transfer between similar environments: building a working copy of an artifact is not easy without access to specific resources, information, skills, and tacit knowledge. In the 1970s, Harry Collins spent some time studying attempts by researchers to build a Transversely Excited Atmospheric Laser, or TEA-laser. One of Collins's subjects, a Dr. Bob Harrison at the University of Bath, tried to make at least two of them for use in his lab. Both lasers were difficult to get in working order, even though Harrison had apparently all of the needed technical knowledge and expertise. Problems included arc breakdowns, sparks as a result of differential charges where there should have been none, and lack of knowledge about the lengths of various wires and flatness of certain pieces of glass (Collins 1992).

An interesting conclusion of this study, confirmed in other studies of technology transfer, is that social contact is needed to make radically new pieces of technology. According to Collins, nobody was successful in building one of these lasers without extensive contact with somebody from a lab in which there was a working laser. That is, formal communication was inadequate; even communication over the telephone was inadequate (1990, 4).

Thus the claim that science is social knowledge is supportable from various points of view. In an important sense, individuals don't create scientific knowledge; they may be nodes in its creation, but what counts as scientific knowledge is created by groups.

TAKING ANTIFOUNDATIONALISM SERIOUSLY

It is now almost a truism that foundationalism is wrong in epistemology and philosophy of science. The Cartesian project of building knowledge on foundations of indubitable premises and incontrovertible reasoning—thus secure against skepticism—no longer seems possible, because there are no rock-solid foundations to be had: sense data can be misleading and do not speak univocally; if there are a priori principles, they are not sufficient to validate empirical knowledge; science and other knowledge-building institutions are solidly human and historically situated and the knowledges they create are marked by their histories. At least potentially, every concept has problematic boundaries, every argument has weak points, and every piece of knowledge can be questioned.

Despite the lack of foundations, there is considerable agreement on facts and justifications, both in scientific and other communities. In practice, social life is such that the complete skeptic is excluded and more moderate skeptics are appeased and answered. Disagreements are regularly and routinely managed and contained. Though skeptical doubts are unanswerable by foundationalist standards, these doubts are in fact answered, assuaged, or avoided, allowing agreement and knowledge to be built up. Recognition of this should force changes in epistemology's questions. No longer tied to foundationalism, epistemology needs to investigate the ways in which agreement is achieved. Therefore, with the collapse of foundationalism, traditional epistemology needs to to be naturalized.

Whereas traditional epistemology asked how we can know, taking as its task the refutation of the skeptic, naturalistic epistemology asks how our best attempts at knowing work and how they fail. According to naturalistic epistemologists like Alvin Goldman (1985), the concepts of traditional epistemology are too narrow to allow for realistic models of actual knowledge production. One result of this narrowness is that traditionalists cannot make the normative claims that they would like, since their models are only applicable to ideal rational agents. To create more realistic models, naturalistic epistemology draws on psychology, trying to match epistemic recommendations and the capacities of humans as knowing agents (see the essays in Kornblith 1985).

Partly as a result of the use of (individualistic) psychology the new epistemology tends to retain traditional epistemology's focus on a small set of cognitive processes and on individual agents as knowers. This is not a necessary feature of naturalistic epistemology, as Goldman points out:

> Actually my conception of epistemics is broader than these remarks suggest. It would comprehend *social* as well as *individual* dimensions of cognition. It would concern itself with the interpersonal and institutional processes that affect the creation, transmission, and reception of information, misinformation, and partial information. Like the sociology of knowledge, it would study not only organized science, but situational and institutional forces that affect the social dissemination or inhibition of knowledge (Goldman 1985, 229, fn.1).

Yet naturalistic epistemology has tended to neglect noncognitive and social features of knowledge production—a fact indicated by the above passage and its placing in Coldman's text. Especially if we are to create reasonable epistemologies of science we have to take Goldman's conception at its most broad, since knowledge production in science is a social process and depends on instrumentation and other noncognitive inputs.[6] Thus the work so far in naturalistic epistemology needs to be supplemented by work in S&TS.

The failure of foundationalism is also a—possibly *the*—central premise for recent S&TS. For example, one of the key roots to current sociology of scientific knowledge is David Bloor's (or the "strong program's") stricture that explanations of scientific knowledge should be symmetrical, that true and false, rational and irrational beliefs should be explained using the same types of resources (Bloor 1991 [1976], 7).[7] The symmetry recommendation is a reaction against an unsymmetrical foundationalist pattern or style of explanation, in which true scientific beliefs require internal, rationalist explanations, whereas false beliefs require external or social explanations. This common pattern of explanation rests on the assumption that there is a relatively unproblematic rational route from the material world to correct beliefs about it. But in a postfoundationalist era we know that there is no guaranteed path from the material world to scientific truths about it and that we cannot identify truths with certainty, so there aren't unproblematic connections between the dualisms of truth/falsity and internal/external.[8] Thus sociology of scientific knowledge, when it remains faithful to its roots, takes antifoundationalism to heart.

Although there are a number of possible interpretations of the recommendation of symmetry, in practice symmetry has been seen as equivalent to agnosticism about scientific truths. Interpreted in this way, Bloor's methodological rule tells us to assume that debates are open when we attempt to explain closure—thus the study of open controversies has been particularly popular, because the openness enforces agnosticism. The advantage of agnosticism comes from its push for ever more complete explanations (Collins 1981a). The less the analyst takes for granted, the more likely she will have to cast a wide net to give a satisfactory account; too much rationalism—and conversely too much externalism, a point that strong programmers usually ignored—tends to make the analyst stop too soon. Establishing the causes of the closure of a debate requires looking at a large number of types of factors. For the empirical study of science and technology, then, multiple analytic frameworks are valuable. These frameworks should be of the same type whether debates are later seen to be correctly or incorrectly closed; that is, the same types of factors are potentially at play in the production of truth as in the production of falsity; for example, since "external" factors—ideology, idiosyncracy, political pressure—are routinely invoked to explain beliefs thought to be false, they should also be invoked to explain beliefs thought true.

Methodological agnosticism has been fruitfully applied to a variety of questions. Demonstrations of the production of consensus on issues of belief are complemented by studies of the production of consensus on methods, questions, boundaries, and authority (e.g., Shapin and Schaffer 1985; Gieryn 1983). Because kinds—human or natural—do not force their own way into acceptance, any and every accepted category or categorization is seen to require analysis. Therefore, S&TS investigates the processes that lead to perceptions of scientific order generally: the "(social) construction of order." In the next three sections I discuss a few representative studies of the social construction of order, to illustrate some points at which S&TS provides a valuable counter to the dominant ideology of science, but at the same time supplements traditional epistemology of science.

OPPORTUNISM IN CONTEXT AND THE PRACTICE OF SCIENCE

The externalist history and sociology of science of the strong program was the first way through which David Bloor's recommendation of symmetry was taken up.[9] Such accounts tend to follow a standard pattern: they identify a scientific controversy in which the debaters on each side can be identified; a social conflict is also identified, the sides of which can be correlated to the sides of the debate; finally, an account is offered that connects the themes of the scientific debate and those of the social conflict, explaining individuals' scientific positions in terms of their social positions. The strong program attempts to fashion S&TS as a form of macrosociology of science; strong programmers assume that large-scale social structures such as class, gender, and nationality determine smaller-scale features such as beliefs—beliefs are superstructural phenomena.

The strong program's analyses typically face a number of problems, stemming from too-simple pictures of scientific controversies and the interests of the actors involved, and from the portrayal of scientists as mindless "interest dopes." These problems are particularly evident if the goal of externalist analyses is to fully explain the results of controversies. Yet such accounts can be convincing, especially when natural and social orders are explicitly connected by the historical actors (e.g., Jacob 1976; Shapin and Schaffer 1985): external factors are most easily seen as causes of scientific beliefs when they are seen as reasons for those beliefs by the scientists in question. So the strong program has had some notable successes, even while it has been overtaken by more internalist studies of science. And though the strong program itself has more or less disappeared as a unified project, analogous work goes on, for example in feminist S&TS: a large number of feminists have identified sexism implicit in scientific beliefs and representations and have connected that sexism with the sexist structures of the wider society. Too simple a social theory and too few interests taken into account are not as much a problem for feminist S&TS as they were for the strong program, because the goals of the feminist history, philosophy, and sociology of science do not generally include creating a full account of science or the creation of a particular piece of knowledge. By not attempting to *explain* scientific knowledge in terms of ideology but only to display and explain the sexism in it, feminist science studies has a much easier task than the strong program. Feminist S&TS involves a more modest epistemological program to go with its more ambitious political one.

Philosophical attention on S&TS often focuses almost entirely on the strong program and problems with it. The strong program, it is argued, ignores "internal" causes of beliefs, those things that get counted as reasons for beliefs by the scientists themselves. Leaving aside potential problems with the internal/external distinction—for example, Nigel Gilbert and Michael Mulkay (1984) show that scientists have different "repertoires," attributing to beliefs different types of causes depending on the context—a focus on the externalism of the strong program ignores discussions of the internal structures of science, its socially situated rationality, and the development of practices, including those that define what we sometimes think of as scientific methodology. The routine dismissal of S&TS misses the extent to which it is an important branch of epistemology.

S&TS portrays science as rational, in the most basic means-end sense: it shows us that scientists use the resources that are available—rhetorical resources, institutionlized power, skills, facts, and machines—to achieve their goals. The notion of a resource depends upon the notion of a goal: I use the term *resource* to indicate anything used in an attempt to reach a goal.[10] If the immediate goal is to convince a colleague of a fact, the resources put in play are rhetorical ones, facts, arguments, and other tools of persuasion. For the production of an experimental result, the needed resources will include machines, skills, and money, among other things. For the creation of theoretical constructs, the needed resources include facts and tools of analysis. Achievements, then, can become resources for further achievements; reaching goals efficiently may depend upon bringing a wide variety of resources into play. The successes of science as a whole depend, then, upon efficient ratcheting of achievements, turning the strengths of past achievements into new ones.

EXAMPLES AND REFINEMENTS: DELOCALIZATION, CREDIT, RHETORIC, AND PRACTICES

There are other ways, besides the externalism of the strong program, to connect the natural and social orders. Steven Shapin and Simon Schaffer, in their *Leviathan and the Air-Pump*, show that disputes about methods are not only about the way the world is, but are also about authority: which methods are valued determines who the authorities are. And they also show us some of the resources that have been put into play to close such disputes, which have in the process helped to define good scientific procedure.

Robert Boyle and Thomas Hobbes are the protagonists of their story, arguing about the value of experimental philosophy and Boyle's air-pump experiments—which became paradigmatic for the category of experiment—in particular. Shapin and Schaffer are interested in the work that had to be done to make those experiments (and experiments in general) valuable and solid. They are interested in the work done and the techniques employed by Boyle to convince his peers that the benefits of experimentation overcome its limitations. Experiments, performed in private, produce particular results about nonnatural situations; how these results contribute to public knowledge and are made to stand for the general and the natural is not obvious. Boyle had to convince other natural philosophers that his experiments were essentially public and universalizable. He had a number of responses to this problem. For example, one of the techniques that transferred his experiments from the private to the public realm was a literary one. Boyle, through detailed description of the experimental set-up and results, created the phenomenon of "virtual witnessing" (Shapin and Schaffer 1985, 60ff.). Readers of Boyle's reports could vividly imagine the experiment and its results and, therefore, were witnesses themselves.

Leviathan and the Air-Pump is about the introduction and consolidation of experimental philosophy as a form of life and the opposition to this form of life. Shapin and Schaffer portray the controversy between Hobbes and Boyle as partly one between different conceptions of the social order—both Boyle and Hobbes saw knowledge as the key to a stable social world, but Boyle found stability in matters of fact and Hobbes found stability in self-evident notions.[11] These two sources of stability imply different social configurations: Boyle's matters of fact needed to be attested to by trustworthy witnesses, and Hobbes's self-evident notions could be judged by his readers. *Leviathan and the Air-Pump*, then, explains the rise of the experimental method as part of the consolidation of authority within the natural philosophy community by gentlemen who, by definition, could be trusted (Shapin 1994).

A lesson that Shapin and Schaffer want us to take from their discussion is the general one that "solutions to the problem of knowledge are solutions to the problem of social order" (Shapin and Schaffer, 332). In particular, the boundaries of sets of legitimate problems, questions, and methods are intimately connected to the boundaries of knowledge communities, the consitution, solidity and legitimacy of which are constantly being negotiated (Gieryn 1983). Knowledge communities need to establish spaces, both physical and intellectual, for themselves; they need to draw lines that exclude and include certain people, problems, methods and materials. The boundaries that are drawn are not dictated by problems given by nature but are negotiated in the context of existing intellectual, institutional, and social maps. Postfoundationalist S&TS, then, displays connections between institutions and the knowledges that they create.

Boyle, like all scientists, faced the problem of turning *particular* into *general* knowledge. A result that is only once obtainable or a machine that functions only in one place or at one point in time is usually not very desirable. Artifacts and results that traverse time and space create power through their stability. Thus generality and stability are goals of both science and technology: the decontextualization and delocalization of an achievement—such as a piece of knowledge—is itself an achievement. A considerable amount of work in S&TS can be seen as showing how decontextualization and delocalization are accomplished.

I mentioned earlier the problems of delocalization of technology. The difficulties in the reproduction of artifacts translate into greater difficulties in replication of experiments. An experiment is the production of an effect using a constructed material system. But whereas "working" and "not working" are often relatively easy to determine for a technological artifact,[12] for interesting experiments the proper results are precisely what are at issue. This creates the problem that Harry Collins calls "experimenters' regress": failed attempts at replication of experiments can be dismissed as inadequate, owing to differences in or improper calibration of the equipment, the competence of the experimenters, and so forth (Collins 1992). According to the original experimenters, the only real attempts at replication will be ones in which the experimenters' tools are created or calibrated so that the results are duplicated (or improved in the appropriate way).

To break the experimenters' regress, a convention is made which determines whether or not the phenomenon in question exists. Of course conventions are arrived at on the basis of a wide variety of factors. Some of the responses to Collins's research are:

> Scientist i: ... he is at a very small place ... [but] ... I have looked at his data and he certainly has some interesting data.
>
> Scientist ii: I am not really impressed with his experimental capabilities so I would question anything he has done more than I would question other people's.
>
> Scientist iii: That experiment is a bunch of shit!
> (Collins 1992, 85)

Collins offers a partial list of criteria of acceptance or nonacceptance of results. The list is derived from interviews with scientists about a set of attempts to detect gravity waves:

> Faith in experimental capabilities and honesty,
>   based on a previous working partnership
> Personality and intelligence of experimenter
> Reputation of running a huge lab
> Whether the scientist worked in industry or academia
> Previous history of failures
> "Inside information"
> Style and presentation of results
> Psychological approach to experiment
> Size and prestige of university of origin
> Integration into various scientific networks
> Nationality. (Collins 1992, 87)[13]

As Collins points out, to close a controversy scientists must draw on all available social resources, including the rhetorical resources represented by such a list. For the scientists involved, judgments based on these factors are important; they do real work, and thus are relevant to a naturalistic study of scientific epistemology.

Collins shows us one place in which closure of controversy is difficult, when the controversy is over competing experimental results. But many of the points that he makes are transferable and have been transferred to other scenarios; the "controversy study" looks at scientific knowledge when it is under attack. In that context the work needed to establish and solidify a knowledge claim is made visible through the challenges that the scientific actors make of each others' claims.

Controversies make visible the work to create knowledge, but some work is always necessary, as is shown by Bruno Latour's distinction between two models of delocalization of results (Latour 1987, 132ff.). The "model of diffusion" has results and technologies forcing their own way into circulation; these artifacts move themselves from locale to locale, on the basis of their own strength. The "model of translation" introduces people and institutions as agents in the spread of ideas and things; facts and artifacts have no power to move themselves, and depend upon the push and pull of humans. The model of diffusion is the model tacitly assumed by the rationalist ideology of science—good ideas will flourish. But while there is some value to that picture, it is an idealization to say that ideas can force assent. The successful dissemination of ideas requires that people be persuaded of their value; delocalization is in part effected by successful rhetorical manoeuvre. (To say that it is rhetorical is not necessarily dismissive. I use the term *rhetoric* in a very traditional sense: rhetoric is the art of persuasion. Especially in philosophical contexts, the term is often used in a normative way, to distinguish *merely* persuasive from logical arguments. If we take rhetoric in its broader sense, the point that closure of an argument requires rhetoric is very nearly circular and, thus, is not surprising. Yet it has proven surprisingly easy to forget that persuasion is an aim of scientific communication and, instead, treat writing as the dispassionate relaying of facts. Putting the rhetorical structure and features of the scientific article in the spotlight can help to create a very different image of scientific practice. S&TS has tended to pay close attention to the rhetoric, as part of the study of the work needed to establish knowledge.)

Bruno Latour and Steve Woolgar's *Laboratory Life: The Social Construction of a Scientific Fact* (1986) is another investigation of day-to-day scientific activities, within a framework that attempts to link those activities to the concrete goals of the scientists involved. Attention to the details of scientific activity has helped to make *Laboratory Life* the best read of the laboratory ethnographies and a paradigm of constructivist S&TS. It is based on observations made by Latour during a stay at R. Guillemin's Laboratory at the Salk Institute in La Jolla, California, where Latour watched and participated in work on neuro-endocrinology. The project is an attempt to understand the activities of the scientist as she tries to "create order out of chaos," from analogical thought processes to negotiations within the laboratory to the establishment of careers.

Laboratory Life, like Collins's *Changing Order*, approaches the laboratory with the irreverence necessary for the symmetrical study of science: Latour and Woolgar are interested in science as an economic activity and also as a collection of language games. Looked at in terms of its inputs and outputs, the laboratory can be seen as a factory: its inputs are raw materials, machines, and labor; the output is a steady stream of scientific papers. Thus the laboratory is a site for the transformation of nature into language (though Latour and Woolgar dispute whether nature really enters this site, as will be discussed in the next chapter). Many of the machines, for example, create graphs, charts, and numbers through the manipulation of material objects; these machines are "inscription devices," producing the data that scientists then study (Latour and Woolgar, 51). Shop talk is similar, a stage in the production (and also evaluation) of papers.

Resources can be bought with scientific credibility. Credibility is gained through having articles cited positively; thus citations are the most important goods for scientists to acquire. In this framework the scientific article, then, is a vehicle for the production of citations: it has to be persuasive as well as useful for the production of more articles. The laboratory is a vehicle for the production of articles: persuasive and useful articles are usually written through the use of expensive machinery and skills. The scientist is involved in a "cycle of credit," attempting to buy material resources with credibility and credibility with material resources (Latour and Woolgar, chap. 5). Interestingly, the credit system is in part a product of the needs of rhetoric. Credit attributions help to establish the seriousness a claim should merit: crediting other authors or publications indicates that one draws on others' evidence and authority—the other authors may be thought of as "allies" (Latour 1987). This is another way, then, that rhetoric plays an important part in the success of science.

Andrew Pickering's *Constructing Quarks* is another contribution to this type of project, a story about scientists making choices based mostly on their expertise. For Pickering, the direction that a theory takes depends importantly on the skills that the relevant scientists have; scientists make choices so that they will be able to use their skills in the process of explication of the theory and accounting for new experimental results (Pickering 1984, 11). On a large scale—and *Constructing Quarks* is about large-scale changes, the establishment of the quark-guage theory—successful choice results in the creation of a paradigm; in Pickering's (1992a) terms this is a redefinition of the culture and practices of the field. Like paradigms, practices can be incommensurable: scientific subdisciplines are largely unconnected to, and occasionally incompatible with, other and previous parts of science. After the quark-guage theory became accepted, experimental practices changed dramatically: "The old physics focused upon the most common processes encountered in the HEP (High Energy Physics) laboratory; ... The new physics instead emphasised rare phenomena" (410). Pickering thus sees the change in scientific practices as involving a symbiosis of experiment and theory, where experiment produces phenomena for theory to explain and theory describes the experimental results that should be attainable.

For Pickering, practices are the accepted patterns of action and styles of work; cultures define the scope of available resources (1992a, 3). Opportunistic science, even science that *transforms* cultures and practices, is an attempt to appropriately combine and recombine cultural resources so as to achieve scientists' goals. Practices and cultures provide the context and structure for scientific opportunism. Understanding this context and structure can allow us to give meaning to proximate goals within a rational choice model of science. Latour and Woolgar's "cycle of credibility" is by itself a crude instrument for the explanation of day-to-day actions because it provides no structure for those actions: it does not help us to understand the constraints on scientific actions that allow scientists to choose *this* action over the myriad of others that he or she might also choose to gain credit. Rational choice models need to be situated in a context in which the choices are narrowed and the outcomes of those choices are more clear.

S&TS describes action in science, then, in terms of the opportunistic use of the resources available to scientists. Understanding these resources is essential to understanding scientific rationality because they structure and contain that rationality.

In claiming that S&TS investigates the rationality of science, I am giving a nonstandard interpretation, but it is not a bizarre one. Clearly today's S&TS is antirationalist in the sense introduced in chapter 1: it does not portray the scientific process as a disembodied and asocial set of applications of a small core of rational principles and procedures. Instead S&TS looks at scientists as pursuing goals, using the resources at hand. "Scientific rationality," I would claim, is a historically situated product of that pursuit; how and why it developed become interesting questions. And science's rationality consists of a loose collection of principles open to interpretation and flexibly applied. Such principles are resources to be used in the process of doing scientific work, rather than merely constraints on proper thinking.

Harry Collins, in his article "Stages in the Empirical Programme of Relativism" (1981b), claims that while the first stage of his program in the social study of science is to destabilize the ideology of science, to show the "local interpretative flexibility," the second stage is to show the "mechanisms which limit interpretative flexibility and thus allow controversies to end" (1981b, 4). It is through the work on that second stage, or a generalized version of it, that S&TS contributes to the epistemological project of showing how communities overcome or avoid the problems of skepticism and produce knowledge. S&TS attempts to understand the interpretive, interactive, rhetorical, and other work needed to establish results.

TOWARD A NON-PANGLOSSIAN EVOLUTIONARY EPISTEMOLOGY

Taken together, the vignettes above contribute to an evolutionary epistemology of science. Scientists' high mutual dependence and low task uncertainty creates a fact-producing cognitive style. Facts are desirable entities because they can be put to use as resources in further work. They are resources skilfully applied in the solution of problems and the achievement of goals. Therefore, useful facts will tend to survive in the pool of scientific resources, and falsehoods and useless facts will tend to be forgotten, refuted, or simply left behind.

Evolutionary epistemologies are hardly new, but their potential merits in the context of the social and political analysis of science are not often recognized: an evolutionary framework can actually *use* the social and political bases of science to show how the system can produce truths. David Hull (1988a, 1988b) does this in his attempt to apply a general account of selection processes to scientific knowledge production. In his account of selection there are two types of entities, "replicators" and "interactors." A replicator is "an entity that passes on its structure largely intact in successive replications," and an interactor is "an entity that interacts as a cohesive whole with its environment in such a way that this interaction causes replication to be differential" (Hull 1988b, 408). Then, by selection upon interactors, replicators become differentially represented in the population. In a given environment these will tend to be the ones whose replication is most facilitated by the interactors.

The replicators of science, Hull postulates, are "elements of the substantive content of science—beliefs about the goals of science, proper ways to go about realizing these goals, problems and their possible solutions, modes of representation, accumulated data, and so on" (1988b, 434). The interactors are scientists. Selection takes the form of *use* by some scientists of the replicators produced by others. By definition, often-used replicators become more prominent in the pool.

There are two further assumptions that we must make to turn this selectionist scheme into evolutionary epistemology—that is, to be able to say that the process leads to good representations. First of all, we must assume that scientists are interested in projects for which representation is useful (Hull actually goes futher than this and attributes to them a natural curiosity). This is needed to ensure that the ideas, data, modes of representation, and the like, that are genuinely useful in finding out about the world—rather than merely the ones that are easiest to remember or the ones that come out of Cambridge—can in some circumstances actually survive. Importantly for us here, this is a relatively unproblematic assumption as long as we take it in the deflationary sense that scientists are at least *sometimes* interested in projects for which representation is useful.[14] Even the production of effects, one goal of scientists and technologists, can be facilitated by knowledge.

Second, there must be high mutual dependence around pieces of knowledge and other ideas; there must be *use* of replicators in order for them to replicate. By definition, scientists are mutually dependent when they need to use each others' resources in order to go about their work, and one way in which they typically get access to those resources is through the use of published ideas, the results that others make available in return for credit. As Hull points out, there is a well-established system of exchange of credit for use that reinforces the production and circulation of replicators. Credit is a medium of exchange; use of other people's ideas is in theory supposed to be acknowledged by attributions, or credit: "nowhere else is the interplay between contributions and credit so finely tuned as it is in science" (Hull 1990, 80).

The system of exchange of credit for use means that the ideas that continue to be prominent in the long run are the ones that prove most useful. And one of the ways in which an idea may be useful is if it represents or contains within itself an implicit representation of some portion of the world. At least some of the time the ideas that survive are pieces of knowledge.

A serious criticism of evolutionary epistemologies of science is that they tend to be Panglossian, they tend to assume that everything in science is for the best, in the long run. Hull, for example, recommends against tampering with present systems of socialization and rewards in science, preferring to leave a well-working institution in place (Hull 1988a, 154). Although there are problems in the detection of fraud (Broad and Wade 1982), he is fairly sure that fraud is rare (1988b, 302ff.). And though—as feminist and other critics of science have shown—bias is a common feature of science, he believes that scientists' interests are sufficiently diverse that they usually overcome bias (1988a, 141). I do not want to make such Panglossian claims here; instead I sketched an evolutionary account of science merely to show that it is at least occasionally possible for science to arrive at some approximately true insights about the natural world. But it should also be a part of an evolutionary account to at least point to ways in which science does not track truth.

Feminist standpoint theory can contribute to an understanding of the place of ideology in science (see, for example, Nancy Hartsock 1983; Hilary Rose 1986; Patricia Hill Collins 1986; Sandra Harding 1991; Rosemary Hennessy 1993). Standpoint theorists argue that science that depends upon or supports oppressive structures will tend to pass more easily unchallenged by scientists who come from privileged groups. Some social structures, like the sex/gender system, look natural to oppressors but unnatural to the oppressed. The oppressed, in trying to freely act, feel the constraints of these structures, constraints that result in the maintenance of hierarchy and injustice. Those who are not oppressed by social structures do not feel their constraints and, hence, are not likely to recognize them, or to recognize them as constraining or oppressive. The difference in actions results in a difference of perspective; the perspective of the oppressed is a revealing and privileged one and, conversely, the perspective of oppressors will typically have blind spots. European and American scientists have tended to be males coming from privileged backgrounds, and so science has tended to exclude the standpoint of others.[15]

For example, biological and medical sciences, studies of biological sex differences, classifications of diseases, characterizations of "natural" behavior patterns, and explanations of all of these in terms of human evolutionary history participate in the construction of gender. Feminist scientists in these areas, and feminist critics of science, have uncovered ways in which sexist ideology permeates inquiry: scientists reproduce, explain, strengthen, and amplify social relations that they see in society (e.g., Bleier 1984; Hubbard 1990; Laqueur 1990; Smith-Rosenberg 1985). In an environment that includes widespread sexism, gender norms are typically confused for genetically determined sex characteristics, and sexual relations are seen as constant and fixed. Both are understood as biological givens. Anne Fausto-Sterling, in *Myths of Gender* (1985), looks at a number of studies of biological sex differences, studies that attempt to show that women and men are biologically different and that those differences allow for evaluation of some sort. She looks at a variety of psychological studies claiming that men and women are biologically determined to have different abilities, leading to differing skills in areas like mathematics. Fausto-Sterling also looks at biological studies aimed at showing the existence and importance of premenstrual tension, another attempt to describe important sex differences. Her work shows how poor routine experiments and studies are when they attempt to reinforce stereotypical gender ideas, a poverty difficult for the researchers themselves and many of their colleagues to see but which is easily visible to feminist scientists like Fausto-Sterling. Thus ideology can contribute to an environment in which, rather than tracking truth, scientific ideas systematically diverge from truth.

The evolutionary epistemologist's analogy to natural selection claims that certain features of the replicators of science—that is, features of problems, methods, propositions, concepts—will cause their differential replication. Evolutionary epistemologists are keen to show that truth, fruitfulness, and other such virtues are among the features selected for, rather than against. But as in natural selection, which characteristics are selected *for* and which *against* depends upon the environment. There are environments, like the ideologically frought environments of some biological research, in which certain epistemic virtues are selected against. In keeping with the idea of a deflationary realism, I do not want to claim that the social structure of science guarantees truth tracking, but rather that it occasionally makes truth tracking possible.

Four

EXPLORING METAPHORS OF "SOCIAL CONSTRUCTION"

EVEN THOUGH SOCIAL CONSTRUCTIVISM and constructivism are popular as approaches to science, it is sometimes unclear exactly what it is claimed is constructed and how. This chapter explores what the "social construction" metaphor means in the S&TS literature.[1] The answer will not be straightforward, because "social construction" and "construction" do not generally mean the same thing from one author to another and, even within the same work the terms are meant to draw our attention to several quite different types of phenomena. Bruno Latour and Steve Woolgar (1986) talk about the construction of both facts and things, Trevor Pinch and Wiebe Bijker (1987) about knowledge (until they apply it to technology). From Karin Knorr-Cetina (1983 and elsewhere) one gets the impression that constructivism is a very specific research program, but Pinch and Bijker call all recent S&TS "social constructivist" (18–19). And the construction metaphor has at least six different interpretations/uses. So what is needed is not to clarify something monolithic but to try to understand and chart out the proliferation of senses of a term. This chapter is a start on that project. Because one of my interests here is with the metaphor of "construction," this chapter will ask What is constructed? and In what sense? And because the two labels "constructivism" and "social constructivism" are often used interchangeably by their adherents, I blend together discussions that go under the heading "social constructivist" and those that are simply "constructivist." I try to point out places in which their conflation might be misleading.

The distinct uses of the construction metaphor I discuss here are:

- The construction, through the interplay of actors, of institutions, including knowledge, methodologies, fields, habits, and regulative ideals;
- In particular, the term *social construction* is often used to draw attention to social processes in the construction of scientific knowledge—the emphasis is on *social* rather than *construction*;

- The phrase "heterogeneous construction" draws attention to ways in which scientists use varied resources to build stable structures, resulting in a further description of the building of some types of institutions;
- Scientists construct theories and accounts, in the sense that these are structures that rest upon bases of data and observations;
- They also construct, through material intervention, artifacts in the laboratory;
- Finally, scientists are said to construct, in a neo-Kantian sense, the objects of thoughts and representations.

Some philosophers have dismissed constructivism quickly, finding it "wildly implausible" that representations are ontologically prior to their associated objects, that scientists somehow construct the world when they arrive at a consensus (Giere 1988, 56ff.). But I hope to produce a reading of some constructivist programs that makes them, or at least parts of them, far more plausible; my explorations and parsings make parts of the programs easily defensible. If constructivism is not unitary and the construction metaphor routinely applies to many different things, then it doesn't seem unreasonable to break it up into a number of smaller programs and commitments and ask about the presuppositions of these. What I conclude is that constructivism is often fully compatible with either empiricism or realism and, thus, that constructivism needs no special defense in a field where these are its competitors. And when it is *not* so compatible, the incompatibilities are created by the parts of the constructivist programs that are least thoroughly argued for, and often least central to constructivist sociologists' and historians' practice, playing a peripheral rhetorical role.

BERGER AND LUCKMAN

The basic ideas behind social construction have been floating around for a long time—since Marx at least, for the main points, and since much before him for some others. But *The Social Construction of Reality*, by Peter Berger and Thomas Luckmann (1966), is the recent source of the *phrase* "social construction" and an important recent source of the interest in processes of social construction under that name. I begin with a discussion of their work because it illustrates one form of construction, the construction of institutions. I claim that this type of social construction is central to, though not a large part of the rhetoric of S&TS. I do not want to imply, though, that Berger and Luckmann represent an important part of the history of sociology of science, or even of constructivism within S&TS, even if they did introduce the phrase "social construction." Indeed, if constructivism is composed of a number of distinct types of claims, any history of that bundle is likely to be extremely complex.

Berger and Luckmann make two bold claims: "that reality is socially constructed and that the sociology of knowledge must analyze the processes in which this occurs." Their title and subtitle promise that these claims are really one; their work is *The Social Construction of Reality: A Treatise in the Sociology of Knowledge*. And their rationale for this is straightforward:

> It is our contention, then, that the sociology of knowledge must concern itself with whatever passes for "knowledge" in a society.... And insofar as all human "knowledge" is developed, transmitted and maintained in social situations, the sociology of knowledge must seek to understand the processes by which this is done in such a way that a taken-for-granted "reality" congeals for the man in the street. In other words, we contend that *the sociology of knowledge is concerned with the analysis of the social construction of reality*. (3, emphasis in original)

But there is something unsatisfying about this. Here "reality" is in scare quotes, as is "knowledge" (except in the emphasized clause, where quotation marks would be repetitive), whereas the words are left unmodified in the title. Are we getting less than we were promised? I think not. Instead it seems to me that Berger and Luckmann were carried away with caution here, or have in mind a larger project to which this book makes only a very small contribution. Their work is as much about the social construction of reality as of "reality," though in making this point we might drive a small wedge between the title and subtitle. It is the distinction between the constructions of reality and of "reality" that I want to explore here, using these terms roughly the way Berger and Luckmann do: "*Reality*" (in scare quotes) refers to subjective reality, or people's beliefs about the world. *Reality* (without scare quotes) refers to the rest of the real world, objective reality, or that which cannot be wished away (Berger and Luckmann's definition).

Their discussion of quotation marks appear in a (now) familiar-looking preamble concerning the scope of sociology of knowledge and the necessity for agnosticism on the validity of knowledge claims.

> If we were going to be meticulous in the ensuing argument we would put quotation marks around the two aforementioned terms ["reality" and "knowledge"] every time we used them, but this would be stylistically awkward. (1–2)

The philosopher is driven to decide where the quotation marks are in order and where they may safely be omitted, that is, to differentiate between valid and invalid assertions about the world. This the sociologist cannot possibly do. Logically, if not stylistically, he is stuck with the quotation marks. (2)

Berger and Luckmann, sociologists rather than philosophers, become agnostics with respect to knowledges and realities, at least for the purpose of doing sociology. They can drop the quotation marks for stylistic reasons while admitting that they remain present in theory. The move is familiar, because it is the methodological agnosticism of S&TS, also found in Bloor (1991), Collins (1981a), Latour and Woolgar (1986), Latour (1987), and other explorations by sociologists of science on the foundations of their discipline. Agnosticism is a useful tool in the S&TS and for sociology; it creates more room for the social.

But *The Social Construction of Reality* is not a precursor to S&TS. Its focus, derived in part from the work of Alfred Schutz, is on ordinary knowledge of the sort that we need to make our way about society. This is an intentional turn away from the emphases of earlier sociology of knowledge, which Berger and Luckmann see "as a sort of sociological gloss on the history of ideas" (4). While they may make room for sociology of science, their interest is in large cultures rather than subcultures, society rather than societies, and their primary interest is knowledge *of* society. Thus the majority of their book is in two large sections apparently as much about society as about knowledge: "Society as Objective Reality" and "Society as Subjective Reality."

In the first of these two sections, Berger and Luckmann discuss two important social processes, institutionalization and legitimation. Here, institutions are thought of broadly, including social roles, customs, and the like. Looking at the literature indebted to *The Social Construction of Reality*, we see that it is these discussions that have borne the most fruit and that have defined for many, particularly outside of S&TS, the scope of the term *social construction*. Thus Berger and Luckmann's discussions may now appear trite and simple: the central point is that institutions have reality. "We recognize [them] as having a being independent of our own volition (we cannot 'wish them away')" (1). But since institutions can in no way be thought of as natural, in the way that water, rocks, trees, and newts can, they have to be human products. This is one way in which people produce reality, not just "reality."

Institutionalization comes about through habitualization, to which "all human activity is subject" (50). When habitualized actions are recognized and involve interactions of more than one type of actor, and these actors play roles with respect to each other, then there exist institutions, by

Berger and Luckmann's definition. The actors have constructed a "background of routine" (54), which constrains behavior through its momentum, and through sanctions when necessary. The momentum of an institution is maintained by socialization and legitimation. Legitimation involves the creation of meanings that integrate institutions. Socialization comes about because children and newcomers to the society see the institution as an objective fact. Knowledge, then, plays an important role in the maintenance of institutions; knowledge of an institution reinforces it, making it more objective: "Knowledge about society is thus a realization in the double sense of the word, in the sense of apprehending the objectivated social reality, and in the sense of ongoingly producing this reality" (62). Sociology of knowledge, then, may be extremely relevant to understanding social construction, though we should note that we did not have to do any interesting or deep sociology in order to accept these constructions. The central point, or at least the central insight, here is one about social metaphysics rather than epistemology.[2]

The second of the two large sections of *The Social Construction of Reality* involves the sociology of knowledge more directly. "Society as Subjective Reality" is a closer look at socialization and the maintenance of knowledge about objective reality. It is a theoretical treatment of the techniques by which a person's perception of society is made to match objective reality. It tells us about the construction of "reality" rather than reality. It isn't necessary to describe this section in more detail here; it is a general, theoretical treatment of the sociology of knowledge, predating the extensive work in sociology of scientific knowledge of the past fifteen years.

Berger and Luckmann have shown us how institutions are human products of an interesting sort. Institutions exist because a significant portion of society knows them to exist, and acts accordingly. This doesn't make them any less real: we cannot "wish them away," precisely because so many other people know them to exist. Thus we must act accordingly, often reinforcing the institutions in the process. This lesson is the important one that people have taken from *The Social Construction of Reality* and is one that appears frequently in the work that appropriates the phrase "social construction" and its legacy.

The emphasis that I am placing on the creation of objective realities like institutions creates a problem for the construction metaphor: it is difficult to see the type of *action* that constructions would seem to require. We think of constructing as a process involving active rather than passive movements, and often goal-directed ones. According to the story that Berger and Luckmann tell, institutions are *accretions,* perhaps only supported by constructions like ideologies, religions, and histories. The accretion versus construction issue is only a trivial problem, though it is indicative of a larger one, stemming from a lack of distinction between the constructions in the two sections of the book. Construction terminology, when dealing with subjective reality (beliefs or knowledge), has a certain history, coming from geometry through psychology. The vehicle of the metaphor has to do with geometrical construction, whereby a figure is created given a few fixed points and some tools. For example, a Greek mathematical game involved the construction of lines of various lengths, given a compass, straight edge, and a line of unit length. In a similar way, for Berger and Luckmann the individual is given a small number of phenomena from which she must construct a workable account of the world. In this they follow the phenomenology of Schutz and Husserl and the work of Piaget, all of whom also use the construction metaphor. But this geometrical explanation does not carry over well to the social construction of objective reality, for *that* process is one that does not need a knowing actor to put all of the pieces together. It is more akin to an evolutionary process, a blind creation of new realities, at least as Berger and Luckmann describe it.

This observation does not mean that we should change our terminology. Sociologists and historians after Berger and Luckmann have put actors more into the picture, thus improving the metaphor. But it does point to a difference between the construction of accounts and the construction of institutions, though how we should characterize that difference might be left open for the moment.

AFTER BERGER AND LUCKMANN: ARGUING FOR SOCIAL OBJECTS

Social construction talk has taken off. It is a phrase now found in the discourses of almost all humanities and social sciences disciplines, though often "socially constructed" means nothing more specific than "of social origin." In some areas and specialties, the connection to Berger and Luckmann's construction of "objective reality" are stronger, and in some cases constructivist research programs have arisen. For example, psychologists and philosophers looking at the emotions and their cultural variation have postulated that emotions are at least partially socially constructed (see Harré 1986 for a collection of such work). There may be a material basis to emotions, but distinctions such as that between envy and jealousy require a moral order. Or, in a different field, Barry Barnes has developed an analysis of power such that power is almost entirely socially constructed (Barnes 1988). At the social level, he claims, power is a function of everybody's beliefs about power; a person is powerful because a sufficiently large number of people believe her to be.

But the field of gender studies is where constructivist ideas have been used most. It should surprise nobody that people studying gender have found the notion of social construction useful. Indeed, once one understands the distinction between the terms *sex* and *gender*, as they are commonly used in recent texts, one understands that gender is a social construction. Gender roles have a history, are reinforced by social knowledge, are given legitimation through connections with other institutions, and cannot be "wished away," as has been shown by the only partial success of the last 150 years of feminist activism. And although *The Social Construction of Reality* was not a work of feminist sociology, Berger and Luckmann clearly saw that gender fit their analysis; a number of their examples involve gender and sex roles (see also Berger and Kellner 1964).

The large amount of research on gender roles has created a rich picture of the ways in which social construction works. Whereas Berger and Luckmann focused on religion as a source of legitimation, scholars of gender have seen the importance of literature, science, history, film, romantic and household roles, and other intellectual and cultural arenas as sources of enculturation and legitimation.[3] Whereas from Berger and Luckmann one gets an impression of fairly simple, uniform roles, feminist scholars have drawn our attention to the multiplicity of competing roles.[4] In short, work on gender and its "deconstruction" has helped to develop the idea of social construction of objective realities.

It should be clear, then, that a great many things can be socially constructed in Berger and Luckmann's sense. To construct an X we need only a few things: (a) knowledge of X has to produce behaviors that impinge on and reduce other people's ability to act as though X does not exist, (b) there has to be reasonably common knowledge of X, and (c) there has to be a method of transmission of knowledge of X. Given these things, knowledge of X becomes "fixed," or virtually ubiquitous in the community. By analogy to institutions like gender and emotions, X exists: it cannot be wished away. Gender is real because we are forced to take account of it in our dealings with other members of our communities. That is, gender structures in society create constraints and resources with which people have to reckon and which have psychological effects: treating people as gendered creates gendered people. Genders have causal powers, which is probably the best sign of reality that we have. Yet they are undoubtedly not simply given by nature, as historical research and divergences between cultures show us.

Likewise many products of science must be taken account of within the scientists' communities, and they have causal powers. And these products are social constructs, created, disseminated, and agreed upon by social groups, as the S&TS literature shows us. But nobody need find this too unsettling. Berger and Luckmann tell stories about the creation of institutions, what one might call "social objects." As Ronald Giere points out, institutions are primarily social realities, rather than purely material ones, and it is social reality that is socially constructed in Berger and Luckmann's sense (Giere 1988). The idea of a social reality isn't particularly new or strange; such social objects as institutions or concepts are a long-standing part of intellectual life. Consequently, rationalist historians and philosophers of science may be bored by this argument for social constructions.

While boredom is a natural response, it is the wrong one. It neglects the extent to which scientists (and others) spend their time and energy dealing with social objects. If there is one lesson that we should draw from S&TS it is that. Seen from another angle, scientists' actions are theory-dependent and their work on theory takes place primarily in a social context, not in a context where influences on them are largely inputs from the rest of the natural world. Even their impressions of these inputs are guided by social objects. Rationalism will not suffice, and philosophers of science should pay more attention to social objects. To make the reasons for this more clear I will give two short examples of areas in which philosophers have tended to leave out the social world, even when it is philosophically important.[5]

When philosophers attempt to characterize scientific arguments, they usually work starting from the model and standards of purely logical arguments connecting data and hypotheses. This isn't to say that they expect science to be fully describable as a set of logical moves, but that those are starting points from which science deviates—perhaps necessarily deviates. But in so doing philosophers might miss the importance of discussions that are outside the scope of evidence relations, narrowly conceived. Discussions of the status and importance of competitors, for example, are an integral part of the evaluation of their claims. Scientists with few credentials can be disregarded, if necessary, and should be disregarded if their claims are sufficiently radical. This is not merely to save time allowing researchers to address the concerns of the important players in the field, but also to deal with that large number of cases in which other standards of evidence do not allow the data to speak univocally. That is, credentials are taken to be credentials of something, namely expertise. Ad hominem arguments, then, are in some cases extremely important in determining whom to believe, even if it seems that most of the work that they do is social, defining the boundaries of a specialty or community.[6]

Another feature of science that philosophers have tended to ignore is experiment. While philosophers of science routinely recognize the importance of experiment, it is usually discussed only in its relation to theory; experiments can refute, provide support for, or lead to, theory. Until recently, experiment was rarely treated as an interesting feature of science in its own light and, even now relatively few philosophers have paid serious attention to it (e.g., Hacking 1983; Franklin 1986, 1990; Galison 1987). One reason is that experiment is treated as though it provides a fairly well-understood window on the world, even as we pay lip service to its complexity and its social dimensions. Experiments are thought of as a supply of data for theorists, and experimenters as mere technicians, applying and testing theories.

To say that experiments are social enterprises is not to denigrate them; techniques, procedures, resources, and organization in the laboratory are clearly part of a social world that is inseparable from the laboratory itself. As such, all of these things deserve further study. But even within the realm of philosophy's standard concerns, the social nature of experiment can be extremely important. For example, one can look at the choosing of controls. This is a complex—and immensely social—process that, among other things, aims to define a list of factors that might influence the subject of the experiment and, thus, aims to define a range of possible "theories" the discipline might consider relevant. Leaving aside complexities arising both from the implementation of these controls and the interpretation of results, experiments provide information only in the context of these lists of social objects, possible causes and theories that the community is willing to seriously entertain. This shows the partiality of experimental tests; these can only be tests in comparison to alternatives already at least partly thought through.

Implicit here is a distinction between social objects and material objects, or between social worlds and material ones. This is a difficult distinction to make sharply. The most obvious strategy—to say that social objects are most of those whose constitution depends on the continued presence of human actors—suffers both from vagueness and from the fact that it begs the question against some of those who are social constructivists about all types of objects. It is likely to go hand in hand with an assumption that there are things that are *not* dependent upon human representation, which some constructivists would deny. The fuzziness of this distinction is unlikely to go away without a considerably more full exploration than I can offer here. But I hope to be able to avoid begging questions, so I will claim that the distinction can be drawn roughly along the line of meaningfulness: social objects must be meaningful, whereas material objects are only meaningful when they are incorporated into the social. Meaningfulness might be one way in which we could characterize the difference between the social and the material. I'll give one short example, which will become relevant again later in this chapter. The example plays on intuitions that large, simple objects exist before anybody has noticed them.

A small uninhabited island in the middle of the Pacific Ocean may never have been noticed before a European or Polynesian traveller saw it. Once it is found it acquires a place on charts, maps, and directions. It thus enters a European or Polynesian world as a meaningful object, placed on such and such a route between other meaningful objects, and offering certain resources. It is thus part of some social world or other. Before it had been seen, however, it certainly must have existed, for our experience with islands is that they are generally enduring objects, their existence having little to do with explorers. Since it was not part of a social world, its existence indicates a difference between social and material objects. By extension of this example, it should be clear how social worlds and material worlds can be conceptually built up.

Adding the dimension of social realities necessarily complicates our accounts of scientists' actions, but I think that it does only that; it doesn't add substantial ontological or metaphysical problems. It creates the task of working out the relationships between these social realities and material ones and between the social realities and scientific knowledge. But adding social realities might help us to work through analytical problems. Bruno Latour's "three little dinosaurs," in which the supposedly real ones seem to change with each change in scientists' representations of them, become simply a puzzle to be worked through, not a "sociologist's nightmare" (Latour 1980).

SOCIAL CONSTRUCTION IN SCIENCE AND TECHNOLOGY STUDIES: A WEAK READING

Use of the term *social construction* in S&TS started to become common in the late 1970s. The earliest uses of it to describe a research program are in the first volume of the Yearbook of the Sociology of the Sciences: *The Social Production of Scientific Knowledge* (Mendelsohn et al. 1977). There, it appears not only in the editorial statement but also as an important part of two articles by Everett Mendelsohn and Wolfgang van den Daele on historiography and on the establishment of a new scientific methodology in the seventeenth century (Mendelsohn 1977; van den Daele 1977).[7] Both articles argue that the institutions of the new science and its epistemologies were heavily influenced by social and political considerations. Certain antiauthoritarian views, for example, were adopted because of a prevalent antiauthoritarian political spirit, especially in Britain. Yet freedom from authority required concessions on subject matter: the Royal Society's restriction of approach to a nonspeculative examination of the natural world (not to meddle "with Divinity, Metaphysics, Moralls, Politicks, Grammar, Rhetoric, or Logick") helped to avoid conflicts with competing institutions and led to an empiricism that we associate with science today.

Mendelsohn and van den Daele argue that modern science and its epistemology are not adequately accounted for by a purely rationalist, internalist history of science. These institutions are not natural, in the sense that they were not read off nature as the best ways of finding out about the world. Therefore they are socially constructed; the causes of their development include social causes. But that is as far as Mendelsohn and van den Daele push the term *social construction*. Internalism about institutions and their methodologies is inadequate. Mendelsohn, for example, says:

> What I have tried to illustrate in this section is the manner in which the forces active in the social order played a critical role (though not the only role) in the establishment of the scientific way of knowing—the epistemology of modern science. The sources of empiricism were clearly present at the cognitive level and perhaps, more importantly, at the practical level among the skilled craftsmen and artist-engineers (identified by Zilsel) who bridged the chasm between scholarship and manual activity. (Mendelsohn 1977, 19)

Today rationalist history of science looks weak and, consequently, these claims themselves look weak. Institutions are created and shaped not to fit a preordained natural space but as a result of the pressures, needs, and interests of the actors involved. Even if we extend the claims to include not only these institutions but also scientific results, this type of social constructivism is relatively uncontroversial in current S&TS; epistemologies and knowledge claims are also human products and thus are generally accepted to be shaped by social forces.

In calling such work "weak" I am not intending to belittle it. This line of research is the backbone of constructivist S&TS, not only in that it is the most common form of constructivism but also in that it has produced a wealth of interesting results. Displaying the social processes that lead to institutions, epistemologies, and knowledges has helped to erase the positivist picture of science. Weak social constructivism is an important part of the postfoundationalist project in S&TS, because it makes science and technology into human, social, and historical endeavors. It shows the contingent nature of beliefs, results, and social configurations.

To see how this use of "social construction" can play itself out, I want to look at one recent example. Greg Myers, explaining each of the parts of his title *Writing Biology: Texts in the Social Construction of Scientific Knowledge* says "*Social construction* allies the book with those sociologists who see science as the product of social processes" (Myers 1990, xi). To be sure that the alliance is complete, Myers gives three of his chapters titles that begin with "Social construction." In each of these chapters he shows how 'social' considerations, mostly considerations of the identities and interests of the readers, shaped the writing of grant proposals, talks, and articles, producing works that were suited to promoting the authors' and reviewers' interests while catering to the readers'.

For example, Myers shows that the review process through which articles submitted to journals pass involves a negotiation of the level and status of the claims made. He argues this in a concrete way, using two articles, each of which was revised and submitted more than once. Leaving aside the fact that in the cases he chooses there was little real negotiation (the authors had nothing to offer in addition to their original articles) there are interesting observations here. At least in articles of the type Myers examines—ones which make large claims on the basis of familiar data—much of what is at issue is the scope of the claim. It can be presented as having more or less generality of scope, and at a more or less theoretical level (Pinch 1985). Authors generally try to make the claim as strong as possible, and, in these cases, reviewers try to weaken it and to reject the paper if the level of scope or theory is not appropriate for the journal. According to Myers, the result of this process is often the publication of a scientific claim that, because of the negotiation involved, is socially constructed.

Given that these are the types of construction processes Myers describes, he is clearly using "social construction" to mean that social processes are involved. For Myers, for a claim to be socially constructed means that before it is published the claim is talked about, changed, and usually weakened. Claims do not just spring from the subject matter onto paper, via passive scientists and reviewers.

This is what Myers generally means by "social construction," not only in practice, but also in his explanations of that practice. For example, he says:

> My stance in the studies so far is to assume that many readers will be surprised by the view that science is constructed in social processes of claims and negotiation, carried out in revisions of articles and proposals and in ironic reinterpretations in controversies. This stance assumes that many readers, especially nonscientists, will start with a different view of the work of science from that which I am proposing, a view that sees the main work of science as passively observing natural facts. (141)

Even his statement of alliance with social constructivists makes science "a product of social processes," which is consistent with a "weak" reading of his use of "social construction." But Myers's position is not unambiguous; when he makes statements such as "The question ... is not how reality is transformed in texts, but how it is made by texts," (98) he seems to indicate that he is interested in a stronger reading. Nonetheless, even if my characterization does not capture all of Myers's intentions (though I think it does capture the dominant ones), it certainly describes his analyses. In short, what social construction means to Myers is similar to what it means to Everett Mendelsohn and Wolfgang van den Daele. It means that distinctly social processes are involved in the construction of institutions and subjective realities.

One core meaning of social construction in S&TS is that the production of agreement depends upon social processes. This is in opposition to the rationalist paradigm in philosophy of science. Because this constructivism is relatively uncontroversial and almost ubiquitous, I will leave it aside and focus on a number of other uses and extensions of the metaphor in S&TS. I look at four important texts or sets of texts, often taken to be exemplars of social constructivist work. They are: Karin Knorr-Cetina's[8] articulations of a constructivist approach published between 1977 and 1983; Bruno Latour and Steve Woolgar's *Laboratory Life* (1979); Woolgar's *Science: The Very Idea*; and *The Social Construction of Technological Systems*, by Wiebe Bijker, Thomas Hughes, and Trevor Pinch (1989). The first two of these are interesting because of their early use of the construction metaphor, the third because it pushes the metaphor forcefully, and the last because it must make the metaphor more definite as it attempts to apply it to a new area, the social study of technology.

KNORR-CETINA

Karin Knorr-Cetina labels her project "constructivist" rather that "social constructivist," perhaps because she wants to avoid having her work placed in the context in which I am placing her here, in a history that includes constructions of institutions or social objects. As we will see, her constructivism does not completely belong in this context. But her work has been influential, and many sociologists, including herself, have not distinguished between her work and "*social* constructivist" work in S&TS (for example, Pinch and Bijker 1987; Knorr-Cetina 1983).

Knorr-Cetina's constructivist program has a number of similarities to Berger and Luckmann's social constructivist one. The most prominent of these is large and general: both programs pay close attention to the microsociological in order to explain the macrosociological. The genesis of features of the social world have to be found in ordinary actions and beliefs.

> The inclination to adopt what can loosely be described as a constructivist perspective is characterized by a concern for the processes by which outcomes are brought about through the mundane transactions of participants. It entails the assumption that

outcomes are the result of participants' interactive and interpretive work. (Knorr-Cetina and Mulkay 1983, 8)

For Knorr-Cetina this focus on the mundane leads her to, or is connected with, an interest in laboratory ethnographies and anthropological studies of scientists. In her discussions, these interests cannot be completely separated, as she argues that anthropological studies are the best way of working on the constructivist program. The anthropological approach involves "direct observation of the actual site of scientific work (frequently the scientific laboratory) in order to examine how objects of knowledge are constituted in science" (Knorr-Cetina 1983, 117). Much of the development of her constructivist position occurs in discussions of her pioneering laboratory ethnography work of the mid–1970s. There Knorr-Cetina's interests are often explicitly methodological and philosophical, especially when she is attempting to promote her new, anthropological approach to the study of science.

An important first premise in Knorr-Cetina's work is that scientific laboratories have been largely misunderstood to be places where ideas are tested and sometimes generated. In contrast to this, she wants to see labs as places where things are made to work. This would have been particularly evident in the projects that she was following, which involved the extraction of plant proteins. It is the process that she wants to emphasize, the production of effects, the refinement of techniques, the calibration of instruments. If processes are given increased importance in our view of laboratory work, then we are allowed to ask: "What if science (and scientific progress) were never primarily concerned with systems of ideas?" (Knorr 1979, 348). Instead of seeing scientific theories in terms of truth and falsity, "scientific activities can also be seen as a progressive *selection of what works* by using what *has worked* in the past and what *is likely to work* under the present, idiosyncratic circumstances" (369). Then we are left with an empiricist (or perhaps pragmatist) view of theories in which "theories are the cocoons left behind when practice is abstracted from the conduct of inquiry" (370). Ideas exist only to facilitate intervention, taking account of the manipulable edges of the material world.

Empiricist roots of Knorr-Cetina's constructivism can also be seen in her occasional use of Bas van Fraassen's arguments against realism (Knorr 1977, 672–73; repeated in Knorr-Cetina 1981). On analogy with the processes of evolution, we need not postulate that scientific theories are true but only that they are successful. The mouse that runs from the cat need not have a correct picture of the danger, though because of the success of mice in general we know that it must have some prompt to run. The mouse, like the activities of science, is the product of a "selection of what works," guaranteeing a certain measure of success. Knorr-Cetina's concern here and throughout much of this period of her work is to establish the merits of her constructivist program over a "descriptivist" one, the latter closely linked to scientific realism. "Rather than considering scientific products as somehow capturing what is, we will consider them as selectively carved out, transformed and constructed from whatever is" (Knorr-Cetina 1981, 3).

Thus one way that we can cash out Knorr-Cetina's metaphor of construction is the empiricist way, the construction of images, accounts, or theories given the data. This takes seriously her picture of theories as cocoons, objects made to facilitate empirical success, but not goals in and of themselves. Science is constructive in the geometrical sense, making patterns appear given the fixed points that practice produces. Van Fraassen explains his choice of the phrase "*constructive* empiricism" as the label for his view through model-building: "I use the adjective 'constructive' to indicate my view that scientific activity is one of construction of rather than discovery: construction of models that must be adequate to the phenomena, and not discovery of truth concerning the unobservable" (van Fraassen 1980, 5). Knorr-Cetina's use of "constructive" owes something to this picture of theories as well.

More than van Fraassen, Knorr-Cetina has a professional interest in the history of theories. Whereas the "constructive empiricist" philosopher wants to show the possibility of the empirical adequacy of theories, Knorr-Cetina, as sociologist as well as philosopher, wants to learn about the way in which the successful scientific practice comes about. The selection process becomes important for her, and "constructed" is equated with "decision-impregnated" (Knorr-Cetina 1982, 126), an equation which has retained some currency. Even with this addition, her empiricist construction primarily involves the construction of conceptual entities. In Berger and Luckmann's terminology, this is the construction of "subjective reality." But Knorr-Cetina is interested in other scientific products as well as the subjective ones. She is interested in the ones that constrain scientists: the certainties, the techniques, the material environments—in short, Berger and Luckmann's "objective reality." Leaving aside the material for the moment, the rest can easily be grouped together as institutions.

The parallels to Berger and Luckmann's primary notion of social construction are generally not explicit in Knorr-Cetina's work, but there is no question that she has an interest in describing scientists as inhabiting a world of their own construction. Knorr-Cetina complicates matters by deliberately lumping together the material, conceptual, and institutional as simply "scientific products," implicitly denying the value of such distinctions. But her interest in social, as well as material, reality comes through in the use of phrases like "objects of knowledge" and "knowledge objects":

> The [anthropological] approach has chosen direct observation of the actual site of scientific work (frequently the scientific laboratory) in order to examine how objects of knowledge are constituted in science. Both approaches [the anthropological and that of the strong program] are social in that they consider the objects of knowledge as the outcomes of processes which invariably involve more than one individual, and which normally involve individuals at variance with one another in relevant respects. (Knorr-Cetina 1983, 117)

Knorr-Cetina is talking about not just the material objects of knowledge, although we will see how they might be included as well. Instead the phrase "objects of knowledge" has a Platonic ring, except that these objects are not permanent, each having a "genesis" and "transformations." Given her protestation that "a constructivist interpretation of knowledge is not to be confused with an idealist ontology" (Knorr 1979, 369) an interpretation of these objects of knowledge as similar to Berger and Luckmann's objective reality looks natural: she can agree that "for participants, established scientific results become part of an independent, technical realm" (Knorr-Cetina and Mulkay 1983, 13).

The construction metaphor now has to be spelled out in terms of the negotiations and transactions that are necessary to transform a claim into a "taken-for-granted object." It is in spelling out these actions that the constructivist program has had some of its successes, showing the literary, rhetorical, and persuasive techniques that are needed to convince the community and, thereby, create an object. Whereas for Berger and Luckmann the creation of objects would be better described as accretion, Knorr-Cetina and other constructivists have added a richness to the description of this process such that that criticism no longer applies. The construction metaphor is adequate if we think of it in terms of large, multiauthored projects like the construction of cities, legislation, or economies where the result comes about because of competition ("individuals at variance with one another") as well as cooperation.

There is another emphasis in Knorr-Cetina's work that provides us with a considerably different reading of the construction metaphor and a quite different type of construction of objective reality. This is an emphasis on the artificiality of the laboratory itself.

> In the laboratory scientists operate upon (and within) a highly preconstructed artificial reality.... But the source materials with which scientists work are also preconstructed. Plant and assay rats are specially grown and selectively bred. Most of the

substances and chemicals used are purified and are obtained from the industry which serves the science or from other laboratories.... In short, nowhere in the laboratory do we find the 'nature' or 'reality' which is so crucial to the descriptivist interpretation of inquiry: To the observer from the outside world, the laboratory displays itself as a site of action from which 'nature' is as much as possible excluded rather than included. (Knorr-Cetina 1983, 119)

This is linked to the concern with selection because "the scientific laboratory consists of materializations of earlier scientific selections; this accounts for its artifactual character"(121). These preconditions of work in the laboratory are also products of science, like theories and techniques, and are equally constructed. But they are constructed in a very different manner, being intrinsically material products rather than conceptual or social ones. The construction metaphor has changed to have something like an industrial or craft interpretation.

The mixing of an empiricist, social, and more material uses of the construction metaphor is not just made by Knorr-Cetina. One interesting and concise example occurs in Stefan Hirschauer's fascinating and otherwise meticulous discussion of surgical practices:

One "leafs through" the three-dimensional patient-body to find the two-dimensional structure of anatomical pictures. Section after section, the proper anatomy of the ideal body is *engraved* on these layers. One *inscribes* the structures which a normal, proper body should have into the patient-body. One removes the idiosyncracies of its "illness," and on the way to this goal one performs exposition and dissection to shape the structures of the anatomical body out of the raw material. In this respect, plastic operations, such as "sex changes," are operations *par excellence*, with the anatomical perspective coming into its own.... *The anatomical body is the result of a sculptured practice.* (Hirschauer 1991, 312, emphasis added)

While attention to the artificiality of the world of the scientist is not new—Gaston Bachelard (1984) and Ian Hacking (1983) are prominent among those who also discuss it—it is something to which relatively little attention had been paid when Knorr-Cetina's work was being done. She forcefully exposes the constructed nature of the laboratory to show us another example of "decision-impregnated" and "decision-impregnating" scientific products and thereby question the extent to which science can describe nature. This insight is interesting enough that it should force us to think about its consequences more fully. What, for example, is acceptable in the production of artificial phenomena such that we still take science to be referring to nature? Or what constitutes the mind-independence tenet of realism?[9]

Because the artificiality of the laboratory is an important insight, I want to give one example of an area in which its implications need to be thought through. People suspicious of reductionism tend to see the issue in terms of questions about the possibility of learning about wholes through looking at the properties of their parts in isolation. Complex systems cannot be studied just by looking at all of their components, for that leaves out interactions. In contrast to that, fans of reductionism claim that there are no features of wholes that are in principle impossible to discover by studying their parts. And they point to the many very real successes that reductionistic research programs have had. In some ways this seems to be partly a debate between people who do and do not want to see nature excluded from the laboratory, in that reductionists advocate studying small things in isolation. But if we take the full extent of the artificiality of the laboratory seriously, the issue becomes more complicated, because what is studied is not examined in isolation but often in situations extremely dissimilar to those found in nature. Endocrinology, for example, does not just study the effects of certain hormones on pieces of tissue isolated from the organism but studies the effects of massive doses of hormones on these tissues, which have themselves been extensively prepared for the study. So scientists engaged in reductionistic research have in some ways been more successful than even their fans give them credit for, because they are more steps removed from whole systems than is commonly presumed. At the same time it seems more likely that properties of wholes are being missed. While this obviously does not decide the reductionism/holism debate, recognizing the artificiality of the laboratory might provide some new types of examples to think about and *might* provide some new insights as to why reductionism succeeds as much as it does.

I mentioned above that Knorr-Cetina glides over the distinction between social realities and material ones. It should now be clear why this is an important issue. Scientists inhabit a world in which both the social and many of the material realities that they encounter are constructed. Many of the social realities are supposed to take account of or mimic the material ones, and some material realities are constructed with help from the social ones. So if we don't distinguish between the different construction processes we find ourselves describing a circle in which any pretense of descriptions of nature disappears:

> The vision behind the constructive programme as I conceive of it is that of a potentially increasing stock of problems created by science in the process of secreting an unending stream of entities and relations that make up "the world." (Knorr-Cetina 1983, 135)

The descriptions that scientists construct are then of the newly created entities, rather than preexisting natural ones.

The material objects that scientists study are different from social ones in *some* interesting ways. They are made from other material objects, rather than just actions. Sometimes, if rarely, they are not even constructed or manipulated by people, as in the case of the objects that some naturalists, geologists, and early astronomers have studied. And Nancy Cartwright is right in seeing them as embodying natural "capacities," perhaps the important objects of scientific knowledge (Cartwright 1989a). Whether these differences are sufficient to get us out of the constructivist circle would have to be argued, but they are suitably striking to show that my distinctions between constructions in Knorr-Cetina's work are not out of line.

LATOUR AND WOOLGAR

Bruno Latour and Steve Woolgar's *Laboratory Life: The Social Construction of Scientific Facts* (1979)[10] has a similar framework to that of Knorr-Cetina, thus allowing me to move quickly over their work to what I see are some difficulties around the products of construction.

Latour and Woolgar put the label of "constructive" on the same types of processes as does Knorr-Cetina. There are the operations involved in the construction of knowledge. For example, Latour and Woolgar chronicle the topsy-turvy fate of the statement "TRF (Thyrotropin Releasing Factor) is Pyro-Glu-His-Pro-NH$_2$" as it moves from being unsayable to possible to false to possibly true to a fact, undeniable by anybody in the field. Along the way, they chart out the different operations that can be done on a scientific paper: ignoring it to detract, citing it positively, citing it negatively, questioning it (in stronger and weaker ways), and ignoring it because it is accepted by everybody. Latour and Woolgar introduce the concept of a "modality"—a modifier of a statement that marks, or in some cases establishes, the level of fact-likeness of the statement—and show how scientists can wield modalities to help push statements in the direction they would prefer.

There is also the construction of patterns and conceptual order (33–38, 168–73). While the construction of theories occupies a less prominent place in *Laboratory Life* than in Knorr-Cetina's work, the creation of patterns, especially through the help of machines—inscription devices, one or more apparatuses that "can transform a material substance into a figure or diagram which is directly usable by one of the members of the office space" (51)—is one of Latour and Woolgar's central concerns. As they point out, inscription devices push the topic of conversation in the laboratory to the inscriptions and away from the material substances, the former being taken to have a direct relationship to the latter.

Latour and Woolgar also recognize the construction of phenomena in the laboratory, and, drawing on Bachelard, call this the "phenomenotechnique."

> The central importance of this material arrangement is that none of the phenomena "about which" participants talk could exist without it.... It is not simply that phenomena *depend on* certain material instrumentation; rather, the phenomena *are thoroughly constituted* by the material setting of the laboratory. The artificial reality, which participants describe in terms of an objective entity, has in fact been constructed by the use of inscription devices. (64)

But this statement, while apparently similar to things that Knorr-Cetina says, contains a significant limitation. Latour and Woolgar, in their enthusiasm for linguistic and near-linguistic activities, focus on the artificiality of phenomena rather than the artificiality of the entire laboratory, and their particular focus is on phenomena created by inscription, and similar, devices. The ellipsis above contains the following:

> Without a bioassay, for example, a substance could not be said to exist. The bioassay is not merely a means of obtaining some independently given entity; the bioassay constitutes the construction of the substance. Similarly, a substance could not be said to exist without fractionating columns..., since a fraction only exists by virtue of the process of discrimination. Likewise, the spectrum produced by a nuclear magnetic resonance (NMR) spectrometer... would not exist but for the spectrometer.

Not only is this claim substantially different from Knorr-Cetina's point about the artificiality of the laboratory, the difference leads Latour and Woolgar to a far more radical constructivism. Knorr-Cetina is interested in all of the technologies and processes a laboratory uses to make its objects, but here Latour and Woolgar are interested in technologies of representation. Whereas it is generally accepted that quantities of TRF sufficient to produce observable effects have to be manufactured ("constructed") in the laboratory (or purified from huge quantities of brain matter, again creating a highly artificial situation) it is not at all clear, and in fact quite contrary to intuition, that TRF wouldn't exist without a bioassay, unless one is talking about the institution TRF rather than the material stuff. That Latour and Woolgar are talking not about the institution but about the material stuff seems to be indicated from their claim not to be idealists:

> We do not wish to say that facts do not exist nor that there is no such thing as reality. In this simple sense our position is not relativist. Our point is that "out-there-ness" is the *consequence* of scientific work rather than its *cause*. We therefore wish to stress the importance of *timing*.... Once the controversy has settled, reality is taken to be the cause of this settlement; but while controversy is still raging, reality is the consequence of debate, following each twist and turn in the controversy as if it were the shadow of scientific endeavor. (180–82)

Rather than recognizing that social objects can be in flux while material ones are not, in *Laboratory Life* Latour and Woolgar attempt to describe a process of the transformation of the social into the material. No mechanism is given; the object is created out of negotiation and eventual consensus. "Before long, more and more reality is attributed to the object and less and less to the statement *about* the object" (177). This is the way that they propose to understand the instability of facts before some point in time, and their apparent stability after the controversy ends.

Latour and Woolgar postulate this transformation from social to material because of their commitment to both an agnosticism about scientists' representations of the world, which they see as a prerequisite for doing anthropology of science (31, 38–39), and a commonsense recognition of the stability of facts and the reality of various products of the laboratory. The former forces them to deny material reality to TRF before 1969 and the latter to accept it after 1969.

Thus Latour and Woolgar introduce a further sense of construction.[11] Here they are talking about the construction of the material world, but not in the sense of laboratory or industrial manipulations. They have in mind a neo-Kantian sense or perhaps a more idealist one, without any commitment to a world of things-in-themselves. In this sense of construction, which its proponents sometimes see as the central sense, science creates the world in adopting theoretical frameworks and not just the social world.

This is the only sense of "construction," of the ones I have identified here, which directly confronts the cores of realism and empiricism. Even the insight that laboratories literally produce the phenomena and artifacts they study, which seems to violate mind independence, can easily be accommodated within those philosophical positions since it rests on causal connections between the scientists and artifacts. But neo-Kantian constructivism does not postulate a causal connection between a representation and its object, or at least any traditionally accepted causal connection. For this reason, most philosophers find constructivism implausible, even when neo-Kantian constructivism is only one aspect of the social constructivist project.

The next chapter outlines some arguments against neo-Kantian constructivism. They are not conclusive arguments—some people have claimed that it is not possible to have conclusive arguments on this issue—but their conjunction should create some substantial doubts about this type of construction. At the very least the arguments are sufficient to push the burden of proof onto the neo-Kantian constructivist, a burden which Woolgar later accepts. But *Laboratory Life* contains no argument for this more radical type of constructivism and, thus, gives us no good reason to accept it. This leaves us an interesting question: How is it that members of the S&TS community come to hold that nature can be literally constructed in this sense?

A sketch of an answer to this question must go as follows: Detailed studies of actual scientific activity seem to indicate that there exists a large amount of contingency in our scientific knowledge before it stabilises. The intuition is that "it could easily have been otherwise." Given this contingency and yet the clear evidence that nature is relatively well behaved once scientists come to some agreement, there is a need to account for this change. The emphasis of contingency is at the root of the justification Woolgar gives in *Science: The Very Idea*, which I discuss below.

HETEROGENEOUS CONSTRUCTIONS

After their collaboration on *Laboratory Life*, Latour and Woolgar's research programs diverged. Latour has worked on a Machiavellian description of the scientist as a node in a network, an accumulator of resources. The Machiavellian scientist gets her strength primarily from the tools of the laboratory and from the use of transportable records (Latour 1983, 1987, 1988). Latour's program is not explicitly constructivist, since he shies away from such labels, preferring to call his approach "actor-network" theory. Nonetheless, some commentators have thought that Latour's and similar work is a "heterogeneous constructivism," a research program that displays scientists' use of varied resources to build networks of power, which in turn represent knowledge, technologies, and other institutions (Taylor 1995a, 1995b). I will not give more than the briefest description of the position here, returning to it in chapter 7. There I argue that this account of science has a distinctly realist flavor, because it gives a part to material objects and their properties in stories of the production of knowledge and artifacts.

"Heterogeneous engineering" is the name that John Law (1986a) gives to the work that technologists need to do to build a successful artifact. They need to combine raw materials, skills, knowledge, and capital, and to do this they must enroll any number of actors, not all of whom may be immediately compatible. Thus the technologist has the task of building, or constructing, a stable network involving diverse components. This program stands in opposition to technological determinism, the idea that technologies have autonomous paths of development, or the idea that the important causal connections between material technologies and societies go in one direction only, from the material to the social.

The 1987 volume, *The Social Construction of Technological Systems*, edited by Wiebe Bijker, Thomas Hughes, and Trevor Pinch officially launched this new *constructivist* research program. The idea of a technological system already contains within it attention to heterogeneity, because such systems contain not only machines but capital, skilled workers, managers, raw materials, and demands. A technological system is exactly the sort of thing that is constructed heterogeneously, because its components are so varied.

Heterogeneous constructivism or engineering applies so easily to technology because it is philosophically mundane; when Pinch and Bijker apply social constructivism to technology they, like some "weak constructivists," adopt the rhetoric of "knowledge is nothing but negotiation" or hint at a neo-Kantian constructivism, but do not need either in practice. Rather than turning our notion of understanding on its head, they are proposing some useful though relatively uncontroversial concepts for the study of technology:

> Key concepts within this approach are 'interpretative flexibility', 'closure', and 'relevant social groups'. One of the central tenets of this approach is the claim that technological artifacts are open to sociological analysis, not just in their usage but especially with respect to their design and technical 'content'. (Bijker, Pinch, and Hughes 1987, 4)

It should come as no surprise that producers of technological artifacts must take into account social facts and "relevant social groups" in the design and manufacture of those artifacts. And it should come as no surprise that different social groups interpret artifacts differently. When Pinch and Bijker apply their ideas to the history of the bicycle, they want to show that the bicycle was a product of trial and error and that new attempts failed because they didn't solve problems identified by one or another social group. They demonstrate that the bicycle is not the product of a straight line of development but that each product was decision-impregnated and that many were decision-impregnating. But again, that an evolutionary view of technological work is useful should be of no surprise to anybody who has seen a few years' worth of new models of cars or computers.

Heterogeneous constructivism can also be applied to science: Bruno Latour and Michel Callon's actor-network theory is a theory of "technoscience" (Latour 1987), in which scientists are seen in the same light as technologists, separated only by traditional disciplinary boundaries. Scientists are in the business of constructing ever larger, ever more stable networks. And the networks are heterogeneous in the sense that they combine isolated parts of the material world, laboratory equipment, "black-boxed" knowledge, patrons, money, institutions, and so on. It is all of these agents together that create the successes of technoscience; no one piece of that network wholly determines the shape of the whole.

In a sense then, heterogeous constructivism is a more detailed telling of the story of the creation of material and social objects. To the more purely textual (including verbal) stories of Berger and Luckmann and weak social constructivism is added attention to material practices, such as laboratory practices. To empiricist constructivism is added attention to larger scale social negotiations. It is thus a combination of other constructivisms, combining them in a rough-and-ready way.

WOOLGAR

Latour's approach to science may be read as a realist one, but Woolgar's has moved as far away from realism as possible. Woolgar is best known for his interest in problems of reflexivity, addressing issues that come about because of the fact that sociology of knowledge is itself a knowledge enterprise and, thus, can be applied to itself. I am going to ignore this strain in Woolgar's work, where some of his main contributions to the field lie, and focus on his explicit discussion of the radical type of constructivism, whereby representations are said to construct the world.

Common sense, Woolgar claims, would have the relationship between representation and object as:

$$\text{Object} \longleftarrow \text{Representation}$$

or, in the case of science:

$$\text{Scientific Knowledge} \longleftarrow \text{Nature}$$

By and large, S&TS has accepted this perspective; it is "epistemologically relativist and ontologically realist" (Donald Campbell, quoted in Woolgar 1988, 54), which Woolgar illustrates with a few quotes by well-known sociologists, such as this one by Barry Barnes:

> Occasionally, existing work leaves the feeling that reality has nothing to do with what is socially constructed or negotiated to count as natural knowledge, but we may safely assume that this impression is an accidental by-product of over-enthusiastic sociological analysis, and that sociologists as a whole would adknowledge that the world in some way constrains what is believed to be. (Woolgar, 54)

Woolgar wants to position himself against this "ambivalence" about representation and reality and "extend the radical potential of sociological studies of scientific knowledge" by reversing the arrow:

$$\text{Scientific Knowledge} \longrightarrow \text{Nature}$$

Reversing the arrow amounts to saying that representations constitute, or construct, their objects. It is in this sense that Woolgar wants to say that the world is constructed, and it is in this sense that he is a constructivist.

Approximately two arguments are offered in favour of reversing the arrow. The first is that objects are unavailable to us without representations; we have no independent access to them. This is a weak argument, Woolgar recognizes, for it doesn't indicate the direction the arrow. We can see this in concrete cases: the fact that we need a microscope to see bacteria is not normally taken to indicate that bacteria are created by microscopes.[12] But while Woolgar's argument doesn't demonstrate the flaws with "objectivism" (as he calls the commonsense view), it shows how difficult it is to prove. "On this basis we are at least entitled to entertain the alternative (constructivist) position as a heuristic" (57). An argument for his version of constructivism that Woolgar does not make, but could at this point make, is that success stemming from the use of this heuristic reflects positively on its truth. It might be interesting to pursue this argument, but, as Woolgar does not make it, and the case studies he presents would not help him to make it (since they don't use the heuristic), I won't examine it here.[13]

The second argument that Woolgar makes depends on two cases of discoveries that he presents. I will look at one of these, the case of the "discovery" of America, which he takes as representative of discoveries in general.

Drawing on a discussion by Augustine Brannigan (1981) of Columbus and the discovery of America, Woolgar points out several problems with the school textbook account of this "event." First of all, the discovery was a process, rather than something that took place at a single point in time. It was a process that extended "in time both before and after the initial announcement of the claim" (59), requiring preparation and planning and requiring extensive negotiation after the claim. Columbus, it is pointed out, didn't claim to have discovered new continents (he believed to his death that the northern islands he saw were off Asia). It took extensive descriptions by Vespucci to make other people believe that the new lands formed new continents. In addition, it takes some negotiation and argument to establish that Columbus should get the credit for the discovery, since it is reasonably well accepted that other Europeans before him had landed on the continents we now call America. "The strength of the successful account—that Columbus discovered America—is its entrenchment. The stability of this particular factual claim is precisely a reflection of the enormous amount of work which is now required to deconstruct it." From this story, Woolgar draws the conclusion that

> the example of Columbus and the "discovery" of America suggests that in our efforts to understand the social basis of discovery we cannot presume the character of a discovered object; the fact of a discovered object and its character is the achievement of the discoverer's (and/or others') claims and definitional work. (60)

> The main conclusion from our examples of discovery is that the existence and character of a discovered object is a different animal according to the constituency of different social networks. . . . Crucially, this variation undermines the standard presumption about the existence of the object prior to its discovery. The argument is not just that social networks mediate between the object and observational work done by participants. Rather, the social network constitutes the object (or lack of it). The implication for our main argument is the inversion of the presumed relationship between representation and object; the representation gives rise to the object. (65)

The problems with the standard accounts of discovery that Woolgar and Brannigan raise are good ones, and their pointing to social factors in the discovery are right.[14] But Woolgar's second argument for the reversal of the arrow—that the variability of accounts should lead us to doubt the existence of anything that the accounts are supposed to be of—is surely unwarranted. To make this jump is to deny the possibility of error and the possibility of different interpretations of the same object. The latter is particularly odd, considering that interpretative flexibility is an important concept in *Science: The Very Idea*. Columbus and Vespucci both tried to define the lands on the west side of the Atlantic, and they had very different ideas and representations of those lands, but there is no reason to conclude from this that their representations constituted the lands. To argue this, as Woolgar does, is not only to jump several steps but also to take a thoroughly Eurocentric point of view, whereby the lived experiences of millions of inhabitants of what we now call America are to count as nothing in the face of two Europeans' (and their allies') representations. This is a place where the "meaningfulness" criterion I postulated above might be applicable: the meaningful social object "America" is created by representations, but the material object is not.

Thus Woolgar's radical style of social constructivism seems unwarranted. At a minimum his arguments fail to establish it and, given the massive contradiction between it and common sense, the failure of these arguments leaves no good reason to believe it. The best possibility for this argument would be to take his talk metaphorically, even though it is fairly clear that he doesn't intend it to be so taken.

LESSONS

The first lesson, and the most obvious one, is that "social constructivism" covers a range of things. It can involve the construction of epistemologies, of theories, of social objects, or of things. It can be an ontological program with the focus on social objects, laboratory artifacts, or one with the focus on the natural world. It can also be primarily an epistemological program, when the focus is on a particular social object, namely scientific knowledge. Outside of S&TS, social constructivist work tends to rest on the first ontological program, the construction of social objects such as genders, power, and emotions. S&TS most often narrows the focus onto knowledge, though it retains a plurality of approaches.

Connected with this diversity, the metaphor of construction seems to have a number of common interpretations. It has interpretations in terms of large social projects, whereby such things as cities, economies, legislation, and knowledge are constructed by many people interacting, possibly with differing or conflicting goals. It has what I see as a geometrical interpretation, whereby conceptual entities are constructed given some fixed points (data). And it has a more physical interpretation, whereby new material objects are made from other ones. Added to these is one that is less plausible and which has little support in argument, the neo-Kantian claim that material objects are constructed out of world views. The next chapter addresses this claim, the only one of the constructivisms that conflicts with realism.

The most common constructivism, however, picks up aspects of and mixes the others. "Weak social constructivism" often adopts the neo-Kantian, radical constructivism as a slogan, yet ignores it in practice. This form of social constructivism usually focuses on conceptual entities or institutions, and makes the claim that at every (or nearly every) step in the construction of knowledge, social processes are at play.

Heterogeneous constructivism creates a different mix, describing the creation of institutions and artifacts through attention to the details of practices. By combining practices and enrolling agents, scientists construct variegated networks, networks that are thoroughly social despite their odd combinations of components. Heterogeneous constructivism is thus a deflationist position: to find out about the origins of an object (social or material) we simply have to look to the practices and resources that had to be combined to create it.

Construction metaphors in S&TS have produced valuable insights, many of whose consequences have yet to be explored. For example, the laboratory in all its artificiality is something more and more people have been examining in recent years. The insight that it *is* constructed remains to be systematically thought through and incorporated into our picture of scientific activity. The sociologists I discuss in this chapter, as well as philosophers such as Robert Ackermann (1985), Nancy Cartwright (1983, 1989a), Ian Hacking (1983), and Hans Radder (1988), have made a start in this direction, but I suspect that considerably more remains to be said. Laboratories are places where nature is systematically excluded. If what the scientist studies in the laboratory is not, strictly speaking, nature, and yet science aims at knowledge of nature, then it is important to understand the bridges between experimental knowledge and knowledge of the wider world. The subject of experimentation is a twisted, contorted, portion of nature and, therefore, we should learn something about the processes of twisting and contorting if we are to learn about scientific knowledge. In other words, we have to learn about the relationship between subjects of experimentation and what they are taken to represent. Thus we may have to rethink the relationship between laboratory knowledge and knowledge of nature. But any such rethinking will recognize that the nature constructed in the laboratory is constructed from other bits of nature, using material techniques; it is not a social construct of the sort that Berger and Luckmann are interested in, nor is it the type that Woolgar is interested in.

One can sum up many of the most valuable social constructivist insights with a simple recommendation: we should more often recognize the existence of social objects in science. As surely as gender, social roles, and emotions exist, social objects in science exist and act as causes of and constraints on scientists' actions. This is something that has always been recognized, of course: explaining a scientists' actions, especially public actions, usually requires reference to knowledge of the time. At the same time, the reality of these objects has often been ignored, and it has often been implied that they can be more easily "wished away" than is usually the case.

Recognition of the importance of social objects is related to the problem of the contingency of knowledge. Scientific knowledge looks underdetermined and contingent while it is being created because there are (often) competing institutions and other social objects, and scientists spend much of their time dealing with these objects. Thus we need a theory of science, or an approach to science, that is consistent with and helps us understand the fact that science is not the purely rationalist and cognitive exercise that some positivists thought it was. Yet to understand science's successes and failures we have to have a theory of science that doesn't make successes and failures into miracles.

Five

NEO-KANTIAN CONSTRUCTIONS

> It is absolutely impossible to be convinced by a constructivist argument for more than three minutes. Well, say an hour, to be fair.
>
> Bruno Latour (1990a, 64)

THE PREVIOUS CHAPTER DESCRIBED different types of things that might be constructed, according to social constructivist science and technology studies. They are: (a) institutions, or social objects; (b) theories, accounts, and representations; (c) new material objects; and (d) the objects of representation generally. That the first three of these are constructed, I argued, is compatible with a deflationary realism and offers important insights into science and society. The claim that the last is constructed produces the neo-Kantian position: representations shape or create that which they represent; no objects of knowledge are independent of our knowing them. Thus, to adjust the picture of constructivism from the first chapter, for the neo-Kantian science looks something like:

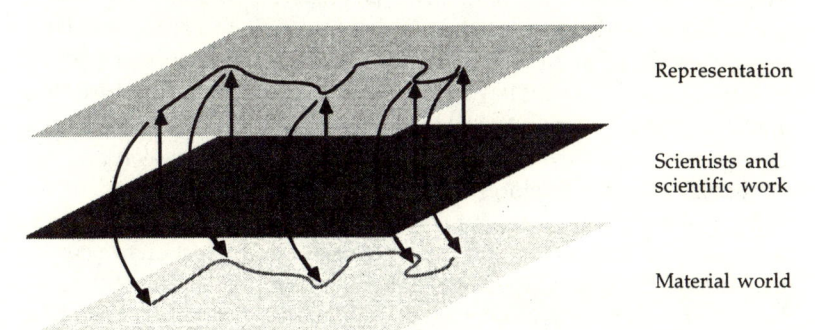

Figure 5.1 Neo-Kantian science

Objects, after manipulation and observation, give rise to data; scientists use data to produce representations; and representations are what give objects characteristics. In this chapter, I argue that if neo-Kantian constructivism is not given a metaphorical interpretation, then it is unjustifiable or untenable.

Neo-Kantian constructivism, and the above diagram, can be read in many ways, just as Kant's own constructivism has been. I want to sort the readings into four broad categories: metaphorical, empiricist, nominalist, and idealist readings. As a metaphor, representations are said to construct their objects because, for example, they focus attention on some characteristics rather than others. Conceptual frameworks shape interests, actions, and perceptions and, thus, shape what we know. But making neo-Kantian constructivism straightforwardly metaphorical removes the conflict with realism, my focus here. Though the constructivisms that fit it best can be interesting and informative, I will leave metaphorical readings aside for now.

The second category of readings puts emphasis on the unknowability of the world. Then the object becomes not a part of the external world, but an already-interpreted phenomenal object. Under this reading the connection between representation and object is clear, since both are part of the conceptual realm. Representations shape these phenomenal objects because they contribute to interpretations, which are a part of any known object. This reading of neo-Kantian constructivism makes it a species of empiricism, an approach to the study of phenomena. It doesn't deny the existence of a mind-independent world, but only claims that we can know little or nothing about it. This new empiricism will be subject to some of the same problems that face the old empiricism; in particular, like the old empiricism it is unable to explain certain types of successes in science without abandoning its commitment to the unknowability of the mind-independent object.

Sometimes the constructivism of S&TS looks like an empiricist constructivism, especially when interpretation is a main focus: when the emphasis is on interpretive flexibility, then practice, which limits flexibility, tends to be ignored. Science starts to look like an entirely discursive activity, and work with and on the material world is left aside. For example, Thomas Laqueur (1990) shows that in Western science and medicine there have been competing models of sex, a one-sex model in which similarities of males and females are emphasized, and a two-sex model in which differences are emphasized. He thus explores the social construction or "making" of sex (not gender); his is a story about how sex is the result of a certain interpretation, one which exists and dominates because of its connection to a particular politics of gender. Greg Myers (1990), in his demonstration of the central role of process of writing in interpretation, sometimes takes himself to be showing how texts participate in the social construction of nature. Texts, and the writing of texts, retrospectively shape what is taken as nature.

To the extent that S&TS gives an empiricist reading to constructivism, then, it accepts too easily positivist presuppositions. Positivism, at least as interpreted in Anglo-American philosophy, was an attempt to create a foundationalist or near-foundationalist picture of science, as a bulwark against skepticism. Positivists thought that knowledge about the real nature of the world was impossible, yet attempted to avoid skepticism by arguing that theoretical knowledge is really a logical manipulation of data—thus knowledge stands firmly grounded in data. While constructivist S&TS derives in part from a rejection of positivist views on science, it is in some ways not a thorough enough rejection of those views. S&TS rejects the possibility of foundationalism while often accepting the foundationalism/skepticism dichotomy. In addition, S&TS sometimes keeps the picture of science as a discursive activity—though the picture is of science as interactive and filled with rhetoric rather than essentially solipsistic and purely logical. The result is a skeptical empiricism: the *noumenal* object is unknowable and, therefore, scientific knowledge cannot represent it; yet scientific knowledge is not merely a systematic codification of data, because data is flexible and open to interpretation.

To avoid collapsing her position into that of the empiricist and to avoid facing the empiricist's problems, the neo-Kantian constructivist needs to erase the distinction between phenomenal objects and the unknowable, *noumenal* ones. That is, realists' successful positive arguments show that scientists do find out about the world, so the neo-Kantian should abandon the unknowability of the world and, hence, the realm of the *noumena*. This takes us to the third and fourth readings of neo-Kantian constructivism.

The third, nominalist, category of readings of neo-Kantian constructivisms takes the issue to be one of whether the world can be said to be structured in the way that the sciences assume it is. Nominalism claims that categories are always human or cultural creations rather than features of the material world and that categories do not reflect any such features. There are material entities and causal interactions in the world, says the nominalist, but they don't have structure in the way that scientific systems of classification do: categories have no reality except that which people give them. Evidence for nominalism about science among sociologists and critics of science typically comes from the diversity of ontologies created by different times and cultures. Given the fact that we cannot compare ontologies directly with the structures that they purport to describe, we have no evidence that ontology is not a wholly relative matter: "specific ontologies flow from cultural practices and hence must be seen as secondary, not primary" (Knorr-Cetina 1993).[1]

Problems of induction show the difficulties that nominalism faces. The massive underdetermination of even our most elementary inductive inferences[2] suggests that for induction to work with any frequency our categories must map approximately onto some important material similarities and differences. Why would the anatomical, endocrinological, or immunological study of one mammal provide information about other mammals, if there were not important similarities between them? The intuition that some information about mammals is transferable and that this is the result of similarities in structure is made stronger because we have an evolutionary theory to account for such similarities. Thus if nominalism is to assume that scientific categories are purely cultural constructs, with no relation to an already structured world, it must either heavily discount our successes in coping, or it must assume that our scientific categories in some way contribute to the structuring of the world, in a material rather than a metaphorical sense.

Thus there is a fourth category, the more radical idealist readings of neo-Kantian constructivism, like Steve Woolgar's, in which the constructivist claim (the arrow from representation to object) is not taken metaphorically and the object is taken to be a part of material reality. Idealist readings take the constructivist arrow at face value, as the strong claim that representations constitute material reality or, in other words, that no distinction can be made between material and social reality, that the material should be incorporated into the more immediate social. In the remainder of this chapter I argue that the positions produced by these readings are methodologically problematic and are just as difficult to defend as those produced by empiricist or nominalist readings.

Probably the most common response to neo-Kantian constructivism takes the form of a transcendental argument for mind independence: mind independence is essential for communication and inquiry and, thus, we cannot decide to reject it without assuming it; mind independence is so central to our way of life that we cannot abandon it, even if we cannot justify it. Nicholas Rescher takes this line, arguing that "it is indeed a presupposition of effective communicative discourse about a thing that we purport (claim and intend) to make true statements about it" (Rescher 1986, 138). But while the transcendental argument has some force against wavering constructivists, the determined antirealist can still try to maintain antirealism and push aside the way of life that seems to contradict it. Jacques Derrida (e.g., 1977) is prominent in doing this, writing texts that, because of their internal contradictions, convoluted style, and openness to interpretation, attempt to avoid statements that unproblematically presuppose a realist framework. Reflexivist sociologists of science, in advocating the adoption of "new literary forms" attempt something similar (e.g., Ashmore 1989; Woolgar 1988).

Other responses to neo-Kantian constructivism have to do with the difficulties in understanding what sort of causal processes are at play when the representation creates its object. If objects in the world are not independent of us and our attempts to represent them, then in what way are they dependent upon us? The bulk of our world cannot be dependent upon us in a material way, the way, for example, a painting is the result of an artist's material actions. Therefore, if representations cause the features of their objects, that cause will in general be a nonmaterial one. Some things that one might call "nonmaterial causation" are perfectly common and well accepted but, as it stands, neo-Kantian constructions are a funny type of nonmaterial causation, because it isn't obvious that they supervene or rest on material connections.[3] Politicians' representations of their opponents can cause certain types of voting patterns, a nonmaterial causal connection of sorts. Nonetheless, we can follow (in a rough sense) a chain of material causal connections on which politicians' hopes depend and supervene: sound and light shows are transformed into magnetic signals, which are transformed into radio and television waves, which are transformed back into sound and light shows, which have peculiar psychological effects on many of those who observe them. These effects involve, among other things, changing beliefs and desires, which supervene on very material changes in brains. The chain goes on. And although causation is nonmaterial, in the sense that nonmaterial things like meanings and beliefs are required for the chain to work, we can understand how there are material signals that "carry" these meanings and beliefs. In the case of neo-Kantian constructions, the material signals seem absent (see Boyd 1992 for another version of this point).

The causal connection problem becomes even larger when we look at science and technology studies' prominent version of neo-Kantian constructivism: *social* constructivism. The neo-Kantian constructivist wants to say that "the limits of our world are the limits of the world." This is typically most plausible when based on an extremely individualistic epistemology. By adopting a strongly empiricist notion of the self—leading perhaps to solipsism—an individualistic constructivist can attempt to justify the causal arrow from representations to material world in terms of the structure of perception. For such a constructivist, the individual's isolation from the material world suggests that it makes no sense to talk of anything lying beyond phenomena; yet phenomena are in part constituted by the frameworks and preconceptions. But because of S&TS's emphasis—a correct emphasis—on the *social* character of scientific knowledge, what is at issue is not merely the representations and preconceptions adopted by individuals, but those adopted by the community: if we take seriously S&TS's interest in rhetoric and consensus-formation, then what matters to the shaping or creation of a material object is the consensus arrived at by the scientific community. But if *our*, in "the limits of our world are the limits of the world," refers to societies, the claim appears unmotivated in a way that it might not be if the constructivism were more individualistic. Why is it that consensus affects material reality, that the convictions of authorities carry weight that the convictions of nonauthorities don't? How does it *cause* changes in the material world? And since there is only rarely complete consensus about issues of theoretical importance, even among authorities, the social constructivist has to understand why particular authorities' opinions carry such causal weight.

Constructivist sociologists present little in the way of argument for neo-Kantian constructivism. Given this lack of argument, a major and counterintuitive addition to our repertoire of causes seems unwarranted. It fails the test of common sense, which would have scientific researchers interested in at least *some* preexisting entities—parts of the natural world ontologically prior to their representation—and consensus irrelevant to the existence of many or most entities. And even though common sense should not be the touchstone of sociology or philosophy of science, major violations of it should require justification.

On the idealist reading neo-Kantian constructivists intentionally commit what some philosophers call the "epistemic fallacy," conflating ontology and epistemology (see Bhaskar 1986, 23ff.): constructivists conflate statements about the world with statements about our claims to know about the world by arguing that because knowledge is socially constructed the objects of knowledge are also socially constructed. But the distinction between the realms of ontology and epistemology can be grounded in the everyday experience of *not* knowing about the world what others seem to rightly know. I do not know very much about what makes cell cultures live or die in the laboratory, nor very much about the workings of my car, but many biologists and auto mechanics do seem to know about these things, and when they apply their knowledge they achieve results that I cannot. At the level of individuals' beliefs, epistemology is separable from ontology, for we often don't know about features of the world that others seem to know about. The epistemic fallacy remains a fallacy at levels above the individual, for the same argument can be made for different levels of social groupings. So neo-Kantian constructivism causes problems for understanding failures in knowledge.

There *are* situations in which representations produce effect on their objects, where the material connections between representation and object are more visible. As was discussed in the last chapter, Peter Berger and Thomas Luckmann show how institutions can be built up on the basis of people's beliefs about them, and actions on the basis of those beliefs. Money, for example, attains value as a result of people's accepting it as a carrier of value (Ruben 1989 discusses this example). Banks are solid in part as a result of people's confidence in them: when depositors lose confidence they withdraw their money and create a cash shortage. And thus traditional bank architecture reinforces stability and attempts to inspire confidence. Gender roles are created by cultural representations of those roles: books, films, art, childhood education, and laws create personae that people try to fit and boundaries that are difficult to transgress. And one last example, this time from the sphere of international relations: wars, animosity, friendships, and alliances are all shaped by the assumption that they exist, though that isn't meant to deny the possibility of underlying causes of those phenomena.

The distinction between social objects and material objects separates some spheres in which representations can shape or create their objects from spheres in which it is plausible that they cannot do so. Clearly social objects, defined as necessarily meaningful, are the type of thing that can be socially constructed. Social objects are meaningful objects, and meaning is intimately connected with representation. Representations and meanings are parts of the same interacting systems. Material objects, on the other hand, are not so obviously part of a tight, interacting system with their representations.

While the above examples show us that some objects can be socially constructed, they do not show us that we should accept neo-Kantian contructivism. Diagram 5.1 is right, at least for many social objects, but the arrow from representation to object is too simple. Without taking a more detailed look at particular situations we cannot assume that representations will create or shape their objects after themselves. What Berger and Luckmann showed is that social objects and their representations are part of a feedback loop: social objects can become stable when many people accept their stability. But they concentrated on cases in which the feedback is positive. There are cases in which the feedback is negative. Secrets, for example, provide a trivial example of a negative feedback loop. The more representation there is of a secret, the less of a secret it becomes. Hypotheses about overcrowding, such as perceptions of traffic jams, may induce people to act so as to lessen the crowding. To see that there may be many other examples, one can look at economics, a paradigm field for social constructions. The equations that an economist produces to describe a certain part of the economy are importantly within the system itself, in the sense that somebody might act upon them. Economists socially construct economies. But it is not obvious whether such equations are in general self-fulfilling prophecies or self-denying ones. Acting on an economist's analysis may change the system such that the analysis no longer applies—neoclassical economists claim this when arguing against the possibility of effective government intervention in the economy. Without further study we cannot tell how particular analysis affects that which it analyzes. This is one way in which the arrow from representation to object is too simple.

There is another way in which the arrow is too simple: it conceals too much. Even for the cases for which it is right that representations help to socially construct their objects, the neo-Kantian constructivist arrow conceals all of the interesting and different reasons why it is right. That is, the constructivist arrow lumps together dissimilar processes and hides all of these processes in such a way as to make them inaccessible to study. For the sociologist this is particularly problematic, because accepting neo-Kantian constructivism makes it difficult to understand how the processes of social construction work, yet these are processes deserving sociological study. The "expectancy effect," in which researchers' preconceptions affect the results of an experiment, is not obviously similar to the maintenance of power through displays of that power. The sociologist (and psychologist) should be interested in the ways in which each of these work. It is all the more odd, then, that sociology of science should be one of the most prominent places in which neo-Kantian constructivism is popular, even rhetorically.

Thus neo-Kantian constructivism poses a methodological problem for the sociologist, because it hides interesting sociological phenomena: other forms of social construction. For the politically motivated critic of science this is equally true. The phenomena that are hidden by the constructivist arrow are sometimes key ones for gaining a political understanding of science, for although that arrow indicates the power of representation it hides the relationships on which that power is founded. Bruno Latour at the same time apparently abandons neo-Kantian constructivism and produces novel descriptions of the power of the scientist, descriptions that attempt to display at a very material level the workings of that power (chapter 7). While neo-Kantian constructivist S&TS should—and usually does—focus on the rhetorical tools needed to establish representations, Latour examines a broader range of scientific activity and is led to say "Give me a laboratory and I will raise the world" (Latour 1983).

For the feminist critic of science, and for the political critic more generally, there is a much more obvious problem with neo-Kantian constructivism. One of the things against which the feminist wants to argue is specific scientific claims about women: this "feminist empiricist" project is not something that any feminist doing S&TS would want to abandon lightly. When nineteenth-century doctors advised pubescent girls to stay indoors, get lots of rest, and do light housework, they were participating in the social construction of middle-class housewives (Smith-Rosenberg 1985). This form of social constructivism few feminists would want to deny. But along with the doctors' prescription came some reasons: these doctors claimed that girls' ovaries would not form properly if the girls received too much exercise, that sterility would result. The strict neo-Kantian social constructivist would have to say that they were right, that their consensus created the truth. The feminist critic wants to argue that these doctors were simply *wrong* in their consensus and that women's bodies are not malleable enough to be constructed so easily by scientific representations of them.

The rift between these two positions is too great to be healed. Neo-Kantian social constructivism in S&TS gives the political critic some tools with which to work: a debunking attitude toward traditional philosophies of science and some interpretative skills for recognizing interestedness. But it withholds a key tool: the concept of *mis*representation. Strong constructivism does not allow for misrepresentation in science, because representations are held to create their objects. For the critic who is particularly concerned about science's attempted representations of herself and her society, the concept of misrepresentation is a crucial tool.

The problems go further than misrepresentation. The political critic certainly does not want to accept that she is constructed to meet science's images, and since she knows that she has not been so constructed (at least in the neo-Kantian sense), she knows that this form of constructivism does a poor job of diagnosing power relations. The bodies, brains, intellects, and societies that science sometimes misrepresents are simply not as powerless in the face of description as neo-Kantian constructivism would have it: they do not simply change with the changing approaches of the biologists, psychologists, and anthropologists. So in this fairly trivial way neo-Kantian constructivism makes the asymmetries of power much larger than they actually are.

SOME LESSONS

Literal versions of neo-Kantian constructivism fail, or may fail, in a number of ways. They may sometimes fail to be reflexively self-consistent, because they argue in ways that presuppose a realist framework. They may fail to make sense of the causal processes acting to shape material objects in the world, to make sense of mind-dependence. They assume that the social construction of social objects can be extended to material ones. They hide processes that should be exposed and lump together very different processes. Neo-Kantian constructivisms fail the political critic because they remove one of the important tools from her repertoire, the concept of misrepresentation. And the constructivist picture misdescribes power relations, claiming that scientists have more power to define the world than they actually have.

If literal readings of neo-Kantian constructivism fail and empiricism is inadequate, then we are left with the metaphorical approach to neo-Kantian constructivism, along with the other more deflationary constructivisms described in the last chapter. These are, however, valuable things to be left with. The others I have already sketched arguments for, and the metaphorical approach is valuable in that it draws attention to the intellectual and material context of inquiry, what is often loosely referred to as "theory-dependence": conceptual frameworks have a tremendous effect on what we can learn, helping to "construct" the worlds that can be known.

Six

THE *STRUCTURE* THIRTY YEARS LATER

INTRODUCTION

FOR THE PAST THIRTY YEARS there has been a persistent reading of Thomas Kuhn's *The Structure of Scientific Revolutions* as a constructivist text.[1] Not everybody has agreed with that reading—it is probably even the minority view—but its persistence is remarkable. The reading is problematic: it attributes to Kuhn a view that is from most people's perspective highly untenable, that scientists in some strong sense construct the world by choosing a paradigm.

Kuhn does not use the term *construct* or any of its immediate cognates to describe his program, and he does not use it in any important way in *Structure*. However, there is still something useful in the term as applied to Kuhn's program, which I will try to bring out. My re-reading is not primarily for the sake of getting Kuhn right, but instead to identify a productive use of the "construction" metaphor. I focus here the relationship between paradigms and ontology—"ontology" in both the sense of what there is in the world and what is claimed to be in the world. As such, I will leave aside questions about incommensurability, the rationality of science, the dynamics of theory change, the constitution of scientific communities, and other contentious issues stemming from *Structure*.

READINGS OF KUHN AS IDEALIST

Kuhn is sometimes thought to hold the neo-Kantian view that scientists, in adopting a paradigm, construct a world (in addition to the social and conceptual world in which they live) where the basic tenets of the paradigm hold true. An early such reading of *Structure* was given by Israel Scheffler, who called Kuhn "an extravagant idealist" (1967). "Idealist" readings of Kuhn's ontological program stem mostly from fairly literal interpretations of Kuhn's talk of different worlds existing before and after a revolution. The scientists in the changed discipline are taken to be not merely seeing the world differently but living in a different world: "When that suggestion [that Herschel's new comet was a planet] was accepted, there were several fewer stars and one more planet in the world of the professional astronomer" (1970a, 115). For Carl Kordig, for example, it is this sentence and ones like it that lead to the conclusion that Kuhn has a "radically idealist theory of perception" (Kordig 1971, 19) and is, therefore, a relativist.

> It must follow that before Lexell there were more stars in the world of the professional astronomer. But if this is true one can no longer say that these astronomers before Lexell were mistaken about the number of stars.... This is because from Kuhn's viewpoint there really were more stars in their world. It is not just that they believed there were more stars in their world. According to Kuhn there *really* was this number of stars. (Kordig 1971, 18)

The position is put by Richard Boyd thus:

> the realist denies, while the constructivist affirms, that the adoption of theories, paradigms, research interests, conceptual frameworks, or perspectives in some way constitutes, or contributes to the constitution of, the causal powers of and the causal relations between the objects scientists study in the context of those theories, frameworks, and so forth.... Realists affirm, and constructivists deny the *no noncausal contribution doctrine*. (Boyd 1990, 182–83)

The "no noncausal contribution doctrine" is meant to distinguish Boyd's metaphysical position from that of Kuhn, his main example of a constructivist (Boyd 1990, 1992).

"DIFFERENT WORLDS" TALK

As Kuhn makes clear, his talk of different worlds should be read in a metaphorical sense. He says, for example, that there is a "*sense* in which [paradigms] are constitutive of nature" (Kuhn 1970a, 110, emphasis added). And, "in the absence of some recourse to that hypothetical fixed nature that he 'saw differently,' *the principle of economy will urge us to say* that after discovering oxygen Lavoisier worked in a different world" (118, emphasis added). The attention here will be placed on the chapter of *Structure* containing the bulk of his references to the changing of worlds. "Revolutions as Changes of World *View*" suggests that changes in the "world" should not be read as more than changes in views. That chapter begins:

Examining the record of past research from the vantage of contemporary historiography, the historian of science may be tempted to exclaim that when paradigms change, the world itself changes with them. Led by a new paradigm, scientists adopt new instruments and look in new places. Even more important, during revolutions scientists see new and different things when looking with familiar instruments in places they have looked before. It is rather as if the professional community had been suddenly transported to another planet where familiar objects are seen in a different light and are joined by unfamiliar ones as well. Of course, nothing of quite that sort does occur: there is no geographical transplantation; outside the laboratory everyday affairs usually continue as before. Nevertheless, paradigm changes do cause scientists to see the world of their research-engagement differently. In so far as their only recourse to that world is through what they see and do, we may want to say that after a revolution scientists are responding to a different world. (111)

Near the end of that chapter, Kuhn clarifies his position again: "Whatever he may then see, the scientist after a revolution is still looking at the same world" (129).

Of course, Boyd, Scheffler, and others recognize that the "different worlds" talk is metaphorical, but they want to read it as a strong metaphor. In this, they are surely right. Kuhn repeatedly says that paradigm changes alter the world of the professional scientist. Not only interpretations but also data change (135). The affected scientists are faced with new problems and must use new techniques to solve them. Thus the world's changes are substantial enough to force a reaction.

HOYNINGEN-HUENE'S READING

Although many people assert that there is some idealism lurking in *Structure*, very few people have argued the case at any length. One person who *has* done so is Paul Hoyningen-Huene, who sees some positive features in the idealism he finds (Hoyningen-Huene 1989a, 1989b, 1993). He argues that there is an ambiguity in the use of "world" in *Structure*, an ambiguity between something "already perceptually and conceptually subdivided" and the more fundamental, unhumanly structured world. Much of Kuhn's discussion, claims Hoyningen-Huene, is about the constitution of the former world, which he likens to Kant's "totality of appearances" or *Erscheinungswelt* (1989b). The latter world bears "great similarity to Kant's thing in itself although it is not identical with it" (1989b, 394), and is relatively unaffected by conceptual changes.

This adds up to a quite limited idealism. Hoyningen-Huene claims that Kuhn's "world of appearances" is material (unlike a dreamt winged horse); its features are not completely dependent on its observers but are shaped by "resistances" that the "world in itself" creates; and the "world of appearances" is not subjective in the sense that the individual observer shapes it, because it is a *socially* constructed world. The social construction comes about because appearances are shaped by held similarity relations, which the community as a whole creates and keeps stable. What we are left with is that the world of appearances is partially shaped by expectations and the frameworks that scientists try to impose upon it, and that these frameworks and expectations are social in nature. This is antirealist only in opposition to a realism that maintains that there is a unitary, best description of the world potentially within reach, a "one-true-theory realism."

However, there is *something* in Hoyningen-Huene's reading of *Structure* that we can identify as incompatible with a more sensitive realism. Kuhn the neo-Kantian idealist asserts that the second world, the world in itself, is not knowable. For example, when describing the sense in which paradigms are constitutive of nature, Kuhn says: "In so far as their only recourse to that world [the world in itself] is through what they see and do, we may want to say that after a revolution scientists are responding to a different world" (1970a, 111). In addition, Kuhn is skeptical of the notion of 'truth', as he explains in the last chapter of *Structure*. Given his wariness about truth, we could guess that he would not be comfortable with a notion of description of the world that implied that science could really know it above and beyond knowing its appearance.

RESISTANCES AND APPEARANCES

Hoyningen-Huene's general picture of Kuhn's philosophy of science is a valuable one, and in the details of his analysis he has much to offer. Yet in its attempt to provide a systematic neo-Kantian interpretation of Kuhn's writing it creates a few problems, which are particularly relevant given recent attention to scientific practice. I am going to examine two problematic areas for this interpretation that will lead us away from talk of worlds of appearances and away from the neo-Kantian Kuhn. The first has to do with resistances and the knowability of the material world, the second with similarity relations. The first is something Kuhn might also see as a problem with this interpretation; the second has to do with his own emphases.

In Kuhn's world of appearances, resistances are everywhere. Nature plays a large role in *Structure*; no more than a couple of pages pass without mention of nature's intrusion into scientists' affairs. Through normal and extraordinary research, researchers chart out the positions and the natures of resistances, so it is not that science doesn't find out about the world. The most important of resistances are those anomalies that may potentially lead to the overturning of paradigms. But Kuhn also mentions resistances that routinely face the scientist working unproblematically within a normal science tradition; they are the shapes of the puzzle pieces with which the scientist must work, the data that normal science collects. When Kuhn describes fact-gathering activities, he is describing the contact of normal science with the resistances of the world. For example, there is

> that class of facts that the paradigm has shown to be particularly revealing of the nature of things. . . . At one time or another, these significant factual determinations have included: in astronomy—stellar position and magnitude, the periods of eclipsing binaries and of planets; in physics—the specific gravities and compressibilities of materials, wave lengths and spectral intensities, electrical conductivities and contact potentials; and in chemistry—composition and combining weights, boiling points and acidity of solutions, structural formulas and optical activities. (25)

This hardly reads like the writings of someone who thinks that science can't find out about the world. Kuhn's stance that scientists don't have direct access to the world seems to be held not because of a deep unknowability of that world but because Kuhn sees the everyday side of scientists. They must live with interpretations and within frameworks, but the world is not necessarily obscured by them.

An example will illustrate one of the ways in which Kuhn thinks that scientists cannot escape the realm of interpretation. When discussing shifts in paradigms and their effects, he draws extensively on analogies to psychological experiments having to do with gestalts. In these experiments, in which subjects perceive the familiar duck-or-rabbit figure, or anomalous playing cards such as a black five of hearts, the experimenter is an external authority on the drawings or cards. But in contrast to that, "the scientist can have no recourse above or beyond what he sees with his eyes and instruments" (114). Kuhn's worry about the knowability of the material world has to do with the absence of any higher authority to adjudicate among scientific claims, not with nature's obscurity.

A second problem with Hoyningen-Huene's interpretation of *Structure* has to do with Kuhn's own emphases on appearances and classification. These emphases create much of the impetus for a reading of "worlds" as "worlds of appearances," which is misleading to the extent that we are apt to forget the actions of scientists in favor of their observations.

In "Second Thoughts on Paradigms" (1974), Kuhn discusses the dependence of classification and identification on similarity relations. He gives a simple example which involves a young boy, Johnny, sorting out over the course of a day the categories "duck," "goose," and "swan." Kuhn claims that it is likely that at the beginning of the day Johnny will not be able to sort out those features that distinguish kinds from those that distinguish individuals: all the ducks, geese, and swans are just so many individual birds at the beginning of the day, and even after a few individuals have been correctly classified, Johnny can't yet know which differences between them are important. By the end of the day, he knows the differences and, hence, the similarities, to pay attention to and can correctly classify these water fowl.

Kuhn's story may or may not be correct. It seems difficult to believe that something like it doesn't apply at some points in our learning of categories. However correct it is, the story would have to be much more complicated to be applied to scientists' learning of classifications, as commentators quickly pointed out (Suppe 1974). One gathers from "Second Thoughts" that the notion of 'paradigm' is to be replaced in part by "learned similarity relations." Hoyningen-Huene takes this a step further and makes similarity relations a central part of Kuhn's philosophy, seeing paradigm changes as changes in held classifications. This explains how it is that worlds of appearances are constructed (to the extent that they are) by communities rather than by individuals; it is communities that hold the rules of classification fixed, in the same way that they hold languages fixed. Individuals can influence a community's similarity relations, but cannot single-handedly change them.

The limitations of the idea of paradigms as held similarity relations becomes clear when we look at some actual examples of paradigm changes, and changes in the world, as described by Kuhn. One that looks as though it might fit the similarity-relation account is the discovery of Uranus, seen at one time as a star, at another as a comet, and then, by Herschel, as a planet. This "minor paradigm change" may have precipitated the discovery of a large number of asteroids, or minor planets (Kuhn 1970a, 116). New objects were potentially more similar to planets than to comets or stars. But the distinguishing features of planets, comets, and stars had changed little. Rather, a class that had previously been closed was now open. There had been resistance to the idea of new planets but, when this resistance was overcome, the categories and, thus, the similarity relations, had not changed. What forced the change was the discovery of a *new* planet, not a different planet.

Other examples are more clear-cut. Roentgen's discovery of X-rays, while changing physicists' conceptual maps, was primarily interesting, and thus erected a paradigm, because X-rays were a substantially new phenomenon. They were a new thing to be investigated, a new tool, and a new source of explanations (59). This probably isn't exceptional; Derek de Solla Price sees most paradigm changes as resulting from new technologies producing new phenomena (1984).

A case that looks even more difficult to reconcile with the similarity-relation account of paradigm changes is that of the major revolution started by Darwin. To a large extent, Darwin left the major categories—species—as they were but changed the relationships between them, and possibly even changed the notion of a biological species (see Mayr 1982). He sought to provide historical explanations for the facts of natural history but he did not change the important categories with which naturalists worked.

As Margaret Masterman pointed out, "paradigm" is not a univocal term: "On my counting, he [Kuhn] uses 'paradigm' in not less than twenty-one different senses in [*The Structure of Scientific Revolutions*], possibly more, not less" (1970, 61). The twenty-one senses can be grouped into three categories: metaphysical paradigms, sociological paradigms, and artifact paradigms (Masterman's categories). Metaphysical paradigms are the "world views" that philosophers have focused attention on, what Gary Gutting has called "super-theories" (1980, 2).[2] Sociological paradigms are centered around exemplars, the shared acceptance of an achievement that structures the activities and the culture of the field. Artifact paradigms are such things as the instruments or techniques that also shape a field. In many concrete situations these three types of paradigms will be intertwined, or at least closely related: for example, an artifact may help to define a metaphysics and be important for an exemplar. Thus changes of paradigms are importantly changes in practice.

So I want to claim that changed similarity relations can make up only a part of what distinguishes paradigms. On the model of Herschel's observations of Uranus, it would seem that one thing that can separate paradigms is new examples of old phenomena. Another separation is the type of explanation that Darwin provided. Perhaps these are both best thought of as sociological paradigms, or exemplars. And some of the most common factors separating paradigms are techniques or artifact paradigms and the interests and directions of exploration that follow from the use of these techniques.

Despite these negative remarks on Hoyningen-Huene's reading of Kuhn the idealist, much of his analysis is surely right: there are some Kantian streams in *Structure*; it is just unclear how much they amount to. Kuhn explicitly uses "world" in an ambiguous way, and given his emphasis on appearances (gestalts, etc.) attributing to him talk of a world of appearances hardly seems unfair. Much of *Structure* is about how scientists' *views* of the world change. To some extent this can be blamed on Kuhn's use of perceptual metaphors and analogies to gestalt experiments, but it is unclear the extent to which he means these metaphors to define the limits of his inquiry. As well as issues about appearances, there is Kuhn's skepticism about the extent to which the notion of 'truth' can be applied in an intertheoretic way, which sounds as though it entails a commitment to a dichotomy between the world of appearances and an underlying reality. None of this should be surprising, because *Structure* was written at a time when another neo-Kantianism, namely positivism, was the dominant philosophical approach to science.

At the same time, something should be added to this reading in order for it to handle the strength of Kuhn's metaphor of changing worlds. While Kuhn places considerable emphasis on the way that scientists' world of appearances can change through revolution, he doesn't forget that scientists act on the world as well. They don't merely observe the world, they also carry out experiments.[3] Revolutions don't just produce new views of nature, they produce new research programs. Thus talk of worlds of appearances is too limiting; it deals with only one aspect of paradigms. The limitations of the similarity-relation account of paradigms point to a limitation of seeing Kuhn's talk of paradigms as being primarily about categories of appearances, steering us away from worlds of appearances and towards worlds in which action and knowledge take place. The ubiquity of resistances takes us even further, questioning the extent to which Kuhn thinks that there is an unknowable realm beyond the worlds in which we live.

PUTTING ASIDE IDEALISM

If Hoyningen-Huene's characterization of Kuhn as an idealist doesn't seem to amount to much that a realist couldn't accept, what about the stronger readings by Boyd, Scheffler, and others? *Their* Kuhn doesn't bear much resemblance to the Kuhn of *Structure*; to argue this, I have to walk through Kuhn's discussion of changes in the world, to show that, for him, the adoption of paradigms makes no "noncausal contributions" to underlying reality.

To start with, we should remember that Kuhn was primarily a historian of science when he wrote *Structure*. This is not to say that he was unconcerned about issues in philosophy of science. On the contrary, he was, and is, interested in philosophy. He claims that it was his "avocational interest in the philosophy of science" (v), and his *dissatisfaction* with it *in the light of historical work*, that prompted his change of fields from physics to history. And it is this historical work that led him to write *Structure*, as is made clear from the first sentence of the book: "History, if viewed as a repository for more than anecdote or chronology, could produce a decisive transformation in the image of science by which we are now possessed" (1). So, while his pictures of science may be informed by philosophical considerations, we should see them as compelled by historical ones.

Historical considerations "tempt" Kuhn to say that the world changes with changes of paradigms; but he asserts that worlds change only in a sense circumscribed by the the fact that scientists' "only recourse to that world is through what they see and do." If we take Kuhn seriously in his qualification, then "world" for him, when he is using it in this sense, means something like the social and perceptual context of human actions. To avoid confusing this new type of world with a Kantian world of appearances, and to avoid claiming that it is identical to the phenomenologists' life-world, I will call Kuhn's new worlds "social worlds," which will help to remind us that Kuhn is talking about professional science, which is a very social activity. As I point out above, the positing of this type of world does not have to lead to the acceptance of the unknowability of a more fundamental one.

After the positing of social worlds, Kuhn wants to turn to their components and scientists' perceptions of them. Here his views are informed by gestalt experiments. His fundamental claim is that real data are not the logical atomists' (and sometimes positivists') "here red now," but instead observations of planets and sunspots, the motion of pendulums, and even electrostatic repulsion and oxygen. This view of data is controversial, which Kuhn recognizes. He sees himself as questioning, though not firmly rejecting, a philosophical paradigm that has existed since Descartes.

Kuhn's view, the historian's view, is prompted by very empirical concerns. What scientists refer to in their papers and notes are not patches in the visual field, but theory-dependent measurements and observations.

> The operations and measurements that a scientist undertakes in the laboratory are not "the given" of experience but rather "the collected with difficulty." They are not what the scientist sees—at least not before his research is well advanced and his attention focused.... Far more clearly than the immediate experience from which they in part derive, operations and measurements are paradigm-determined. (126)

If we accept this view of data, which doesn't even deny the existence of traditional sense experiences, then we can immediately see how the adoption of a paradigm can change the social world. The adoption of paradigms changes exactly those things that count as existing—the things that can be data—and with it changes the definition of good research. Once one has gained a great deal of experience with the new ontology, one might even only perceive *it*, and find it extremely difficult to perceive alternate entities. And under a new paradigm, the places one looks to verify and falsify propositions are new places.

There is no noncausal contribution of paradigms to the world, then, either to the social world or to what lies behind it. The adoption of new paradigms makes definite causal contributions to social worlds, in that they define for the scientist what entities do and do not exist. That is, they are social causes of new phenomena.

THE WORRY ABOUT 'TRUTH'

Besides Kuhn's "other worlds" talk, probably the main reason he has been seen as having an unusual metaphysical picture has had to do with his perceived attitude toward truth. The concept is pretty much avoided throughout *Structure*, introduced only to be dismissed as unnecessary (170). In particular, it is unnecessary to see paradigm changes as bringing science closer to the truth. Science is an evolutionary process, Kuhn claims, but not one towards a goal. There is even progress, but not truth. For many, this view serves to make Kuhn an antirealist, if not necessarily an idealist. Realism seems to entail some commitment to truth, a commitment to the idea that scientific statements are sometimes true. Yet in *Structure* Kuhn seems to avoid making any such commitment. So it might be imagined that his apparently iconoclastic ideas about truth are connected to a more radical constructivist, or possibly even idealist, metaphysics.

There are a couple of reasons why Kuhn's disdain for truth need not be linked to idealism or even constructivism. First, skepticism about truth in no way implies constructivism,[4] and, if anything, the two do not sit well together. The constructivism that Kuhn is taken to espouse depends heavily on the notion of truth, because under that view paradigms establish what is true about the world. Constructivism's theory of truth is presumably not a traditional theory, but it is a theory of truth. In contrast, Kuhn would rather not use the term at all. So he cannot both be a constructivist and deny truth any value.

Second, the position that Kuhn rejects is a scientific realism that today looks like a caricature. He objects to the position that holds that "there is one full, objective, true account of nature and that the proper measure of scientific achievement is the extent to which it brings us closer to that ultimate goal." Kuhn may have been objecting to that position for the same reasons that most realists today would: the idea that there is only one true account of complex phenomena is dependent on a reductionism (probably to the physics of elementary particles) that is outdated and almost certainly wrong.

Though Kuhn doesn't ever describe his views on truth very fully, there are short discussions in the "Postscript" to the second edition of *Structure*, and in "Reflections on My Critics" (1970b) that help us to understand his position, or at least his position at the end of the 1960s. Kuhn presents several problems with 'truth', which lead him to reject it as a measure of progress in the sciences, at least over the long term. There is a historical problem:

> I do not doubt . . . that Newton's mechanics improves on Aristotle's and that Einstein's improves on Newton's as instruments for puzzle-solving. But I can see in their succession no coherent direction of ontological development. On the contrary, in some important respects, though by no means in all, Einstein's general theory of relativity is closer to Aristotle's than either of them is to Newton's. (1970a, 206–7)

Kuhn's professional opinion as a historian leads him to believe that truth is not a measure of progress. This is partly because he is still thinking of a limiting truth, a single, best theory that science is said to be steadily approaching (1970b, 265). That type of truth is not to be found in history.

There are also at least three philosophical problems, though Kuhn does not separate them out in this way. The first is closely related to the historical problem: in his opinion, there are no characterizations of truth adequate for application to whole theories and none that allow us to say that one paradigm is more truthful than another. This is essentially the same as what he says in "Reflections": "Granting that neither theory of a historical pair is true, [many philosophers of science] nonetheless seek a sense in which the latter is a better approximation to the truth. I believe nothing of that sort can be found" (1970b, 265). The nature of paradigms prohibits talking about their overall truth value. They are not the sort of things to which truth can apply, being more like ways of life, or ways of establishing truth. Among other things, they set some of the criteria for establishing truth, but that doesn't allow them to be themselves true.

The second philosophical problem with truth boils down to an issue of language. For Kuhn, following Tarski, 'truth' is "truth in a language." Since scientists separated by paradigms operate in different languages, applications of the predicate *true* across paradigms are possible only insofar as we can translate. Therefore truth is a concept that can be applied locally, but not globally; it is reasonably well defined intratheoretically, but not intertheoretically. To see this, all we have to do is remember that translation is a difficult enterprise for Kuhn and that paradigms are incommensurable. Of course if we completely reject incommensurability, as many philosophers do, then we will reject this difficulty with truth.

The third philosophical difficulty is an epistemological one. There is no way of escaping frameworks or paradigms; researchers are always within one or another. Therefore they cannot escape the paradigm they are in to establish the extratheoretic truth in what they are saying. "There is... no theory-independent way to reconstruct phrases like 'really there'" (1970a, 206). Once again, this problem divides truth along intra- versus intertheoretic lines, because when scientists attempt to talk about truths from another paradigm, they do so only from within a paradigm—theirs. So there is a sense in which truth is inaccessible if we take it to be more than intratheoretic truth. The fact that this is an epistemological problem means that we don't have to put too much weight on it. There is little difficulty in claiming that there are truths without being able to establish particular truths. But for the practically minded historian, this epistemological problem might mean that for practical purposes we should dispense with the notion of truth, at least in its extratheoretic and correspondentist flavors.

Some people may still find antirealism in things that Kuhn says about his rejection of truth. The passage quoted immediately above, for example, continues: "the notion of a match between the ontology of a theory and its 'real' counterpart in nature now seems... illusive in principle." Intuition would have it that there can be no realism without such a match. This seems right, but limited; Kuhn would be taking an antirealist stance here were he talking about everyday, local applications of truth. But if we remember that Kuhn's disquietude is about truth as a theory-independent concept, then this rejection is a simple corollary of Tarski's views on truth or of Kuhn's appreciation of the theory dependence of method. The fact that there can be no theory-independent truth in no way implies that there can be no truth at all. We are simply limited to a "partial perspective" (Haraway 1991b).

At least some people will find this picture plausible. It is, for example, similar to the one defended by Hilary Putnam in his more recent guises (e.g., Putnam 1981, 1987). Putnam separates truth into two different concepts: the local concept—truth within a framework, or language—and the global concept—framework-independent truth. About the former he is a straightforward realist. About the latter he has Peircian views—which may or may not be antirealist—of truth as the ideal limit of inquiry. For my purposes here it doesn't matter too much if it is the right or wrong picture to hold, but only that Putnam sees it as capturing what was right and important in realism. And the first part of it—for Kuhn is no Peircian—is a reasonable reconstruction of what little Kuhn says on the topic of truth. If it is, then the Kuhn of these texts doesn't come out a scientific antirealist. Kuhn agrees that science tracks reality; he just doesn't believe that that tracking of reality can be a measure of progress. He believes that some scientific statements are true; he just doesn't believe that it makes sense to talk about the truth of larger packages, and he doesn't believe that there is a God's-eye truth.[5]

One can find other reasons why Kuhn, as a historian, might find 'truth' an unuseful concept, though these are not explicitly given. It is not hard to see that one of the targets of *Structure* is "Whig History," that history which attempts to construct the past as a series of steps toward or away from present positions. The introductory chapter, "A Role for History," claims that the book comes as a result of a small revolution in historiography. This revolution challenged several assumptions, the most important of which is the assumption that science is a steady accumulation of facts, theories, and methods. Instead, history of science, particularly history of science after Alexander Koyré, has shown that science is anything but steady and is in many senses not an accumulation. The "new"—now old—history of science had new goals, goals that put an increased emphasis on specifying the causes of particular views and episodes and on displaying the "historical integrity" of science (3). Given these goals, truth becomes less important as one of the historian's tools. The causes of a belief, for example, while they might include inputs from the world, do not include the truth of the belief. And a sequence of events in the history of science cannot be explained simply by the fact that they represent progress toward the truth. These are points that have been made repeatedly in recent years in the context of the strong program and other work in S&TS. While they in themselves do not provide reasons to reject the idea of truth, they do show how history of science usually does not require scientific truth in order to go about its business.[6]

There are, then, a number of reasons why Kuhn may have been objecting to wholesale application of the idea of truth that don't require him to be an antirealist. But even if Kuhn *is* best read as an antirealist, his antirealism is not the constructivism which is sometimes read into *Structure*, because that constructivism requires 'truth.'

RE-INTERPRETING KUHN'S "CONSTRUCTIVISM"

This chapter started with a claim to be about the metaphysics of Kuhn's position. But with the collapse of an idealist reading of *Structure*, it seems that Kuhn doesn't really offer any interesting metaphysics. What is constructed is the social world, which we already knew. In this section I propose that although there may be no interesting nonrealist metaphysics in Kuhn's philosophy of science, he can be read as saying something about the way the world is. On this reading, the term *constructivist* becomes less misleading as applied to Kuhn, since there is a metaphorical sense in which scientists construct the world.[7]

Many of Kuhn's remarks about his philosophical positions are ambiguous, some of them purposefully so. Part of the reason for this ambiguity lies in the fact that, particularly in *Structure*, Kuhn may have other priorities from the ones that we normally attribute to him and may have decided not to commit himself to definite positions on some issues that interest philosophers. After all, some of his intuitions stem from his position as a historian and as a reader of history. Considerations such as the theory-dependence of what counts as data and good methodology, a recognition of the strength of consensus about a field, and skepticism about uniform progressiveness are part of what what guides positions in *Structure*. The importance of these factors, and ones like them, is also one of the things we can learn from Kuhn.

The ambiguity comes out when Kuhn says things like: "In a sense that I am unable to explicate further, the proponents of competing paradigms practice their trades in different worlds." In responding to a paper by Richard Boyd, he says:

> Both of us are unregenerate realists.... [N]either of us has yet developed an account of [realist] commitments. Boyd's are embodied in metaphors which seem to me misleading. When it comes to replacing them, however, I simply waffle. (Kuhn 1979, 415)

and

> Boyd's world with its joints seems to me, like Kant's 'things in themselves,' in principle unknowable. The view toward which I *grope* would also be Kantian but without 'things in themselves' and with categories of the mind which could change with time as the accommodation of language and experience proceeded. A view of that sort need not, I think, make the world any less real. (418–19, emphasis added)

These passages reinforce points I've already made, but they also serve to emphasize that the comments that follow represent only one possible development of the constructivist position—Kuhn saw his own position as indeterminate.

If the natural world were tremendously simple in the number and type of different entities and causal relations it contained, then for each subject matter it would only take a little time before a theory were constructed that accounted for everything that people wanted it to. If, on the other hand, the natural world were spectacularly complex, then we would expect that each theory constructed would be at best barely adequate for a short while, until interests changed. We, and the scientists involved, would probably lean toward nominalism, as each set of categories would turn out to be artificial and inadequate.

One option for a constructivist metaphysics is to claim that the natural world is likely to be on the complex end of the spectrum, but not so far that science is nearly useless. When scientists adopt a good position, or a paradigm, they would often be adopting it for its value in helping them to steer around the entities and relations that exist. It would tell them which entities to pay attention to and which ones not; it would even help them by convincing them that large numbers of entities don't, can't, exist. It would prescribe a way of life, by telling experimenters which bits of machinery to put into their laboratories, and it would proscribe ways of life that don't involve manipulating, and finding out about, the preferred entities. In a very concrete way adopting a paradigm would construct a social world.

This is a picture of paradigms given repeatedly in *Structure*. For example, to argue for a paradigm might be to "provide a clear exhibit of what scientific practice will be like for those who adopt the new view of nature" (94). And,

> [the paradigm] functions by telling the scientist about the entities that nature does and does not contain and about the ways in which those entities behave. That information provides a map whose details are elucidated by mature scientific research. And since nature is too complex and varied to be explored at random, that map is as essential as observation and experiment to science's continuing development. (109)

There is nothing in this picture that is antagonistic to realism. So the constructivism that I am proposing be explored becomes a species of realism, a realism committed to a certain amount of complexity in the natural world. This seems appropriate as a description of Kuhn's views, given his self-description as an "unregenerate realist."

I call this position "constructivist" because it mimics the position that holds that the world is constructed by scientists' ideas or by social convention. This "Kuhnian" constructivism or "constructive realism" sees the possibility of a number of highly successful, yet competing, world views. That is, it takes as a premise the notion that there is no unique, correct description of the natural world. It sees science's interactions with nature partly determined by world views, and scientists' categories partly influencing what they find, even what they observe. In this way it takes seriously Kuhn's emphasis on the theory-dependence of observation and method.

An example is called for. Compare the following two excerpts from articles on animal behavior. The first is from the first volume of *Behaviour* (1948); the second from a more recent issue (1990).

Stage 2 begins when they [mice] react to one another's squeaks by little jumps and by adopting a position of "readiness for action," made up of the postures mentioned earlier. If, however, one such mouse is approached by another, it either attempts to run away or adopts a "defensive posture" towards the approacher. This posture bears a close similarity to that adopted by a mouse in "submission" to another mouse after defeat in a fight, described by Ginsberg and Allee (1942). The report that "the chased mouse rears on its hind legs, draws one fore-leg close to the body, extends the other stiffly, remains motionless, and squeals when touched by the other mouse. (Chance 1948, 65)

Female parasitoids have to decide which hosts to accept for oviposition and which ones to reject. These decisions are often described with static optimal diet models in which a single parasitoid searches in a non-depletable patch [references]. However, patches will often be depleted in nature. In addition, parasitoids may have to search a patch in the company of conspecifics.

When patches are depleted, and when a parasitoid searches for hosts in the presence of conspecifics, these models do not apply. The optimal decisions of one parasitoid will depend on the decisions made by the others. Therefore, an evolutionary stable strategy (ESS) approach is necessary. In this paper, we investigate the oviposition decisions of *Leptopilina herotoma* (Hym.: Eucoilidae), a solitary larval parasitoid of *Drosophila*, as these are influenced by the number of parasitoids depleting a patch. (Visser et al. 1990)

There are numerous differences between these two papers. The first is a fairly empirical treatment of an artificial situation. The second is a more theoretical treatment of a situation seen in the wild. But what I want to draw attention to is the difference in the attitudes toward the respective behaviors. The first article, having no model or theory into which to fit the behavior, displays an interest in describing the details of the behavior. The behavior in question is made up of a series of movements. The second article treats the behavior as a given, not needing extensive description. The authors are interested in distributions and timing of oviposition. Which movements make up that oviposition are relatively unimportant.

I want to claim that this difference separates the majority of today's articles in this field from those of forty years ago. It certainly doesn't separate all, but the two are representative of their times in a general way. What has changed in the study of animal behavior? Almost everything. People studying behavior today have economic models that allow them to explain many more patterns of behavior in evolutionary terms; they have a long list of categories of behaviors, like oviposition, that can be thought of as more or less the same across many species. These changes have resulted in changes in the type of things that can count as data. Whereas in 1950 small movements were more likely to be data, today statistics on the number of times, and when, certain "behaviors" occur are more likely data, where the behaviors are thought of as units. Clearly this different idea of what counts as data will influence, among other things, what the researcher looks for and sees in the field. And those who collect this data will be intending to fit it into an optimization or game-theoretic model.

In short, the type of thing that the modern researcher in animal behavior looks for, how this data is collected, its meaning, and how it is used, is all often different from those of their counterparts forty years ago. How the world is divided up in practice has changed, and it is a short step from that to saying that these researchers have constructed a new world in recent years.

THE POSITION AFTER KUHN: SCIENCE AS PRACTICE

(i) *Feminist Grounds for Constructive Realism.* On this reading, Kuhn is both a constructivist and a realist. But Kuhn is not alone in occupying that position; other philosophers, historians, and sociologists have said things that would seem to place them in this constructive realist camp. For example, Evelyn Fox Keller finds some constructive realism in the geneticist Barbara McClintock's thinking:

> To McClintock, nature is characterized by an a priori complexity that vastly exceeds the capacities of the human imagination. Her recurrent remark, "Anything you can think of you will find," is a statement about the capacities not of mind but of nature. (Keller 1985, 162)

And this becomes Keller's position, too:

> I take this world of "residual reality" to be vastly larger than any possible representation we might construct. Accordingly, different perspectives, different languages will lead to theories that not only attach to the real in different ways (that is, carve the world at different joints), but they will attach to different parts

of the real—and perhaps even differently to the same parts. (Keller 1992, 74)

From this and some other assumptions Keller is led to look at the "forms" of scientific practice in terms very much like those of my reconstructed Kuhn.

Donna Haraway's postmodernism is another such position, one that I want to describe and display in more detail: she adopts constructivism to emphasize the interpretative flexibility of science, but realism to match her feminist goals. The resulting position is a perspectivalist one.

I start with the theme of textualization. Postmodernists have placed texts, broadly defined, at the center of societies, and interpretation as the central category of social action. Critical theory becomes about representation and redescription; in the postmodern world, experiences are replaced by texts. Scientific texts are treated as containing stories, and it is the stories Haraway wants to sort out, finding their points of reference, finding out how they work.[8] Haraway is interested in the metaphors that science imports, naturalizes, and then exports to other cultural domains. That science is "stories" highlights plurality: one can tell many different stories connecting a given group of facts. Thus Haraway explores some of the stories told and the metaphors used in the past thirty years that concern primate sexual politics and the relative roles of males and females in human origins: this exploration comprises a large part of her *Primate Visions* (1989), under the heading "The Politics of Being Female: Primatology is a Genre of Feminist Theory."

The emphasis on stories is methodologically motivated. Haraway applies the lessons of recent literary theory to scientific stories, to see their rhetorical techniques, their metaphors, in short to be able to *read* them. But she does not want to demean them (or all of them) in so doing: "To treat a science as narrative is not to be dismissive, quite the contrary. But neither is it to be mystified and worshipful..." (Haraway 1989, 5). Calling science's texts "stories" allows ambivalence about them; thus the move plays a role similar to that played by "symmetry" or "methodological relativism" in constructivist science and technology studies (e.g., Bloor 1991; Collins 1992).

> Analyzing a scientific discourse, primatology, as story telling within contested narrative fields is a way to enter current debates about the social constructions of scientific knowledge without succumbing completely to any of four very tempting positions [constructivism, standpoint theory, realism, and race and gender analyses], which are also major resources for the appoaches of this book. I use the image of temptation because I find all four positions persuasive, enabling, and also dangerous,

especially if any one position finally silences all the others, creating a false harmony in the primate story. (Haraway 1989, 6)

Ambivalence is a methodological tool for the person interested in the social production of knowledge; it allows one to find the social in unexpected places without endorsing judgmental relativism. The political problems in judgmental relativism are enough to push Haraway away from it, though not so far that she is unwilling to treat it as a resource. But as it stands ambivalence is not a coherent position and, for this reason, she attempts to forge some coherence in her essay "Situated Knowledges: The Science Question in Feminism and the Privilege of Partial Perspective" (Haraway 1991b).

As its subtitle indicates, "Situated Knowledges" originated as a commentary on Sandra Harding's *The Science Question in Feminism* (1986). In that book, Harding presents a dialectic of feminist positions on science, a dialectic that appears to lead to a "postmodernist" position. Feminist empiricism undermines itself because feminists are too successful at uncovering sexism in science. Sexist scientific research is thus not "bad science" but "science as usual." Empiricism gives way to standpoint theory. Standpoint theory claims that women, or feminists, in some versions, have a privileged perspective because of oppression. But there are many forms of oppression and, hence, there must be many privileged perspectives. To the Harding of *The Science Question*, that is problematic;[9] thus she is led to a postmodernism that, among other things, denies that there can be "one true story" about reality.

Haraway backs away from her earlier (and Harding's) postmodernism and constructivism, on political grounds: "the further I get in describing the radical social constructionist program and a particular version of postmodernism, coupled to the acid tools of critical discourse in the human sciences, the more nervous I get.... It shouldn't take decades of feminist theory to sense the enemy here" (185). But if it shouldn't take those decades to see political problems with relativism, its recurrence in feminist theory needs to be explained, which Haraway does in terms of the history of feminist science and technology studies. Relativism's attractiveness, she claims, comes from two things. First is the fact that feminists want a strong tool for "deconstructing the truth claims of hostile science." And second is that feminists want to go about that deconstruction by showing the contingency and historical situatedness of science. Strongly relativist forms of social constructivism accomplish both of those goals, but they don't leave feminist critics with the tools to construct *better* accounts than the scientific ones.

> So, I think my problem and "our" problem is how to have simultaneously an account of radical historical contingency for all knowledge claims and knowing subjects, a critical practice

for recognizing our own "semiotic technologies" for making meanings, and a no-nonsense commitment to faithful accounts of a "real" world. (187)

The solution is to abandon hopes for a "God's Eye" perspective, and settle for "partial perspectives" and "situated knowledges." The metaphor that Haraway wants to use is the visual, perspectival, one whereby knowledge is obtained by actors and groups with a definite perspective. Their social positions will both highlight and obscure different parts of the world, and will tend to create certain types of knowledges. Perspectivalism allows us to leave behind both relativism and objectivism, the two being opposite sides of the same coin. It allows us to accept the historical contingency of scientific knowledge while maintaining that it is knowledge *about* something.

This is a reinterpretation of what Harding calls postmodernism. Harding says, for example:

> Once the Archimedean, transhistorical agent of knowledge is deconstructed into constantly shifting, wavering, recombining, historical groups, then a world that can be understood and navigated with the assistance of Archimedes' map of perfect perspective also disappears. As Flax puts the issue, "Perhaps 'reality' can have 'a' structure only from the falsely universalizing perspective of the master." (Harding 1986, 193)

> There are as many interrelated and smoothly connected realities as there are kinds of oppositional consciousness. By giving up the goal of telling "one true story," we embrace instead the permanent partiality of feminist inquiry. (194)

Truth is not a casualty of these positions: Harding's postmodernism and Haraway's perspectivalism agree in rejecting the idea of "one true story," and they agree in opening up the possibility of telling many true stories. The world that disappears is the one that can be perfectly described. There are perspectives, but only partial ones.

Finally, for Haraway constructive realism comes in the form of assuming agency in the material world: nature is a "Trickster" who cannot be fit into our categories.[10]

> Acknowledging the agency of the world in knowledge makes room for some unsettling possibilities, including a sense of the world's independent sense of humour.... The Coyote or Trickster, embodied in American Southwest Indian accounts,

suggests our situation when we give up mastery but keep searching for fidelity, knowing all the while we will be hoodwinked. I think these are useful myths for scientists who might be our allies. (Haraway 1991b, 199).

If nature is the "Coyote" then we cannot expect our science to create perfect representations, even from a limited perspective, but only to represent that face that the Coyote chooses to show us.

(ii) *Philosophical Grounds.* One philosopher for whom the natural world is more diverse than it is for Kuhn (and thus he might be more of a *constructive* realist) is Paul Feyerabend in the recent article "Realism and the Historicity of Knowledge" (1989). It is worth looking at this article briefly as an example of an eloquent exposition of the type of constructivism that we sometimes have missed seeing in Kuhn. It should be pointed out, though, that Feyerabend does not use and, in fact, rejects the term *constructivism* to refer to his own views; he says that the "dichotomy between descriptions and constructions is much too naive to guide our ideas about the nature and the implications of knowledge claims" (Feyerabend 1989, 405).

Feyerabend starts from an apparent conflict between two assumptions that many people take for granted. The first of these is "that the theories, facts, and procedures that constitute the (scientific) knowledge of a particular time are the results of specific and highly idiosyncratic historical developments" (393). There is little doubt that this has been conclusively established by work in the history of science. "The second assumption is that what *has been found* in this idiosyncratic and culture-dependent way ... exists independently of the circumstances of its discovery" (394), which Feyerabend calls the "separability assumption." Presumably Feyerabend means this to apply only to the true part of what has been found, or means to qualify it in some other similar way. I take this second assumption to embody the "realism" of the title to his essay.

After arguing against some of the more common ways to support the separability assumption and concluding that it is wrong, Feyerabend presents his realist synthesis. There is a level of conventionality to our metaphysics, even to successful metaphysics, that makes us act in and see the world in a particular way.

> Scientists are sculptors of reality—but sculptors in a special sense. They do not merely *act causally* upon the world (though they do that, too, and they have to if they want to "discover" new entities); they also *create semantic conditions* engendering strong

inferences from known effects to novel projections and, conversely, from the projections to testable effects. (404–5, Feyerabend's emphasis)

Of course, to create semantic conditions is to act causally, but it is substantially different from the type of acting *upon the world* that we normally see scientists as doing. For Feyerabend the creation of these conventions is a cognitive matter with implications for the way in which the world is approached.

One thing that distinguishes Feyerabend from most other realist philosophers of science is his insistence on the rightness, in the appropriate environments, of many rejected views. Greek gods, for example, are for him part of a way of "sculpting" the world that could potentially make as much sense as atomistic materialism does. In this, most would regard him as eccentric; but this eccentricity does not necessarily result in an antirealist metaphysics.

> I do not assert that any combined causal-semantic action will lead to a well-articulated and livable world. The material humans (and, for that matter, also dogs and monkeys) face must be approached in the right way. It *offers resistance*; some constructions (some incipient cultures—cargo cults, for example) find no point of attack in it and simply collapse. On the other hand, *this material is more pliable than is commonly assumed*. Molding it in one way (history of technology leading up to a technologically streamlined environment and large research cities such as CERN), we get elementary particles; proceeding in another, we get a nature that is alive and full of gods. (406, Feyerabend's emphasis)

Feyerabend's aggressive assertions that scientists "are sculptors" and "manufacture atoms" may lead commentators to see in his view something like idealist constructivism (e.g., Boyd 1992). But *this* constructivism, like Kuhn's, does not rely on any "noncausal contribution" to the world, except insofar as effects of our languages can be thought of as noncausal. Our languages (and beliefs and lifestyles) affect our interactions with the world, and thereby change what we find there.

A DIAGNOSIS

Kuhnian constructivism can draw attention to the *practice* of science. Frameworks, questions, tools, and methods shape what scientists do and say.

This is a pluralist position in its recognition that there are many potential scientific practices and that some of these compete for resources and status; scientists and scientific communities compete for recognition as privileged represeners of some piece of nature. But Kuhnian constructivism is also realist in its recognition that sometimes the scientists engaged in these practices are successful in knowing about and describing entities and structures in the world.

There don't seem to be good grounds to see in Kuhn the kind of idealism of which he is sometimes accused. Why is it, then, that people have been eager to read some idealist antirealism (or constructivist antirealism) into *Structure*? Why is it that Kuhn's imagery has been often conflated with more genuine expressions of idealism? There are two important reasons.

The first stems from the fact that at the time Kuhn was writing, realism was not always disentangled from positivist reductionism—even today the two are occasionally equated. Thus realism may have been more like the type of position that Kuhn does criticize, the position that there is a uniquely correct ontology that science is approaching. Kuhn would have *become* a realist only as scientific realism changed and was articulated. The old Kuhn would have seemed about as radical a constructivist as they come.

The second reason concerns the lack of attention to what I term social worlds, the genuinely constructed worlds that scientists inhabit on a day-to-day basis, which includes the ontology they accept, the experiments that are permissible, and the institutions with which they must deal. For those not accustomed to thinking about these worlds, Kuhn's metaphors will seem strange. Philosophy of science has inherited from positivism a fairly small vocabulary with which to describe science. It includes such words as *observation, theory,* and *experiment,* but tends not to include vocabulary that reflects the range of things that may be observations, theories, or experiments. For example, the concept of a protocol, a routinized sequence of manipulations designed to achieve a very specific end, such as isolating a particular protein, is not a part of the normal vocabulary of philosophy of science, even though it is a broad category of procedures that are a standard part of the laboratory scientist's day-to-day life.[11] Protocols produce data or clean samples, though by means not necessarily understood by the people who follow them. They are interesting because they are, to a greater or lesser extent, taken for granted. They are a necessary part of the scientist's social landscape.

Without keeping in mind the importance of social objects it is difficult to appreciate the potential value in saying that scientists' worlds change when paradigms do. We are apt to forget that a change in theory can result in the complete reorganization of the laboratory and the lives that intersect with it. It can change the meaning and relative importance of different types of observations. Thus, even when a particular type of resistance is undoubtedly shared by two consecutive paradigms, for example a type of resistance that precipitates a change of paradigms, the lives of the users of those two paradigms might have changed sufficiently that they would give completely different meaning to those resistances. So instead of being something that unites their worlds, it might be something that divides them. It is this type of observation that might make it fruitful to talk of scientists inhabiting different worlds.

Seven

CREEPING REALISM:
BRUNO LATOUR'S HETEROGENEOUS
CONSTRUCTIVISM

> Solutions to the problem of knowledge are solutions to the problem of social order.
> —S. Shapin and S. Schaffer (1985, 332)

IN THEIR "ROLE AS GUARDIANS OF TRUTH AND RATIONALITY" (Gutting 1984), philosophers attempt to abstractly distinguish good and bad thought, and good and bad science in particular. Good science and good thought the philosopher tries to describe and explain within her own terms. Explanations of bad science and bad thought are left to sociologists and psychologists. Sociology of science is saddled with the dregs, left to study second-class phenomena. The strong program in the sociology of knowledge was the result of an attempt on the part of some sociologists and sympathizers to rectify the imbalance. It made the claim that all of science is a potential area of study for the sociologist, or for social analysis. David Bloor says,

> Can the sociology of knowledge investigate and explain the very content and nature of scientific knowledge? Many sociologists believe that it cannot.... They voluntarily limit the scope of their own enquiries. I shall argue that this is a betrayal of their disciplinary standpoint. All knowledge, whether it be in the empirical sciences or even in mathematics, should be treated, through and through, as material for investigation. (Bloor 1991, 1)

For sociology of science, or for the social study of science more generally, to successfully study *all* of scientific knowledge, it probably has to identify as social all of the important causes of scientific knowledge. Realism is then perceived as an obstacle to a full social study of science because, if a material entity has a substantial effect on the choice of theory, then a complete account of the choice of theory will involve at least one apparently non-social factor. Sociology could accept this limitation, and does when the inputs are of a different, for example psychological, nature; but such an acceptance would leave nagging doubts that the sociological causes involved in any theory choice were secondary to old-fashioned empirical causes. And since sociology has in general no tools for interrogating natural phenomena except those of the sciences it studies, it has no independent standard of truth and falsity with which to compare scientific judgments and, thus, no clear method of sorting out the relative importance of social and empirical causes in the making of a scientific judgement. S&TS then, has found it easier to attack realism directly (e.g., Barnes and Bloor 1982).

There are other reasons for this attack, having to do with the connection between realism and truths of nature. Harry Collins argues that only something like his Empirical Programme of Relativism (EPOR) can provide a sound methodology for the sociological study of scientific knowledge (Collins 1981a). EPOR is a particular interpretation of David Bloor's recommendation of symmetry, an interpretation that makes social causes the only ones. The reasons for symmetry are simple: truth, rationality, success, and progress cannot provide the grounds for an explanation of the adoption of a theory because these can only be fully known with hindsight.[1] Arguing that a scientist adopted a particular theory because it was true, for example, invokes a judgment that could not have been validated in the course of a controversy. Thus real features of the material world do not look as though they can contribute to an explanation of the theory choice. Also, for symmetry, reliance on such factors as truth, rationality, and progress has the tendency to convince people to stop looking at social interactions too quickly; conviction that a certain scientific discipline consistently maps the world might steer the sociologist away from interesting sociology. For these reasons Collins recommends that sociologists (and philosophers and historians) adopt for methodological purposes a position of skepticism with respect to scientific knowledge or, as he puts it, assume that relativism is correct. It should be pointed out, though, that for the Collins of the early 1980s EPOR is justified *only* as a methodological strategy; although it is incompatible with rationalist accounts of science Collins does not see it as incompatible with "hidden-hand" accounts that lead to realism. A more recent Collins (1992) is willing to make stronger claims for his methodological skepticism.

This chapter points to some limitations of the skeptical methodological strategy and describes the modification of it by the Bruno Latour of *Science in Action* and *The Pasteurization of France*. I argue that there are difficulties for the strongly antirealist position taken by S&TS in the early 1980s and that Latour's interesting moves—his heterogeneous constructivism—deal with these difficulties. I don't want to claim that Latour's solutions are

Creeping Realism 115

the only ones that have been put forward: Andrew Pickering, Karin Knorr-Cetina, Peter Taylor, and others have their own positions, focusing, like Latour, on practice.[2] In mock-Latourian fashion, we will take some detours and digressions before turning to our central actor.

In his article "Creeping Surrealism" Joel Achenbach describes a society (ours) in which the unreal is given considerably more importance than the real. An advertisement for the importance of the Constitution cannot use the Army office where military recruits take their oath—it is too "small, sterile, poorly lit." In order to interest people the ad was filmed

> in a majestic vaulted room at a Catholic College.... Light streamed in from windows on high. Smoke machines filled the room with dense, tangible atmosphere. The actors—attractive, demographically diverse—were spaced apart in the room, each one perfectly erect, hand over heart, illuminated in chiaroscuro. (Achenbach, 116)

Or, tours of Disney and MCA-Universal studios take people past studios that were built for the occasion.

> So they're even building old-fashioned backlots, with a simulated New York street, a Middle America courthouse square, and quiet Leave-It-to-Beaver neighborhoods.... The sets are for tourists. Façades like these are inherently fakes, but these are a step beyond—They're imitation fakes, built to create the illusion of façades. (115)

The Disney studio is a "simulacrum" (e.g., Baudrillard 1983), a representation that is better than the original, which may not even exist. It is Dan Quayle getting into an argument with the television character Murphy Brown, and then trying to make up by sending Brown's baby a present. But the lesson I want to take out of this is simpler—in short, Achenbach sees everywhere a "creeping surrealism," with original realities becoming increasingly unbelievable and irrelevant.

S&TS sometimes seems to be in a world in which the surreal has already conquered. For sociologists such as Steve Woolgar (1988) the entities scientists study have only the reality those scientists give them. Not 'unreal', the natural world becomes constructed through scientists' efforts and negotiations. This strategy has been remarkably successful on many fronts, allowing work in S&TS to produce a number of fascinating insights and studies. For example, this strategy probably helped Harry Collins to identify the problem of "experimenter's regress": what counts as a replication of an experiment is not clear-cut, and has to be negotiated. The strategy has also allowed people like Andrew Pickering to identify scientists' interests that might otherwise go unnoticed (Pickering 1984). It would be tiresome to run through these and other examples of successes of strongly antirealist S&TS, so I merely wish to emphasize that there *have* been successes, and notable ones, and move on to a few failures. Of course some guardians of truth and rationality (e.g., Brown 1989) disagree that there have been successes.

One failure is straightforward. Antirealist S&TS fails to give a satisfactory account of technical success, the achievement of technical goals. By this I mean not just technological goals but also more mundane laboratory successes. This is a variant of problems to do with causality: antirealist S&TS fails to give a satisfactory account of why the structure of the world should depend upon scientific consensus. To give it credit, it *has* tried to disarm this objection. The objection assumes that science is implicated in at least some technical successes, which seems fairly unproblematic. However, it might be possible to explain a great many technical successes without reference to "science." That is, many pieces of technology might involve not much more than trial and error and might involve very little that should be called scientific "knowledge" of the world. This is one of the things that the volume *The Social Construction of Technological Systems* (Bijker, Hughes, and Pinch, 1987) was intended to accomplish, though it's not obvious that that goal was achieved. For example, Edward Yoxen's account of the development of ultrasound technology (Yoxen 1987) depends as much as any history of technology on an assumption that the actors saw problems and had knowledge of nature that helped them to achieve solutions to those problems. Yoxen neither tries nor (inadvertently) succeeds in writing the history of this episode without reference to knowledge of nature, and the same applies to others of the contributors to *The Social Construction of Technological Systems*. So accounting for technical successes remains an important problem for any analysis of science.

A second failure of antirealist S&TS (or sociology of knowledge) is more complicated. David Bloor presents us with four tenets for a sociology of knowledge: It should be "causal,... impartial with respect to truth and falsity, rationality and irrationality,... symmetrical in its style of explanation,... and reflexive" (Bloor, 5). If one is to take seriously these tenets for a sociology of knowledge as a programmatic manifesto and accepts the interpretation that they are normally given, one would expect that in principle a scientific consensus or decision could be causally reduced, at least roughly, to purely sociological factors. But in fact no plausible such reduction has been presented, nor has even an indication been given of how one could make such a reduction. What we see instead is that sophisticated accounts deliberately eschew the use of reductionistic causal connections and reductions to social interests. For example, Donald MacKenzie in his *Statistics in Britain* (1981) gives functionalist explanations for people's beliefs and actions, arguing that they are "appropriate" for these people's social positions.

The case against reductionism is a strong one. Harry Collins even uses this strength to make room for social explanations (Collins 1992). He argues on various grounds—including problems stemming from Nelson Goodman's new riddle of induction, the underdetermination of theory by data, and Wittgenstein's problems about following rules—that an "algorithmic model" of science cannot work. There is no methodological canon that can simply be applied. In place of the algorithmic model Collins wants to establish an "enculturational model," which puts more emphasis on tacit knowledge.

Collins describes his "enculturational model" in terms of some concrete case studies, such as his examination of the difficulties in building a laser, described briefly in chapter 3 (Collins 58ff.). The TEA-laser (Transversely Excited Atmospheric pressure CO_2 laser) is a relatively simple machine invented and developed in the late 1960s and early 1970s. Yet efforts to duplicate this simple machine were plagued with problems. For example, the final problem that Collins describes his subject as facing, "anode marking," was only solved by a telephone call to an informant in a lab where there was a working laser. It was suggested that the experimenters change the polarity from his energy source. In the end, a TEA-laser was constructed.

If the enculturational model is to work, we have to posit some regular features of the world with which the culture manages to successfully deal. If anode marking can be stopped by reversing polarity and if this can be learned, then there is some knowledge of nature (even if not any deep understanding) floating about the TEA-laser community. That is, to build a successful laser (it can "vaporize concrete" [Collins 51]), there has to be some knowledge of a nonhuman nature. I don't want to argue here that a social reductionism should simply be supplemented by one in terms of observations and rationality; the underdetermination of theory by data shows that that cannot work. But sometimes it seems as though a reasonably thorough *explanation* of scientists' behavior is possible and, hence, an *approximate* reduction of that behavior to its causes is possible. I want to claim that in many such cases the material world, in the sense of an external reality and its manifestations, should be among those causes.

At first glance, that material world doesn't look as though it is part of a social world, which leaves (even an approximate) *social* reduction unaccomplished. Of course, not everybody will see the failure to reduce scientific decisions to traditional social factors as a failure at all. But it seems that until such a reduction can be made Bloor's manifesto (Bloor, 5) for sociology of science will be unfulfilled.

In *Science in Action* and *The Pasteurization of France* Bruno Latour solves the two problems above (that is the failure to explain technological success and the failure to be reductionistic to social factors) by radically shifting viewpoints on science and its objects of study. What follows is a selective summary and interpretation of his model. The examples are Latour's.

Knowledge is tightly connected to power. We might therefore imagine scientists as politicians or generals, who try to create alliances large enough that nobody can question their power within their domains. Scientists contest each other's power mostly through argument; at that level contests are textualized. At other levels scientists muster material strengths. Science as a whole works through the interplay of strengths.

In a scientific paper the author attempts to establish, to a potentially hostile reader, a fact and her claim to the power to do so (Latour 1987, chap. 2). In order to ensure that the reader cannot question her power, the author arrays lists of her allies in the form of citations (31ff.). In questioning a particular point within the paper, the lone reader may find himself face to face with one of the author's allies, who will in turn have allies, and so on. So when I cite "(Latour 1987, chap. 2)" I claim to have built an alliance with that author, and if you, the reader, question my claim you will have to contend with him. Latour sees the scientific paper as "one player's strokes in [a] tennis final" (46) with a potential reader supplying the other strokes. Or, in keeping with his metaphors in *Pasteurization* the scientific paper is a battle plan ready to greet an opponent. The opponent's thrusts are already thought out, the scientist's parries already chosen.

Behind the author and her paper lies another great ally or alliance, the laboratory. This is the center of Latour's model of science, as his Pasteur boasts "Give me a Laboratory and I will Raise the World" (Latour 1983). It is the laboratory that gives scientists power other people do not have, for "it is in the laboratories that most new sources of power are generated" (Latour 1983, 160). The laboratory, with its inscription devices and its tools for changing scale or for keeping nature under control, provides the scientist with power over nature (Latour 1988). It provides the scientist with enlisted allies (nature) in the process of gaining power over the readers of articles.

Scientists have great powers of rhetoric (Latour 1987, 61) but besides this they are much like other people—medium sized and of medium strength, being far larger than microbes yet far smaller than mountains. This is why inscription devices and the change of scale is important. Inscription devices allow the scientist to deal with nature on pieces of paper, which are also medium sized, durable, and transportable: such representations are "immutible mobiles." Microscopes and telescopes change the sizes of things, making them also human in scale. Once nature is brought down or up to the scale of the scientist, and once it is brought into the laboratory or "center of calculation," then it is much more easily manipulated. For this reason "epistemologists had chosen the wrong objects, they looked for mental aptitudes and ignored the material local setting, that is, laboratories" (Latour 1983, 160).

All of this sounds mysterious perhaps, but it has a straightforward interpretation. We can see this in Latour's study of Louis Pasteur and the Pasteurians. When faced with an epidemic of anthrax, the Pasteurians move to the place where anthrax can most easily be found, namely the farm. There they attempt to sift through the many phenomena of the farm to extract the phenomena with which they can deal most strongly, the microbe.

> But a Pasteurian does not linger on the terrain of his hastily constructed laboratory. Indeed, the knowledge thus accumulated is almost always weaker at this stage than is that of the men in the field, veterinary surgeons or physicians. The whole Pasteurian strategy, now that they have extracted a few aspects from the macrocosm, is to gain strength by making a long detour to their central well-equipped laboratory. (79)

Inside the laboratory the extracts are defined, manipulated, and domesticated. The definition process consists of a series of trials of strength: "In the laboratory any new object is at first defined by inscribing in the laboratory notebook a long list of what the agent does and does not do" (80). The processes of manipulation and domestication are familiar; the microbe, now defined, is subjected to more trials of strength until the scientist can use it for his own ends.

Finally there must be a demonstration of the power of the scientist. To show to the world what he has accomplished the Pasteurian takes his alliance with the domesticated microbe and uses it to vanquish the wild microbe. In a time when heroic gestures are necessary, the Pasteurian may even go so far as to take his laboratory and his new alliance back to the farm (Latour 1988, 87–88 and Latour 1983, 166). At later times, when the public has already accepted the power of the scientist this may not be necessary.

The boundaries of scientists' power are not entirely *internal* to science, in the traditional way of using that word. Pasteurians had the power to move governments, hygienists, farmers, and others. This they accomplished by "translating" others' interests: one translates using rhetorical and other techniques to transform people's goals and interests so that they are one's own. For example, Pasteur might try to convince the French army that in order to achieve their goals they must *first* help Pasteur achieve his. This makes his activities "obligatory passage points" (Latour 1987, 156).

We must return to the process of definition. The new object "is defined by what it does in the laboratory trials, *nothing more, nothing less*.... The new object is *named after what it does*" (Latour 1987, 87). Thus, for example, when Pierre and Marie Curie are experimenting with a new object, they subject it to numerous tests, distinguishing it from other, already-defined elements.

> It defeated uranium and thorium at the sulphurated hydrogen game; it defeated antimony and arsenic at the ammonium sulphur game; and then it forced lead and copper to throw in the sponge, only bismuth went all the way to the semi-final, but it too got beaten down during the final game of heat and cold! At the beginning of its definition the 'thing' is a *score list* for a series of trials. (Latour 1987, 89)

In some way, Latour wants to claim, it is through these trials that the scientist *constructs* new actors: they are actors that exist in the laboratory and other artificial situations, but not straightforwardly in the natural world.[3] They are pieces of the natural world displaced, to reveal their interests.

Latour's model, then, does not simply see science as consisting of networks of human alliances, in straightforward analogy to politics. The model describes a "heterogeneous network," because it includes actors who would normally be excluded from other models. We have seen how new scientific objects are tested to find out what they can and cannot do. But this is also a series of tests of actors, to find out which alliances can and cannot be built with them. That is, the microbe can be seen not just as an entity which Pasteur studies but as an actor with whom Pasteur builds an alliance. The feats performed by microbes are *interests* to be managed and used by the clever scientist. For example, Latour describes the efforts of Diesel:

> At the start, Diesel ties the fate of his engine to that of *any* fuel, thinking that they would all ignite at a very high pressure.... But then, nothing happened. Not every fuel ignited. This ally which he had expected to be unproblematic and faithful betrayed him. Only kerosene ignited, and then only erratically.... So what is happening? Diesel has to *shift his system of alliances*. (Latour 1987, 123)

The system of alliances that Diesel and other scientists have to manage include entities as diverse as kerosene, air pumps, engineers, financiers and entrepreneurs, and possibly the consumer market. The scientist, especially the one involved in technology, must be constantly aware of many or all of these different actors if he is to succeed.

It is in these unorthodox actors that we find realism creeping into our framework again. For antirealist S&TS the entities scientists study are constructions, and nothing more. For Latour these entities become agents and, though we assume that scientists in some way define or construct them, we take their interests as determined. Nature is socialized, made part of the social order. With this incorporation, Shapin and Schaffer's claim, at the head of this chapter, acquires a new meaning. Solutions to the problems of knowledge are exactly solutions to the problems of social order.

The determined nature of these interests comes out in Latour's sad stories of Diesel and the Curies. Diesel's goal is to design and market an engine following Carnot's principles of thermodynamics. In order to build his alliance he must discover what the interests of various fuels are. When he inquires, he discovers that only kerosene is willing to ignite at a low temperature and high pressure. He must redesign his alliance so that the kerosene's interests are met or controlled, without losing the support of other parts of the network he is building. In the end Diesel does lose the support of his financial backers and his technical partner. Without these crucial parts, the network he is attempting to build falls apart and the engine does not come to exist. Diesel's network fails because of his inability to manage all the interests of the participants. But we can also say that Diesel's network fails because the fuels are unexpectedly demanding. Their interests cannot be satisfied without alienating the rest of the network. Therefore there is no easy way to hold together this alliance.

Pierre and Marie Curie's investigations on "substance x"—later "polonium"—represent an episode in more basic science. The Curies *define* polonium through a series of tests, yet at the same time they are *inquiring* as to whether substance x has interests a, b, c, and so forth. They *discover* these interests so that they and later chemists can be more powerful. In this they succeed. But in the end, polonium betrays them, for they do not learn of its interest in producing deadly radiation.

We can see this creeping realism in another part of Latour's work. The second, theoretical, part of *Pasteurization* consists of an ordered series of points, a parody of rationalist philosophy. Here Latour greets us with a world of pure actors, actants, or entelechies (Latour 1988, 159), much like Leibnizian monads. There is some question as to whether everything else is reducible to these actors, for Latour's first injunction is against reduction: "Nothing is, by itself, either reducible or irreducible to anything else" (158). Actors gain strength by forming associations, by speaking for others, and having others speak for them.

> A force becomes potent only if it speaks for others, if it can make those it silenced speak when called upon to demonstrate its strength, and if it can force those who challenged it to confess that indeed it was saying what its allies would have said. (197)

Between the paradoxes, jokes, and reminiscences, the world that Latour is describing requires S&TS to look at actors and their networks, either of which may take *any* form.

> Entelechies cannot be partitioned into "animate" and "inanimate," "human" and "nonhuman," "object" and "subject," for this division is one of the very ways in which one force may seduce others. (194)

Though Latour does not want to allow it—"There is no difference between the 'real' and the 'unreal,' the 'real' and the 'possible,' the real and the 'imaginary'" (159)—realism is creeping in. If the student of science is to accept Latour's model, then it seems that the actors, or at least their interests, will have to take on a degree of reality and constrain events.[4] Therefore what was traditionally seen as Nature, or at least her properties, will have to take on a degree of reality and determine events. This is why we see Latour hedge:

> Did the microbe exist before Pasteur? From the practical point of view—*I say practical, not theoretical*—it did not. To be sure, Pasteur did not invent the microbe out of thin air. But he shaped it by displacing the edges of several other previous agents and moving them to the laboratory in such a way that they became unrecognizable. (Latour 1988, 80, my emphasis)

However we divide the practical and the theoretical here, we are left with the implication that from the "theoretical" point of view, the microbe did exist before Pasteur.

I don't want to claim that Latour is consistent in his realism. In his "Clothing the Naked Truth" (1989) he is explicit about his distaste for scientific realism (or more often, what he calls "rationalism"):

> If Russian historians claim that there had never been any Trotsky and that he had never been the head of the Red Army, rationalists are incensed by this tinkering with history; but if someone asserts that electrons have always been there even before Millikan tied his fate to theirs, or that spontaneous gen-

eration had never been there after all, they swallow those lies hook, line and sinker. (Latour 1989, 120)

He justifies this position on the basis of a structuralist semantics, which makes *electron* a word with constantly changing meaning—hence electrons didn't exist before Millikan. But on the other hand, in another recent article, "The Force and the Reason of Experiment" (1990a), Latour recognizes his commitment to knowledge of the material world and announces that "A little bit of constructivism takes you far away from realism; a complete constructivism brings you back to it" (71). Recent essays (Latour 1990b, 1992; Callon and Latour 1992) reveal a search for a consistent position behind the apparent contradiction, which he wants to locate in an "amodern" (1990b) or "nonmodern" (1992) perspective that denies a nature/society divide and goes on from there. Latour sees the spectrum between the strongest constructivisms and the strongest realisms as uni-dimensional—nature is more or less constructed depending upon one's position on the continuum. In contrast, his amodernist network theory adds to the one-dimensional "modern" yardstick measuring constructedness of things a dimension measuring stability, allowing us to follow trajectories. It is not clear whether Latour's new philosophical position can be made plausible and workable; in any case, I have here only been interested in drawing out the realism implicit in his network approach. Networks consisting of both human and nonhuman actors need to combine to produce stable technologies and useful scientific representations.

There is a lesson in this about certain types of critiques of science. One of Latour's goals is to naturalize science and bring it into the dirt with most of the rest of our institutions, to show how being a scientist is akin to being a politician, a general, or a capitalist. Unlike strong programmers, Latour is interested in the processes of science over its products, internal relations of science over external causes of scientific results (though he claims to reject the internal/external distinction). And unlike neo-Kantian constructivists Latour does not assume that representations construct their objects but, instead, looks at the material processes that connect representation and the world and shows us some ways in which scientists materially shape the things with which they work. Latour's internal critique displays several ways in which scientific knowledge is inseparable from power: laboratory knowledge is (at least often) a description of the relative powers of subjects and artifacts in the lab, and knowledge arising from publications, discussions, and exchanges involves complicated and subtle power games. To make these points, especially the first, Latour has to accept the reality of some objects of scientific study and powers of artifacts; his critique of the processes of science hinges on their effectiveness, as will any similar analysis of processes. So one lesson is that this type of analysis will tend to be allied with realism.

Latour's model should be of interest to the political critic of science for it, in a sense, reduces everything that goes on in the laboratory to power, the currency of politics. And if he is right that we can make sense of science when we view it through the lens of power relations, we can understand why it is that scientific knowledge has often proven so easy to apply. Scientific knowledge is already designed to produce effects, to be a tool in the hands of the scientist, before it even leaves the laboratory: according to Latour, one task of the laboratory scientist is to force substances to do what is needed, and the laboratory sciences' methodologies are in part designed around that task.

In addition, Latour's model should be interesting because it doesn't sacrifice the successes of science to the analysis of rhetoric. Rhetoric and reasoning become one and the same, both efforts to win intellectual battles by gathering allies and superior force. So when the political critic wants to point out that the interior dynamics of science are not necessarily the ideology-free realm of rational discussion that is part of science's self-adopted image, that challenge to traditional forms of scientific rationality does not become a challenge to science's pragmatic successes.

Now I can claim that Latour has put forward at least a sketch of a solution to two problems which face antirealist S&TS of science: its inability to account for the successes of technology and its inability to reduce scientific decisions to traditional social factors. The first problem is now a problem of explaining the cleverness of the technologist. This is so because a piece of technology is now seen as a tight alliance. The person who constructs it is somebody with a good understanding of the interests of the various actors involved, and an ability to manage those interests. This understanding comes from the technologist's ties with the scientist, who is always inquiring about and forcing confessions of interests from potential actors. This in turn can be accomplished because of the strength that that great alliance, the laboratory, gives the scientist.

The second problem dissolves. On the one hand, Latour does not wish us to reduce anything to anything, let alone scientific decisions to social factors—his "irreductionism" is something with which I have not dealt here—and, on the other, he has provided us with a whole universe of new social (f)actors or agents to which we can reduce things. For those of us who do not appreciate or understand Latour's irreductionistic bent, the second half of this will be more useful. We need no longer try to reduce scientific decisions to class struggles, political platforms, or national goals, as we can more convincingly try to reduce those decisions to the interplay of atoms, microbes, meteorites, experimenters, theoreticians, microscopes, entrepreneurs, *and* class struggles and political platforms. To pervert a line from

David Bloor, for sociologists not to take these actors into account is to voluntarily limit the scope of their own enquiries.

What Bruno Latour is proposing is a new alliance. Where S&TS and scientists and antirealism have failed, or not yet succeeded, S&TS, heterogeneous actors, a thoroughly deflationary constructivism, and a disguised realism might have a chance. If it does succeed it will not be without costs. Realism creates methodological problems by introducing some objects, or actors, to which S&TS has little access. Scientists define the interests of these new actors, and there is little way of circumventing their definitions. This places us in the position of depending on a few of our subjects for all of our information about the others. Thus, the costs of this alliance may be prohibitive for an interesting S&TS. Whether they are or not remains to be seen, though we can now appreciate the wariness toward Latour (e.g., Collins and Yearley 1992).

There is wariness that comes from other directions, as well. Latour, in flattening the social landscape into networks of monadic agents, leaves no space for individual psychology. Peter Taylor, in his attempts to reshape heterogeneous constructivism, has been highly critical of Latour's actors' impoverished psychologies (1995b). Those actors are simply rational. The same flattening of the social landscape means that all features of culture have to be interpreted as particular configurations of the network. But that seems to do violence to norms, ideologies, and other nonlocalized parts of culture. Textures of social life disappears.

Thus heterogeneous constructivism probably needs an enriched vocabulary for talking about actors and cultures. But with such enrichment I think that the new alliance is a strong one. An appreciation of the power of natural actors is necessary for S&TS to escape the difficulties connected with antirealism, and Latour's alliance includes an appreciation of that power.

AN AFTERWORD ON THE SUCCESSES OF S&TS

Although Latour solves some of the problems that antirealist S&TS faced, what happens to the successes of that S&TS? In the "Afterword" to the second edition of *Changing Order* Harry Collins makes the following claim:

> Just as the empirical success of descriptions of the world based on Euclidean geometry encourages us to think that parallel lines never meet, it is the fruitfulness of sociological case studies that leads us to reevaluate the nature of science. If truth, rationality, success, and progress ... are not found to be the driving forces of science when discovery and justification are described in as

> much detail as possible, then, it seems, science does not need them to explain its development. (Collins 1992, 185)

This positive argument for antirealism is a form of the abductive argument from success: we should believe the theory implicated in successful methodology. The success of (neo-Kantian) "constructivist" accounts in providing good descriptions of scientific activity and in showing us new phenomena should convince us to believe the premises or "theory" on which those accounts are based.

When I presented the abductive argument for realism, I made an important qualification, which applies again here: the argument doesn't automatically tell us what a practice's success gives us warrant to believe. What is implicated in successful methodology *may* be a grand, overarching theory that researchers keep in the back of their minds, but it may also be a collection of simple causal hypotheses that are employed in everyday work. Similarly, when we look to the success of constructivist S&TS we have to decide which premises are implicated in that success.

Latour's work rests on an assumption of the reality of the many actors and their interests involved in scientific productions. His descriptions assume that the power relations between scientists and the material world are a key to understanding the success of science. Most work going by the name "social constructivist" in S&TS doesn't actually employ neo-Kantian constructivism as a methodological resource—this form of constructivism is usually just a gloss overlying accounts. What this work does employ, on the other hand, is a recognition of the social and political activity of science, a recognition of the artifactuality of the materials of the laboratory, and a recognition of the stability and causal force of social objects.

If we take Collins's abductive argument seriously—and I think that we should—the conclusions suggested by it are neither that scientists construct the material world through their theories nor that the material world is irrelevant in scientific work. Instead, the argument suggests that science uses the material world in interesting ways. And among other things it suggests that science is social relations: politics plays an important role in science, stretching from the material politics of the laboratory to the politics of human societies.

Eight

METAPHORS AND REPRESENTATION

RECENT WORK IN S&TS shows that scientific models and descriptions are replete with explicit metaphors and analogies.[1] And when we look at larger theoretical frameworks we find metaphor even more centrally placed—according to Mary Hesse (1966) and Donna Haraway (1976), almost *every* major paradigm depends upon one or a few key metaphors. For some (e.g., Gergen 1986; Jones 1982; Papin 1992) this provides a strong argument against realism in the sciences: if metaphors are so prevalent, how can we say that scientific theories describe reality rather than construct frameworks? In particular, how can inquiry influenced by metaphors current in the wider culture, as so much of science is, be taken as representing? Metaphors are perceived as an unstable part of language and, hence, an unstable place in which to find good representations; it is often assumed that metaphors are not the sort of thing that can refer, or be true or false. This chapter is an answer to claims like these. My aim here is to present an account of metaphor which can be used to understand metaphors in science as more than mere literary flourishes or rhetorical devices yet, at the same time, showing that they can be part of representations.

WHY SO MANY METAPHORS? THREE REASONS

Various researchers have shown that metaphors in science are valuable as heuristic and conceptual tools (e.g., Hoffman 1985; Nersession 1988) and, as such, often serve important descriptive and referential functions (Boyd 1979; Ackermann 1985; Cummiskey 1992).[2] It has even been argued that science is impossible without metaphorical thinking, because metaphors are needed to provide the cognitive resources to explore new domains (Martin and Harré 1982). The central point here is made by Richard Boyd, for example, in "Metaphor and Theory Change" (1979). Boyd argues that metaphors can be valuable conceptual tools, and can define research programs rich with questions, insights, and agendas for research—he calls such centrally placed metaphors "theory constitutive." For example, the mind-as-computer analogy has played "an indispensable role in the formulation and articulation of theoretical positions" (Boyd 1979, 361). The ubiquity of metaphor and analogy in the sciences can be taken as evidence that literal language lacks the resources for (at least easy) applicability to new realms. Robert Ackermann (1985), among others, makes a similar point, emphasizing the fact that research instruments produce novel *types* of data that have to be accomodated; metaphors are necessary because they enlarge conceptual resources.

A second reason for the ubiquity of metaphor has to do with the structure of theories. The traditional or "received" view of scientific theories sees them as formal structures, a list of axioms on the model of Euclid's axioms for plane geometry, connected to the world via definitions and "bridge principles." But this view fails to make sense of the way that scientists use, reformulate, revamp, and extend theories when faced with new problems or when creating new avenues of inquiry. One place where it fails is in reifying the formal structure; the formalism is never completely abstractable from the goal of representation.

Mary Hesse (1966) argues that what connects theories and the material world is a set of metaphors and models; these give the theorist tools with which to extend the theory. This is not simply a reiteration of the claim about the need for new conceptual resources; instead metaphors and analogies are essential parts of theoretical activity in that they provide the "growing points" for theories. The traditional view of theories as formal structures makes them near-tautologous redescriptions of data (or perhaps of phenomena), providing little space for exploration. If theories were merely formal structures, anomalies would provide as much reason for the overthrow of the entire system as of any part of it. Theories concretized in models and metaphors, on the other hand, can provide guidelines for new experiments and new theoretical innovations; the metaphors or analogies on which they are based provide strategies for dealing with anomalies in ways that formal systems cannot. Metaphors are necessary because of their fertility.[3]

A third reason for the central place of metaphors in scientific theorizing draws on the fact that theories and models are abstractions within a framework. Models approximate away from the truth: the usefulness of these models and the abstractions they employ indicates that too-tight correspondence is something to escape from. Nonetheless, or perhaps because of this, scientific representations aim at elucidating *structures* of relations in the material world. Representations are idealizations or abstractions precisely because these structures tend to be more permanent; they are also easier to represent, if harder to discern. But they aren't *merely* abstractions, because they have to take place within a framework, a lens through which to choose elements to idealize. Abstraction and conceptual approximation so often lead to explicit metaphors because theorizing and modeling are closely analogous to the creation of metaphors in their attempts to find terms in which to represent structures.

Thus some work on modeling has looked at the ways in which structures are mapped. For example, Dedre Gentner (1982) groups together scientific models, analogies, and metaphors to look at them as maps of structures, bringing out features that serve to make them better or worse maps of things and the relations between things. An extremely simple model, such as the Rutherford model of the atom as a solar system, is a mapping of structure. It asserts that nucleus and electrons stand to each other in some similar relations—mutual attraction, asymmetry of masses, revolution of the former around the latter—as do sun and planets. What is valuable about this simple model, however inadequate it later turned out to be, is that it mapped some of the supposed structure of the atom in familiar terms—what a simple metaphor should do. Theoretical work is metaphorical work and, hence, it is no surprise that explicit and familiar metaphors are common. That is, I want to move from saying that metaphors are essential resources for scientific theorizing—my first two reasons for the ubiquity of metaphor—to saying that scientific theories *are* essentially metaphorical descriptions. The following section takes a detour through some examples, to illustrate and further explain this point.

ABSTRACTIONS AND IDEALIZATIONS

Game-theoretic models in evolutionary biology provide illustrations of the importance of idealization in theoretical activity. Game theory consists of a small set of assumptions and mathematical techniques designed to model competition among strategies; the strategies are assumed to be genetically coded for; it is the strategies, rather than their individual instantiations in organisms, that compete or play the game. For example, an early and well-known application of some of the core ideas involved attempts to model aggression, the Hawk-Dove game (Maynard Smith and Price 1973; Maynard Smith 1982). Here the attempt is to model—with obvious human correlates—responses to intraspecific conflict. Conflicts are assumed to take place between two (generic) organisms, over a resource of determinate value. The modeler imagines some possible responses to the conflict; in this case they are either to fight or to retreat—the Hawk and Dove strategies respectively. The task of the modeler is to find a stable ratio of Hawks to Doves, a ratio that is locally optimal in a sense defined by the theory.

Game-theoretic models depend upon idealizations and abstractions from the material world in order to work. Most uses of game theory assume that reproduction is asexual, that strategies are directly correlated with genes, and that the population is infinite and unstuctured; also, game-theoretic models aim at stability (a surrogate for optimization), even though there are good reasons to believe that the evolutionary process leads consistently neither toward optimization nor stability. And most importantly, the strategies available to the "contestants" are assumed to be among the ones that the modeler presents (Maynard Smith 1982). In the Hawk-Dove game, two strategies are abstracted from among the countless variations of conflict responses seen in animals and erected as ideal types: either aggression or flight in the event of a conflict. Thus, there is a sense in which game-theoretic models are straightforwardly false when compared to animals in the wild. They are nonetheless attractive falsehoods, providing elegant characterizations of the pressures on at least the idealized strategies.

This is not an extreme example: as has been pointed out many times in recent years, scientific theories and models are idealizations and don't actually describe the world as it is. For example, Nancy Cartwright, in *How the Laws of Physics Lie* (1983), examines a number of models which are in some sense approximations of physical situations, but Cartwright chooses to see them as convenient fictions, or as lies—because they are approximations away from the truth as we know it.[4] Especially "laws," like the law of gravitation, never accurately describe how bodies behave, other forces always being in play. The law of gravitation may not even be approximately correct in the sense of being a few units of measurement off some correct figure: it is an idealization in the sense that it imagines bodies and gravitational forces in an isolated state that may never be obtained. At the same time it clearly describes something, which Cartwright calls a "causal power" (1983) or "capacity" (1989a, 1989b).

These idealizations and abstractions are not unrelated to those that go on in the laboratory. Laboratory experiments are performed on constructed objects in constructed settings: usually the materials are entirely artificial or many times purified before they are let into the laboratory, and they are placed in situations in which they would never be found in nature. This is a necessary move if experiments are to create generalizable knowledge, because the material world, unpurified and unchanged, is overly idiosyncratic; its most regular and constant features are Cartwright's causal powers and capacities.

There is another aspect to representations of this sort, an aspect one could call "conceptual approximation." Conceptual approximations are models in a general sense, including such explicit models as the game-theoretic ones of behavior. Like such models, they aren't merely idealizations but attempts at description in very specific terms. Game theory portrays animals as consisting of a suite of strategies that play an evolutionary game. The idealized animals are seen through the lens of the framework, which helps to define the appropriate idealizations.[5]

To take a different example, Konrad Lorenz's psychological models of instinct depend on an energy metaphor which provides another such lens through which to view organisms. For Lorenz an instinct is a "fixed action pattern," a specific set of actions that are relatively invariable within and between individuals of the same species. Lorenz emphasizes invariance through detailed descriptions of behavior:

> If the specific excitation of fighting is elicited in a male of the genus *Haplochromis*, a cichlid . . . , the fish first responds by spreading its median fins and assuming "nuptial" . . . coloration. Then the fish approaches the releasing object—a dummy or a live rival—and orients in such a way that the largest contour of its body is presented at a right angle to the adversary's line of sight. . . . In this position, the fish extends the gill flap or branchiostegal membrane downward so that it forms a broad, black crest enlarging the fish's contours when seen from the side. . . . (Lorenz 1981, 112)

His central question has to do with the internal releasing mechanism for fixed action patterns such as these. His model—similar to a Freudian one—posits the build-up of "action-specific energy"; that is, energy that in normal situations only applies to this one particular instinct. Energy builds in two ways: by slow accretion or by application of the appropriate stimuli. When energy levels reach certain critical points, the pressure forces the energy's release through the instinct.

Though ethologists have found it useful and, intuitively, parts of it have some appeal, the model suffers a great number of empirical problems, which are probably problems for any energy model (Klama 1988). It is, at best, approximately true—a conceptual approximation.

If conceptual approximations are approximations at all, that is, if they genuinely represent the world, then they are the bread and butter of scientific theorizing. One way to see this is to look at Hilary Putnam's well-known problem of the disastrous meta-induction: "What if all the theoretical entities postulated by one generation (molecules, genes, etc., as well as electrons) invariably do not exist from the standpoint of later science?" (Putnam 1984, 145). Or in terms of representations: what if all of the representations (such as theories) of one generation invariably are false from the standpoint of later science? This is more than an idle question because every field sees some conceptual innovation, and earlier representations are often inadequate after this innovation. If we consider those earlier knowledges false then hopes that present knowledge holds some truth are unwarranted, whatever good arguments there might be for them. Conceptual approximations exist in proportion to the truth in knowledge and, thus, it is important to be able to make some sense of them. But understanding how a model can be a conceptual approximation to the truth is not difficult once we see the way in which models function as metaphors: models represent the world through a lens that identifies some structures as the relevant objects of study.

Understanding how metaphors represent structures without creating exact correspondences, then, can show us one way in which scientific representations do the same. The theories-as-metaphors analogy helps us to understand conceptual approximations if an account can be given of metaphors such that they do some approximating work. The next section provides such an account.

If the theories-as-metaphors analogy is a good one the realist need not be committed to the *literal* truth of theories or even to too-strict versions of bivalence—that theories are literally true or false. Thus, as McMullin points out, van Fraassen sets up the wrong target when he defines realism:

> *Science aims to give us, in its theories, a literally true story of what the world is like; and acceptance of a scientific theory involves the belief that it is true.* This is the correct statement of scientific realism (van Fraassen 1980, 8).

Instead realists need only claim that science aims for fruitful metaphors, which capture something of the structure of the subject matter. These metaphors will be approximately true in the sense that they represent something of that structure.

If this idea can be used to defend realism against empiricism, as McMullin would like, I think that it is more useful in defending something of realism against some standard relativist accounts. Historians of science, aware that scientists' ontology does not seem fixed, are led to the conclusion that scientists do not "cut the world at its joints" (Kuhn 1979); instead scientists impose structure on an unknowable world. "Theories as metaphors" gives us a framework from which to see how different theories can be approximately true yet contrary; two metaphorical descriptions of a subject matter can be dramatically different yet nonetheless both can be fruitful representations. A metaphorical view of theories can accommodate the ontology change that sometimes motivates a neo-Kantian impulse without accepting any ultimate unknowability on the part of the world; it provides another analogy through which to see the perspectivalism that realism probably needs.

A REPRESENTATIONAL ACCOUNT OF METAPHOR

Philosophical interest in metaphor has a long history, though most of it is filled with wariness and suspicion and recommendations for metaphor's nonuse. Thomas Hobbes, a master of metaphor himself, says, in a discussion of absurdities, that

> the sixth [cause of absurdity], to the use of Metaphores, Tropes, and other Rhetorical figures, instead of words proper. For though it be lawfull to say, (for example) in common speech, the way goeth, or leadeth hither, or thither, ... yet in reckoning, and seeking of truth, such speeches are not to be admitted (Hobbes 1968 [1651], 114).

Metaphor did not become respectable in English-language philosophy until the work of Max Black (1981 [1955]), though since then there has been a veritable explosion of interest in metaphor. This explosion is largely due to the appearance of theories of metaphor that recognize that, contrary to Hobbes, Locke, Kant, and others, metaphors are not merely tools that deceive or give pleasure, but are important to understanding. Philosophers, psychologists, and linguists, in their attention to reasoning and understanding, have found something valuable and interesting in metaphor. Nonetheless, there does not seem to have been a resolution of major issues. Although we have learned much from Black, Searle, Davidson, Ortony, Lakoff, Johnson, and others, the community is still divided on at least one central issue: how to interpret the meaning of metaphors, with Davidson, Rorty, and others defending a "noncognitivist" view (Davidson 1981; Rorty 1987), and Goodman, Hesse, and others defending something like Black's "interaction" view (Goodman 1981; Hesse 1987). Davidson and Rorty argue that metaphors do not mean anything more than their words say: "My computer has a virus" means nothing more than that there is something called a "virus" infecting my computer. It may call to mind much more, but that should not be confused with meaning. Black, Goodman, and Hesse are more willing to say that metaphors have real, interesting meanings. In Black's interaction theory these meanings arise through an interaction between predicates of the comment and topic terms of the metaphor. In "Anthropologists are grave robbers," commonplaces associated with grave robbers, the comment term, interact with predicates applied to anthropologists to create a meaning.

The account that I present here is a descendant of the "interactionist" views of Black and I. A. Richards (Richards 1936), but taking advantage of some of the enormous amount of work done on metaphors in the past twenty years. My questions will be among those that have characterized philosophical discussion on metaphor: How does metaphor create meaning, if it does? What sort of meaning does it create? I won't try to answer those questions for all metaphors but will, instead, try to sketch some answers for a class of metaphors, a class that I claim includes those that are particularly important for science. The answers take the form of two claims, the first of which is:

(i) *Metaphors can take structure from one domain and apply it to another.* Complex analogies point our attention towards similarities in structure. Sonar in bats is analogous to radar in airplanes. They perform their respective tasks in remarkably similar ways. There are similar problems and similar solutions. But most importantly, their places in their respective environments are extremely similar: sonar and radar both map the surroundings when normal vision isn't adequate.

Many metaphors do much the same thing as analogies. They compare structures, but in an asymmetrical way. They take structure from one domain and apply it to another, normally taking from the vehicle and applying to the tenor. I am using Richards's (1936) terminology here, the standard terminology from literary criticism. The "tenor" is the topic, the ground, the primary reference, or the nonmetaphorical part of the metaphor. The "vehicle" is that which shapes or gives new perspective to the tenor. In "Sam is a pig," the tenor would be Sam and the vehicle pig. The situation quickly becomes more complicated with more interesting metaphors, and when we start asking questions about whether it is words, things, ideas, or systems of any of these to which our terms should apply.

In some cases the application of structures across domains may involve considerable conceptual reorganization. In others the domains are already perceived to be similar enough that they amount to no more than pointing out similarities. But in the best of metaphors, the restructuring "filters" (Black 1981) our thoughts so that we see the domain of the tenor in terms of the structure of the domain of the vehicle. This idea has been worked out in some detail by Eva Feder Kittay (1987), who uses the metaphor of "metaphor as rearranging the furniture of the mind." But before discussing Kittay's work, I would like to draw on some simple cases to make the point plausible.

In *Metaphors We Live By*, George Lakoff and Mark Johnson look at metaphors which obviously play with structure. "We understand experience metaphorically when we use a gestalt from one domain of experience to structure experience in another domain" (Lakoff and Johnson 1980, 230). They show us clusters of clichés and dead metaphors, which are all related by one central structural metaphor, often spatial. A basic one is HAPPY IS UP; SAD IS DOWN:

> I'm feeling *up*. That *boosted* my spirits. My spirits *rose*. You're in *high* spirits. Thinking about her always gives me a *lift*. I'm feeling *down*. I'm *depressed*. He's really *low* these days. I *fell* into a depression. My spirits *sank* (Lakoff and Johnson 1980, 15).

What the central metaphor does here is place a familiar one-dimensional spatial orientation on top of an array of emotions, allowing us to quickly navigate our way around an emotional structure. As Lakoff and Johnson point out, there are many metaphors similar to this one, accomplishing roughly the same thing: giving a simple structure to things that are abstract or difficult to talk about. The best-known example coming from *Metaphors We Live By* is only a little more complicated. The ARGUMENT IS WAR metaphor includes the following instances:

> Your claims are *indefensible*. He *attacked every weak point* in my argument. Her criticisms were *right on target*. I *demolished* his argument. I've never *won* an argument with him. If you use that *strategy*, he'll *wipe you out*. He *shot down* all of my arguments (Lakoff and Johnson 1980, 4).

Again, it is fairly plausible that the structure of one domain, war, is being applied to another, arguments. All of the above statements depend upon one central metaphor, which we use to help us analyze (and win) arguments.

As well as looking at large groups of statements, we can look at a single image. On the cover of the September 3, 1990 issue of the *New Republic* was a picture of Saddam Hussein, touched up so that the sides of his moustache had been trimmed, making him look like Adolf Hitler. In putting this doctored photograph on the cover, the *New Republic* was participating in and supporting a metaphor that was starting to gain some currency: Saddam Hussein is Adolf Hitler/1990 is 1939 again. American journalists, editors, politicians, and commentators were asking their audiences to bring forth a package of images of the war against Nazi Germany and apply them to the war against Baathist Iraq. But it wasn't merely images that were called forth; the images had to have some structure and coherence. We can see this from the fact that people were routinely asked to make decisions on the basis of the metaphor. The situations were thought to be sufficiently parallel that lessons learned from World War II were thought to be applicable to the war on Iraq.

Kittay calls her theory of metaphor a "perspectival" theory, because it emphasizes metaphor's creation of a new stance. Metaphors, she claims, involve the interplay between two semantic fields, roughly those of the tenor and the vehicle.[6]

> Metaphorical transfers of meaning are transfers from the field of the vehicle to the field of the topic [tenor] of the relations of affinity and opposition that the vehicle term(s) bears to other terms in its field. More precisely, in metaphor what is transferred are the relations which pertain within one semantic field to a second, distinct content domain (Kittay 1987, 36).

Because of this transfer of relations, the person who understands the metaphor sees the semantic field of the tenor in a new way, producing the new perspective.

Kittay's theory is worked out within both a linguistic and a philosophical framework, in too detailed a manner to be summarized here. What I wish to draw from it are a few points concerning structure and the relation of metaphorical meaning to literal meaning. First of all, Kittay makes a fairly sharp distinction between the literal and metaphorical meanings of a sentence. Metaphorical meaning is "second-order meaning," something we look for because of an incongruity, given the context, the utterer, the prefaces, and so on. The literal meaning of a metaphor participates in the incongruity. Yet Kittay does not want to indicate that there is a huge gulf between metaphorical and literal meanings. The processes by which we determine each of those are quite similar; in both cases Kittay relies on a relational account of meaning derived from Saussurean linguistics and Dretske's information theory. Whether or not the account of meaning works, it looks right to argue that metaphorical meaning and literal meaning are not substantially different in kind (Gibbs and Gerrig 1989; Glucksberg 1989).[7] Once the restructuring of the domain of the tenor is done, figuring out the metaphorical meaning of a sentence should involve the same processes as figuring out literal meaning.

One potential problem with her theory that Kittay points out concerns structure. The notion of structure that she uses is very much like the notion of "conceptual scheme" that Donald Davidson (Davidson 1974) has argued is incoherent: Kittay claims that metaphors change our perspective, but don't *necessarily* give us any new facts. Davidson's argument is basically that it makes no sense to distinguish between structure and content; the structure of thought can always be described in terms of the facts that we believe. His goal is to show that incommensurabilty is incoherent; he is particularly concerned with the large-scale incommensurability that Kuhn and Feyerabend believe exists. But along the way, he argues that the notion of "scheme" is suspect, if it is thought to be other than the content that the scheme supposedly organizes.

> Someone who sets out to organize a closet arranges the things in it. If you are told not to organize the shoes and shirts, but the closet itself you would be bewildered. How would you organize the Pacific Ocean? Straighten out its shores perhaps or relocate its islands or destroy its fish (Davidson 1974, 14).

Kittay responds that it is not at all hard to make sense of the notion of structure or of the organization of the closet itself or the Pacific Ocean (Kittay 1987, 314–16). We can add a shelf or hang shoe-holders. "We might want to 'organize' the ocean according to thermal differences at different depths, or according to the habitations of sharks" (315). I think that this response is correct, but I don't want to pursue this line.

Davidson's claim (or at least this interpretation of Davidson's claim) goes too far. We can make at least *some* sense of the distinction between structure and content by looking to paradigm cases, to mathematical axioms, to grammar, to subway maps. But he is right that the distinction between structure and content is not a sharp one, and perhaps is relative to context. Relations can be recast in terms of monadic predicates, given a rich enough set of predicates. And in practical terms the distinction may be very fuzzy: was having invaded a smaller neighbour a common attribute of both Nazi Germany and Baathist Iraq, or was it a common structural feature of the two situations?

In fact the fuzziness of the boundary between structure and content can help to deal with another criticism. The most trite of metaphors, for example "Her car is a real gas-guzzler," or "Richard is a fox," don't seem to be about large numbers of relations and associations. Rather, they are conventionalized to the point that only one (or at least very few) of the properties of the predicate are being applied to the subject. Structure doesn't enter into this at all and, thus, it seems as though my (and Kittay's) picture might be overly elaborate for many metaphors. But Davidson's blurring of the line between structure and content helps us, in that it allows us to see the break between simple or conventionalized metaphors and the ones that map structures as a small, rather than large, gulf. The two types of metaphors blend into each other. The perspectival account might describe one side of a spectrum, or best apply to some limiting cases. Other students of metaphor would agree. Both J. J. A. Mooij (1976) and Dedre Gentner (1982) have shown how the interaction of structures might apply to only a subset of metaphors, though possibly the most interesting subset for many purposes.

The second claim is more complicated, and is itself compound:

(ii) *Metaphors make assertions that have meanings, of two different kinds. First of all, they make the assertion (or proposal) that the structure/ideas brought from the vehicle to the tenor are fruitful. Secondly they use the new structure to make a descriptive truth claim.*

(a) *That metaphors mean.* I have mentioned emotivist theories of metaphor without describing them. They become important when one discusses metaphorical meaning because those who hold emotivist theories deny that there is any such meaning. The two best-known emotivists are Donald Davidson (e.g., 1981) and Richard Rorty (e.g., 1987), whose views on this issue are extremely similar, both being based on the same semantic theory, Davidson's. I'll sketch Rorty's discussion of the view, because it puts matters in a larger perspective.

Rorty starts from the premise that semantics has only been successful when applied to artificial representations of the most dry of literal languages. Accepting this, we can have two attitudes toward the concepts of semantics, a conservative and a radical one. The conservative attitude takes "'cognitive claims' as the most important claims which can be made for a given sort of language" (Rorty 1987, 284). It tries to "broaden our use of terms like 'truth,' 'refers to a world' and 'meaning' so as to make them relevant to metaphor"(284). The radical attitude (his) places much less emphasis on cognitive claims and, consequently, is willing to accept the limitation of these semantic terms to literal, scientific language, the "relatively uninteresting uses of words." The rest of language becomes a matter of pragmatics. To argue for the radical attitude, Rorty nudges us to have the Davidsonian intuition that meanings must be intimately related to truth conditions, and shows us some metaphors for which truth conditions don't seem to be forthcoming.

But scientific language, which Rorty puts in the "uninteresting, cognitive" category, has been shown to be shot through and through with metaphors, many of which are not easily dispensible. Thus the radical position might be more radical than it at first looks: it might turn out that semantics applies only to artificial languages. In addition, there is a problem having to do with the applicability of Rorty's argument, though it doesn't tell against Rorty and Davidson's position. Metaphors aren't purely linguistic phenomena. Clearly not just literary artists but also visual artists make use of metaphors. If 1939 can be metaphorically related to 1990 partly through a picture in a magazine, then language is not the only thing at issue in metaphors. And if Lakoff and Johnson are right that a whole pile of clichés can be grouped into one unstated conceptual metaphor, then metaphors need not be contained in sentences.

But there are good reasons for dismissing not only Rorty's argument but also his and Davdson's overall position. Timothy Binkley, among others, has shown that metaphors can be true or false for readings other than their literal one. Binkley asks us to imagine the following conversation concerning a lawyer.

> A: That Richard is a fox, isn't he? Did you notice how he slyly equivocated on the defendant's statement?
>
> B: Oh, I don't think he's a fox. It was probably just a lucky blunder. You should have seen him last week and you'd find it hard to believe he's a fox too (Binkley 1981, 141).

Here we have a not unimaginable, though slightly wooden, conversation between two people, where the central assertion being discussed is undoubtedly metaphorical. (It's a trite, common, overused metaphor, but it's a metaphor nonetheless.) Yet the conversation indicates that what is at issue is whether it's true as a metaphor, not just literally true. But if it's potentially true or false, then it has to have a meaning; this is explicit in Davidson's semantic program.

Another reason why we need recourse to metaphorical meaning is that it can help us to understand dead metaphors. Nelson Goodman (1981) points out that when metaphors die they often acquire quite straightforward meanings. The new literal meaning of a dead metaphor, like "turning a blind eye," is related to its old metaphorical meaning; it is a subset or a simplification of the old meaning. But we would have to posit a fairly interesting process of meaning creation if there were no such thing as metaphorical meaning. The old *emotive value* of turning a blind eye would have to be transformed into a *meaning*. That is, a feeling or an image would have to become a meaning, and it would have to be a gradual process because dead metaphors are rarely completely dead, and there are many dying ones. In contrast to the problem that the emotivist faces, Kittay's account can handle dying metaphors:

> The experienced superiority of a new ordering (or perhaps something more random and less rational, such as laziness, special interests, or new habits) allows it to become entrenched and to replace the old ordering. As it takes hold, we forget that the furniture was ever differently ordered.... It is now the literal truth (Kittay 1987).

So we can see that for a variety of reasons the perspectival theory is preferable over the emotivist theory for many common metaphors and, thus, at least these paradigm metaphors can have meanings.

(b) *How metaphors mean.* I make claims about two different ways in which metaphors "mean." The first is that they assert that the structure and associations of the vehicle is appropriate for talk about the tenor. The second is an active statement about the tenor. (There is a third meaning, too, but I am going to ignore it: the literal meaning of the sentence involved. This becomes more important when we ask how we recognize metaphors.) To see the interplay between the two metaphorical meanings, we should follow Timothy Binkley's example and ask how we can deny metaphors.

Until the nineteenth century it was common to think of the vagina in terms of the penis (Laqueur 1990; Tuana 1989); the vagina was seen as a mirror image of the penis, though it was a "less perfect" version. Yet there were constant disagreements about exactly how this metaphor should be applied, stemming from disanalogies between male and female anatomies. A late example has to do with the place of the clitoris in the metaphor, for it is on the one hand a site of female pleasure and, thus, itself a "female penis," and on the other an organ for which there is no obvious male homologue, given the vagina-is-penis framework (Laqueur 1990, 64ff., 137ff.). Thus, there were disagreements about specific uses of the metaphor and its limits. Approximately at the beginning of the nineteenth century, however, the vagina-is-penis metaphor was overturned; given new anatomical observations and new gender politics it was rejected as inappropriate. This is the second way of denying a metaphor, denying not a specific application or use of it but denying that it provides any valuable insights at all.

We could also look at a simpler metaphor. Imagine that in the exchange about Richard the lawyer, the second person (B) says: "Oh, don't say that; Richard's not nearly that straightforward a character." Here B is objecting to something quite different from what she objected to in Binkley's version. She is claiming not just that Richard's not a fox, but that the terms of the metaphor are somehow inappropriate. She's denying the first of my two metaphorical meanings, whereas in the other conversation she was denying the second.

There is a small amount of carelessness in calling the first type of metaphorical meaning "meaning"; it is sloppy because this meaning could be just as easily viewed as a proposal or, sometimes, a bullying act. The first metaphorical meaning of "S is P" says something like "The structure of P is appropriate for talking about S." To read it as a proposal it says something like "Imagine the structure of P applied to S." And as a bullying act (we could here remember the constant media bombardment of "Saddam is Hitler/1990 is 1939 again") it says "Right now, P's structure is appropriate for S-talk." Whether or not we view it always as a meaning is probably not too important. Even if we don't, it is still a cognitive matter.

The second meaning of the metaphor, the actual description, is what is new in this account, although what I am doing that is new is placing some emphasis on it, rather than noticing it. This second meaning is important because many metaphors don't just assert similarity, they also tell something about the tenor. In Kafka's "Metamorphosis" the insect can be a metaphor for an old or ill person, but Kafka also tells a story. Like the tenors of many metaphors, the insect *does* things.

Though it may be obvious that many metaphors have this second type of meaning, pointing it out is necessary for any account of metaphors aimed at understanding their use in science. The two meanings in metaphors show us that not only are there better and worse metaphors, but they can be better and worse by virtue of what they say about the world.

METAPHOR AND THE POLITICS OF SCIENTIFIC KNOWLEDGE

The political critic demands that in accounts of science more of the important aspects of science be placed within the realm of the social. Neo-Kantian constructivisms allow for that within a respectable philosophical position, by claiming that causal structure is imposed by minds on the world, rather than vice-versa. The theories-as-metaphors analogy accomplishes the same thing by recognizing that to some extent people do impose structure on *what they take as* real, through the language with which they describe it. They construct perceptual and social worlds. This still allows that metaphors can capture something of the structure of things-in-themselves: metaphors do often refer and represent, and their value may lie in bringing to the fore hidden features of that which they represent.

"Theories as metaphors" allows us to see more clearly how perfectly good—and possibly correct—science can carry the markers of ideological and other conflicts both external and internal to science: metaphors capture an aspect of the structure of their topic, but what aspect it is, and how it is "filtered" depends upon the specifics of the metaphor. That theories latch onto the world in only very particular aspects is commonly accepted. But seeing theories as metaphors helps to make it more clear and important: it creates a continuum from explicit metaphors through theory-constitutive metaphors to the theories themselves. Thus it allows us to see how scientists' understanding of the world is filtered through metaphors, through perspectives on and approaches to the world. But the activity of creating and maintaining these perspectives is a social one, heavily steeped in the interests and ideologies that affect such a social process.

I would like to give a few examples of important metaphors that structure fields and, simultaneously, perform important social functions. These metaphors participate in the construction of social worlds. From today's vantage point the first of these examples is less obviously good science and more obviously ideological, the second is the converse. Together, however, I think that they show a range of the effects of scientific metaphors.

In the nineteenth century an analogy was developed that linked gender and race: women's features were seen as almost identical to those of non-white men. Nancy Stepan says that "lower races represented the 'female' type of the human species, and females the 'lower race' of gender" (Stepan 1986, 264). The pair of metaphors were easily accepted by the scientific community; they fit well into standard stereotypes and perceptions of the social and natural order. Stepan points out that although this may seem like pseudo-science today, it certainly did not a century ago; almost all of the important scientists doing anthropological work accepted and used the race-gender metaphor. Once accepted, they were even productive, as brain, skull, jaw, pelvis, and limb measurements revealed a number of correlations between the bodies of women and men of "lower races."

> By directing attention to exactly those points of similarity and difference that would bring women and lower races closer to apes, or to each other, the race-gender metaphor generated data, many of them new, which "fit" the metaphor and the associated implications carried by it. Other aspects of reality and human experience that were incompatible with the metaphor tended to be ignored or not "seen" (Stepan, 274).

The ideological value of this race-gender metaphor is so clear as not to need spelling out. The establishment of a natural scale of race and gender justified the extension of social hierarchies from race to gender and vice-versa.

The second example concerns a group of metaphors describing the relation of DNA to the rest of the organism, a group that Evelyn Fox Keller describes as the "master molecule" theory (Keller 1985). It asserts that genes "control, determine, code for..." development. DNA as a master molecule in a totalitarian biology increases the importance of genetics among the disciplines that study the structures of organisms, because genetics, and particularly molecular biology within genetics, becomes the study of that which ultimately determines all else biological. But DNA as a master molecule doesn't only affect power relations among biologists; it contributes to top-down models of development, including human development, and, more generally, to reductionistic technical solutions of problems. And finally, the model of authority that "DNA as master molecule" employs is one that coheres with traditional models of power in the state and the (male-centered) household, the models of power that Foucault (1990) labels "juridico-discursive."

Both of these examples show effects of ideology. A common way in which "ideology" has been used in connection with science is to contrast "ideological" with "pure": scientific knowledge is ideological when it has been distorted by issues of power and pure when it has been unaffected. If sociological and political critics of science are right, then there is no such thing as "pure" science in this sense; DNA as a master molecule need not be a *distortion*, though it comes from a specific perspective and reflects common models of power. Even in cases in which scientific debates and beliefs do not reflect debates and beliefs in the wider society, the sociology of science can show us the ways in which those cases hinge on internal struggles, the alignment of allies, and rhetorical devices. And this applies as much to true beliefs as false ones. So ideology, if it is to remain a useful concept, cannot be thought of in terms of distorting influences; the production of truth cannot be distinguished in a general way from the production of falsity through the "pure/ideological" contrast.

But there are other models for a notion of ideology that can allow one to maintain politically engaged critiques of science. Whether the term is used or not, many recent feminist critiques of science have identified ideology not by its ability to produce falsehood but by its potential social effects. That is, a concept or a belief can be ideological if its effect is to change or entrench the power relations of social groups. Thus ideological statements can be a type of speech act, if they describe the world—possibly even describe it well—at the same time as they perform a social function. This is a notion of ideology with a history as long as that of the notion of ideology as falsehood (Eagleton 1991; Lynch 1994). It spreads the concept widely, since many ideas will have effects on power relations, but it has the advantage of focusing attention on the relations between beliefs and the social and material world.

On my account metaphors, also, are one type of speech act: they are performative in that they bully us into seeing the structure of the tenor through the structure of the vehicle; and yet they are also descriptive, perhaps asserting a comparison, perhaps representing some putative fact about the tenor.[8] Once inside the game-theoretic framework biologists start to see Hawk-Dove interactions, and they start to see all behavior in terms of competition among strategies. Inside the master molecule framework they see development as the following of a set of instructions, the body as a locus for information exchange. Metaphors are complicated speech acts because, not only do they both perform and say (they are "performative" and "constative" in J. L. Austin's [1962] terminology), metaphorical meaning is not given by the literal sentence meaning. Recognizing both the performative and the constative aspects of metaphors helps us to understand how they can serve ideological functions while serving as representations. This helps to tie together many critiques of science: the authors of those critiques can be described as saying that scientific language and actions can do more than one thing at once. Given this, good science that is straightforwardly political becomes a routine possibility.

One unobvious reason that metaphors can be seen as ideological is that according to interactionist views metaphors change some of the structure of associations of the vehicle, not just of the tenor. To say that the world is a machine is not just to shape our conception of the world, but also, eventually, to reshape our conceptions of machines; we make the world appear a little more machinelike and machines a little more worldlike. Similarly, to call some forms of copulation in animals "rape" is to comment on human "rape."[9]

We can use this discussion to redescribe aspects of the pervasive sexism and androcentrism in science that feminist empiricists have worked to make visible. Some sexisms and androcentrisms that feminist historians, philosophers, and sociologists have identified in scientific knowledge are such because of their metaphorical bases. Theoretical activity in science adopts common sexist metaphors in part because those are the metaphors most available in a sexist society; they appear natural and valuable. Feminists are well positioned to uncover the sexism of these metaphors because, as standpoint epistemology argues, feminists are in a position to question the naturalness of sexist metaphors: disputing the naturalness and hierarchy of gender is a central part of the intellectual and political activity of feminism. Literary analysis of science, which has proven itself useful to feminist scholars of widely differing theoretical orientation, becomes an obvious tool in feminist science studies, because it identifies gendered aspects of scientific knowledge and the processes that lead to its creation.

"Theories as metaphors" helps us to understand and sympathize with relativist and neo-Kantian impulses without giving in to them, and it leaves a place for ideology and politics within good science. In short, following McMullin, the theories-as-metaphors view can be part of a realist philosophy of science, capturing some of the relativist notions of "ways of seeing" but viewing them as conceptual approximations. By doing this, it also helps us to understand ideological components of empirically valuable models and theories: scientific arguments, theories, and positions are expressed in and pursued within the framework of ideology-laden metaphors and assumptions. In this sense scientific research is not separate from the societies in which it is embedded; the scientific community participates in, repeats, and reflects struggles in larger society.

Nine

POWER AND KNOWLEDGE

THE POWER IN/OF KNOWLEDGE: SOME BACONIAN MAXIMS

RECENT EMPIRICAL RESEARCH in science and technology studies shows a marked absence of the rationalist values traditionally associated with science, an absence of, for example, Robert Merton's normative values of "universalism, communism, disinterestedness, organized skepticism" (Merton 1973, 270). Today's socially oriented scholars find no impersonal criteria for evaluating claims, and they find scientists fiercely competitive, interested, and often unskeptical about at least their claims and those of their allies. S&TS also comes to another antirationalist conclusion, that science—and engineering, of course—is *active*. It is a game played on an agonistic field; its results are the results of the *agon*. Research follows patterns or practices defined in an environment of resistances from the material world but also cultural resources and constraints, such as concepts, tools, exemplars, allies, and ideologies. In these environments scientists are involved in projects of "heterogeneous engineering," rather than purely conceptual work. Thus S&TS pays attention to power in attempting to understand knowledge.

Theoretical discussions of the politics of science also focus on the connections between knowledge and power. Joseph Rouse, for example, argues in his *Knowledge and Power* that scientific knowledge is a *form* of power (Rouse 1987). Drawing from views of Nancy Cartwright, Bruno Latour, and particularly Michel Foucault, he argues that science enables people to cope with the world, but not more than cope; in particular science does not find out what the world is really like. Knowledge *is* power, plain and simple. Thus Foucault's term *power/knowledge* might be emblematic of the discussion of the politics of science (Foucault 1980). It brings together, though also hides, important connections between knowledge and power.

I am going to follow Rouse and Foucault in taking power/knowledge to be central to understanding science, but I want to break the concept up into some constituent dimensions. My question is: what should the "/" mean? I want to show some ways in which knowledge and power produce each other and, therefore, that we should resist any temptation to take power/knowledge as a unitary concept. Instead we should take power/knowledge as a reminder of the many connections between powers and knowledges. One power can produce knowledge, which can then be translated into another power. A will to power can become a will to knowledge. Therefore, in discussing the politics of science I will be sketching a properly epistemological picture of science: science produces and depends on both powers and knowledges, moving like a ratchet from one to the other.

To make these points I hang the discussion on some hooks provided by Francis Bacon; in this I am participating in a long tradition in philosophy of science, which has over and over found in Bacon expression of the ideas of the day, whether that day be in the seventeenth or the nineteenth century (Pérez-Ramos 1988).

To connect knowledge and power is to deny of science that it meets an ancient ideal, that of knowledge as contemplation; the *vita contemplativa* has almost always been held—particularly by philosophers—to be more noble than the *vita activa*. The ideal of knowledge as contemplation affects most descriptions of science and, thus, science is distinct from and above (or prior to) technology not only in the public imagination but also in scientists' and philosophers' hierarchies. Until the past decade history, philosophy, and sociology of science focused almost exclusively on theorizing as the paradigmatic scientific activity, and on theorists (Einstein, Darwin, Newton, Galileo, etc.) as ideal scientists, making science appear much more a contemplative enterprise than an active one.

Though the *vita contemplativa* was and is a philosophers' ideal, it was notably not Bacon's, he considering himself a man of action. Bacon's sciences center around such active pursuits as natural magic, technology, and alchemy. Probably the most important analogy he makes for natural philosophy is a sometimes strained geographical one, allowing him to emphasize movement. The exploration and conquest of the Americas represent for Bacon a break in the history of Europe and European learning. With knowledge of the Americas, Moderns gained knowledge that Ancients had never had; Bacon uses geographical knowledge to show that ancient knowledge can be surpassed or overturned in other realms, to construct a modern philosophy that will give rise to more new useful inventions like gunpowder, the compass, and the printing press. With this in mind, he has a somewhat fanciful account of Columbus:

> Columbus, before his wonderful voyage over the Atlantic, gave reasons of his conviction that new lands and continents might be discovered besides those already known; and these reasons, though at first rejected, were yet proved by subsequent experi-

ence, and were the causes and beginnings of the greatest events. (Bacon 1902a, 1, Aph. XCII)

The frontspiece to his *Instauratio Magna* is an engraving of ships sailing through the twin pillars of Hercules out to sea, below which is written "Multi pertransibunt and augebitur scientia"—"many shall run to and fro, and knowledge shall be increased." Bacon's use of the Biblical prophecy (Daniel 12, 4) identifies the modern age as the last one (Whitney 1986).

The geographical model of knowledge has a number of effects. One of them is to start to identify the work needed to produce knowledge. Whether or not Columbus had good reasons for sailing westward—he certainly didn't have the ones Bacon attributes to him—European knowledge of the Americas required travel and exploration and was not to be gained by contemplation and speculation. "Though a much more faint and uncertain breeze of hope were to spring up from our new continent, yet we consider it necessary to make the experiment" (Bacon 1902a, 1, Aph. CXIV). This leads to the first way that Bacon connects knowledge and power: *knowledge is produced by power.*

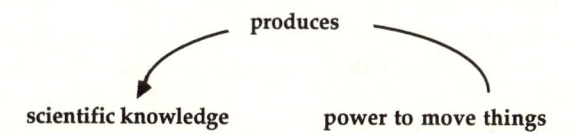

$$\text{scientific knowledge} \xrightarrow{\text{produces}} \text{power to move things}$$

For Bacon, knowledge of the forms of nature, which should be the goal of natural philosophy, is difficult to achieve largely because nature keeps herself hidden. He is quick to adopt metaphors of seduction of female nature:

> Join with us; that when he [the true son of science] has left the antechambers of nature trodden by the multitude, an entrance may at last be discovered to her inner apartments. (1902a, 10)

> The present discoveries in science are such as lie immediately beneath the surface of common notions. It is necessary, however, to penetrate the more secret and remote parts of nature, (1902a, 1, Aph. XVIII)

and her torture and rape:

> The secrets of nature betray themselves more readily when tormented by art than when left to their own course. (1902a, 1, Aph. XCVIII)

> For you have but to follow and as it were hound nature in her wanderings, and you will be able when you like, to lead and drive her afterward to the same place again.... a useful light may be gained, not only for a true judgement of the offenses of persons charged with such practices [witchcraft, etc.], but likewise for the further disclosing of the secrets of nature. Neither ought a man to make scruple of entering and penetrating into these holes and corners, when the inquisition of truth is his whole object. (quoted in Merchant 1980, 168)

> For like as a man's disposition is never well known or proved till he be crossed, nor Proteus ever changed shapes till he was straitened and held fast, so nature exhibits herself more clearly under the trials and vexations of art than when left to herself. (quoted in Merchant 1980, 169)

Bacon's misogynist thinking and metaphors overshadow an important insight: useful information can be gained from observing a piece of the material world in isolation or in contrived situations, often more than can be gained from watching it in its natural environment.[1] Bacon is thus the first philosopher of experiment, before there was a tradition of experiment about which to philosophize. Both the insight and the metaphors in which it is couched continue to represent the experimental tradition because, ever since Bacon male experimenters have tortured female nature to force her to reveal her secrets (Merchant 1980; Leiss 1972).

S&TS has taken up the insight, not directly from Bacon, and usually without the misogyny. Students of experiment today, such as Robert Ackermann, Ian Hacking, Karin Knorr-Cetina, and Bruno Latour, show how the entities experimented upon and the phenomena studied are usually not even parts of nature, since they are many times refined, twisted, contorted, and placed in situations in which their natural ancestors would never normally be found. As much as possible, nature is barred from the laboratory. The laboratory is thus a place—a *factory*—for making new facts. Ability to manufacture new relations among the parts of the material world and, thus, to learn something about old ones, depends upon possessing tools and techniques for unmixing, controlling, and reshaping things. The laboratory, the exemplary site of science, is filled with machines for and people skilled in manipulating nature. Knowledge of the *forms* of things—in the Baconian sense forms are potentialities—depends upon having the power to place those things in contexts in which scientists can see those forms.

Even once the experiment is done the production of knowledge depends upon other tools that provide the power to simplify, to abstract, to amass data, and to sort fact from artifact. As Bacon says, "the unassisted hand and the understanding left to itself possess but little power" (1902a, 1, Aph. II). Bruno Latour tells us about "inscription devices" and "centers of calculation"; H. E. Le Grand about how important (and difficult) the production of a convincing and useful diagram can be (Le Grand 1990). And there are many more tools for the establishment of knowledge: statistics is a set of powerful techniques for the refinement of data; mathematics more generally turns useless statements into useful ones by reshaping and combining what is known. The new products of scientific tools and techniques should be more convincing, more powerful, or applicable to a wider variety of problems, allowing scientists to pursue epistemic objects more efficiently.

Talk of techniques and tools points to the context in which these resources can be used. Generally the tools available to the scientist are the ones developed, understood, or accepted by the community within which she works. It is important to keep the *community* focus because, among other things, these resources have to be sufficient to convince audiences of the strength of the research: the long-term fate of a proposed fact is in the hands of the discipline as a whole. A technique whose fidelity can be easily questioned is of little use to the researcher, the research being only as strong as its weakest link. Nonetheless, this allows a wide, though not infinitely flexible latitude: accepted within the community of population ecologists, for example, are statistical techniques that are neither commonly understood nor indigenous—they are instead sanctioned by another field and thus acceptable for use in a number of fields. There is a pragmatic dimension to this process. The tools and techniques acceptable in a field are the ones that have been shown to work with some consistency, however one wants to define "work." New resources and new uses of resources tend to be scrutinized until their worth to researchers is sufficiently well established, at least if it is perceived that much hangs on them. Thus, the standard tools in a field can be expected to succeed in transforming the less useful into the more useful.

Bacon's insights about experiment can be expressed as insights about knowledge production more generally: the object is to reform what you have so that it will be useful. This leads to the next power/knowledge association: *power is produced by knowledge.*

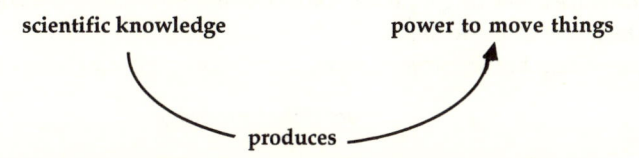

scientific knowledge   power to move things

— produces —

Knowledge translates into usefulness and usefulness into power. And indeed this is the claim often made by scientists searching for funding and support:

scientific knowledge, even the most basic scientific knowledge, can often be applied productively to create technologies, the technical power of which can in turn create state or corporate power. Thus, the claim goes, basic science deserves support because of its potential applications. We have "good reason for the hope," says Bacon, "that a vast mass of inventions yet remains, which may be deduced not only from the investigation of new modes of operation, but also from transferring, comparing, and applying these already known" (1902a, 1, Aph. CX). Thus, Bacon and many more recent advocates for science have argued for the public support of science because of the technological benefits it supposedly brings.

Some historians and philosophers of technology have questioned this claim, arguing that many technological developments owe less to basic science than is commonly presumed, or that scientific knowledge is not applied but *used* by technologists.[2] That is, technologies and the construction of artifacts are not driven by new scientific facts, though they may involve scientific knowledge. Students of technology sometimes claim that the important relation between science and technology may be the one falling under my first Baconian hook, that scientific knowledge is possible because of the application of, and sometimes simply the study of, material technologies. The slogan of these historians of technology is "Science owes more to the steam engine than the steam engine owes to science." They attempt to reverse, or at least erase, the standard hierarchy of scientists and engineers.[3]

The difference between use and application is not too important here; whether knowledge is usable or applicable it is productive of power in the same sense. The form of scientific knowledge, particularly experimental knowledge, is often such that it tells how to do things: experiments on aphid migration can show how to slow down aphids; recombinant DNA research (now "biotechnology") produces knowledge of how to manipulate genetic material. By its very form—causal descriptions of different effects—experimental knowledge often provides tools to dominate that about which experimenters know. And on the other side of the issue, successful technologies depend on knowledge, even if it isn't all basic scientific knowledge. To build a new piece of machinery technologists need to combine a number of different types of knowledge: tacit technological knowledge, scientific knowledge, and knowledge of the reception and use of the machinery. So knowledge can create the power to move things.

Knowledge has the power to move or not move people, as well as things.

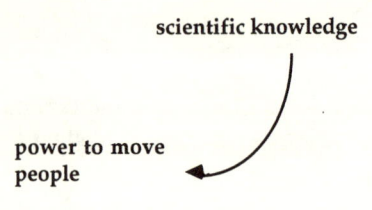

scientific knowledge

power to move people

If experimental, technical, and even theoretical knowledge can be used to control and manipulate nature, then a scientist, especially in a technocratic society, can use her knowledge of the material world to try to make herself more powerful in the social world. Though Bacon supported the sole and arbitrary power of Queen Elizabeth I and then King James I in his overtly political actions, his philosophy of science and his utopian treatise, *The New Atlantis*, reveal a more subversive tendency toward technocracy and meritocracy. For example, Bacon claims that the noblest of ambitions is not selfish or nationalist, but the ambition to further human control over nature:

> It will ... be as well to distinguish three species and degrees of ambition. First, that of men who are anxious to enlarge their own power in their country, which is a vulgar and degenerate kind; next, that of men who strive to enlarge the power and empire of their country over mankind, which is more dignified but not less covetous; but if one were to endeavor to renew and enlarge the power and empire of mankind in general over the universe, such ambition ... is both more sound and more noble than the other two. Now the empire of man over things is founded on the arts and sciences alone, for nature is only to be commanded by obeying her. (1902a, 1, Aph. CXXIX)

And then, when describing the leader of the scientific class in his utopia, Bacon does not forget to mention all the trappings of power he displays:

> He [one of the fathers of Salomon House] was clothed in a robe of fine black cloth, with wide sleeves and a cape: his under garment was of excellent white linen down to the foot.... He had gloves that were curious, and set with stone; and shoes of peach-coloured velvet.... He was carried in rich chariot without wheels, litterwise, with two horses at either end, richly trapped in blue velvet embroidered; and two footmen on each side in the like attire. The chariot was all of cedar, gilt, and adorned with crystal; save that the fore-end had panels of sapphires, set in borders of gold, and the hinder-end the like of emeralds of the Peru colour. (Bacon 1864, V, 395–96)

Bacon's technocratic utopia has never been completely instantiated, but a political economy of knowledge has evolved in which knowledge of the natural world can be used to reshape society and to make the scientist indispensible in its new configuration. Power is given to those who are thought to know. Jürgen Habermas describes trends toward a technocratic society in the increasing power of experts to define the terms of political debate, thus alienating the public from the political process (Habermas 1970). Bruno Latour's *The Pasteurization of France* shows how Louis Pasteur and the Pasteurians reorganized human societies on the promise that they could thus control nature. The pasteurization of milk requires the reorganization of agriculture; vaccination requires discipline and control of large populations; healthy soldiers require new power entrusted to the doctor. The Pasteurian doctor or researcher becomes central, becomes an "obligatory point of passage" for the achievement of goals (Latour 1988, 43ff.). Similarly, Foucault, though he would be wary of such a formulation, shows in his studies of the prison and asylum how people are reshaped through the distribution of power across the social and medical sciences. Describing the project of his *Discipline and Punish*, Foucault says "what I wanted to show was how, from the seventeenth and eighteenth centuries onwards, there was a veritable technological take-off in the productivity of power" (Foucault 1980, 119). In the same way that knowledge in the natural sciences can be a source of power over the natural world, social scientific knowledge is sometimes applicable and a source of power in the social world; the application of that knowledge makes social scientists "obligatory points of passage" for social projects. Foucault's study of normalization, in his works of the 1970s, can be seen as describing the power of the scientist, particularly the social scientist and doctor, in shaping populations.[4]

In a more general way, the accepted fact reshapes the field within which researchers work, creating and blocking off new research projects, adding to and subtracting from the ingredients available for the construction of arguments. In extreme cases an established fact can create many new fields of research, new spaces for inquiry: the fact that DNA can be manipulated has had these repercussions and has changed standards of argument in a variety of fields. The establishment of scientific knowledge has social effects within research and other communities. We have had to treat scientific facts as to some extent analogous to material objects, to pay attention to the pragmatic aspects of these objects. Knowledge is a social object: it is socially meaningful and, in the right context, has to be reckoned with. An accepted fact is fully real, because we cannot "wish it away" (Berger and Luckmann 1966, 1).

The dependence of technology on knowledge means that consistent success in any "technological" field has to indicate truth in its knowledge-base. Therefore another Baconian hook is: *power is a sign of knowledge.*

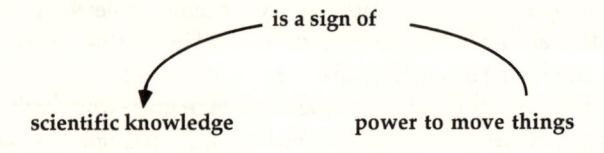

is a sign of

scientific knowledge   power to move things

Bacon, in an argument for realism in technological knowledge, says:

> Of all the signs there is none more certain or worthy than that of the fruits produced, for the fruits and effects are the sureties and vouchers, as it were, for the truth of philosophy. (1902a, 1, Aph. LXXIII)

> Other signs may be selected from the increase and progress of particular systems of philosophy and the sciences; for those which are founded on nature grow and increase, while those which are founded on opinion change and increase not.... the sciences still continue in their beaten track, and nearly stationary, without having received any important increase.... But we see that the case is reversed in the mechanical arts, which are founded on nature and the light of experience, for they seem full of life, and uninterruptedly thrive and grow. (1902a, 1, Aph. LXXIV)

This argument, like more recent simple abductive arguments for scientific realism, depends upon the premise that success in human actions is usually the result of basing those actions on correct information (Putnam 1975). From that Bacon takes himself to be justified in concluding that success, or power over the material world, is a sign of truth or knowledge.

As we saw in chapter 2, this argument is not adequate as it stands: empirical success (power) for a theory requires only empirical adequacy, not truth. A theory need not be true to be useful, but only a good predictor. To counter this empiricist point the realist argument was developed further, locating signs of truth not in the mere use of theory for prediction but in the successful use of theoretic knowledge for the creation of new empirically adequate theories. Discrimination among hypotheses to identify the empirically successful ones is only possible given knowledge of the grounds for discrimination. Thus what is true or what is real is "what is implicated in instrumentally reliable methodology" (Boyd 1990, 186).

Boyd's slogan is a weak one, in that it leaves open which supposed assumptions to believe. For example, in the context of my discussion here a skeptical worry might arise. "Success" might be a result of the power of entrenched beliefs to move people rather than things. That is, how can we tell the difference between knowledge that is genuinely successful at representing and that which, because of its entrenchment or ideological value, creates the appearance of success? How can we identify the specific knowledge responsible for power? These questions cannot be answered by application of a simple rule, because what is implicated in instrumentally reliable methodology may not be obvious. We have to do interpretative work and triangulation to distinguish between the implicated and the nonimplicated; we have to look for knowledges that are *actually* productive of power, rather than knowledges that are claimed to be. This is often a difficult task, producing fallible answers, but it is certainly not an impossible task. Power is a sign of knowledge without being a transparent sign.

My last Baconian hook opens up a complex set of power/knowledge relations, with the simple equation: *knowledge is power.*

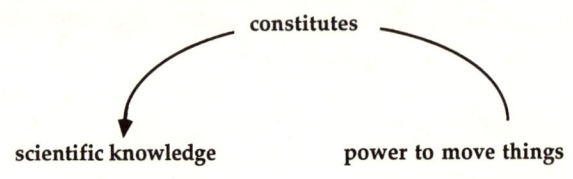

```
                    constitutes
         ┌─────────────────────────────┐
         ▼                             ↘
  scientific knowledge          power to move things
```

Bacon says in a number of places that "knowledge and human power are synonymous," and that "truth, therefore, and utility, are perfectly identical" (Bacon 1902a, 1, Aph. CXXIV). His reasons are straightforward; real knowledge of the natural world is of "forms" of substances, underlying natures which express the potentialities of those substances. For him, the only knowledge possible is of how to produce effects:

> It appears to us that scarce anything in nature can be fundamentally discovered, either by accident, experimental attempts, or the light of physical causes, but only by the discovery of forms. (Bacon 1902b, 169).

> Nature is only subdued by submission, and that which in contemplative philosophy corresponds with the cause in practical science becomes the rule.... Man while operating can only apply or withdraw natural bodies; nature internally performs the rest. (1902a, 1, Aph. III–IV)

> The form or true definition of heat—Heat is an expansive motion restrained, and striving to exert itself in the smaller particles.... With regard to the operative definition, the matter is the same. If you are able to excite a dilating or expansive motion in any natural body, and so to repress that motion and force it upon itself... you will beyond all doubt produce heat. (1902a, 2, Aph. XX)

Bacon has taken the first relation of power and knowledge to heart. Knowledge is only produced through the application of power, and thus the only type of knowledge you can have is that the application of this force on that object produces such and such an effect; so his fundamental claim is a pragmatic one.[5] The position is echoed today, with Joseph Rouse holding a particularly strong version.

> Power relations permeate the most ordinary activities in scientific research. Scientific knowledge arises out of these power relations rather than in opposition to them. Knowledge is power, and power knowledge. Knowledge is embedded in our research practices rather than being fully abstractable in representational theories. Theories are to be understood in their uses, not in their static correspondence (or noncorrespondence) with the world. Power as it is produced in science is not the possession of particular agents and does not necessarily serve particular interests. (Rouse 1987, 24)

Science allows people to manipulate the material world remarkably well, and for this reason Bacon's emphasis (and more so Rouse's) is a valuable counter to a model of science as achieving distanced understanding of the natural world. Aspects of scientific practice *and theorizing* can be seen as instrumental in the sense that their primary uses are to enable manipulation: of facts, things, and people.

Whether or not the pragmatic position was adequate to describe early seventeenth-century science, it is not fully adequate today. In Bacon's simplified version of the pragmatic view of scientific knowledge, all that can be known is how substances behave, or what powers scientists have over them. Yet it is clear that experiments produce evidence of structures over which knowers have very little power: knowing that the difference between the human X and Y chromosomes is productive of differences in sex does not translate into power to produce differences in sex, or at least it didn't for the first seventy or more years after it was established. In focusing on the first power/knowledge relation, Bacon is not describing some of the strength of the experimental sciences: the application of a variety of different tools to a particular problem yields far more than merely pragmatic knowledge. In Rouse's more sophisticated version, theories and other scientific knowledge are *tools*, and we shouldn't look at them as representational knowledge. The pragmatic view of scientific theories fails when it runs into areas of science that are clearly successful and yet are utter failures at manipulation. And there are theories, perhaps not very good ones, which are such failures at manipulation that they have no observable consequences, nothing to latch on to. This was the case of string theory in physics for the first half-dozen or so years of its life; similarly, much of ecological theory can make no hard predictions about natural environments.

The pragmatic attitude toward scientific knowledge, that it is only power in the form of discourse, is really part of a pragmatic attitude to language as a whole. Rouse treats all scientific language as purely performative, doing rather than saying. A more moderate description of scientific language, which accepts the speech-act premise that statements often do more than one thing at once, allows us to take the insights that Rouse proposes without having to claim that *all* knowledge is power in this sense. Rouse is right to emphasize the often neglected pragmatic aspects of scientific knowledge but wrong to then ignore representation; knowing how is usually, though not always, connected to knowing that, and knowing that can sometimes be unconnected to knowing how.

There is a slightly different way of interpreting the knowledge-is-power equation that gives it more universality. Because a scientific claim is the product of the use of a number of tools—laboratory, mathematical, rhetorical—it remains backed up by those tools when it is made as a claim in a public setting. The claim is to some extent a stand-in for the powers that support it. So for you to challenge my claim you have to demonstrate that your resources are more powerful than mine, or at least that there is a weak spot in my resources, that one of my tools accomplishes less than I think. Thus, a challenge is a show of force, even in a purely intellectual arena. In this sense knowledge is not power in what it accomplishes, but in its origins and its stability. Knowledge is a social object; it acquires object status—it is *knowledge* to be used or reckoned with rather than somebody's opinion to be ignored—because of the solidity of its creation and acceptance. The authors of a proposed fact try to build a structure that cannot be challenged. Acceptance and use of the proposed fact can strengthen it further, if it is found useful and makes its way to the center of a discipline: its centrality makes it more difficult to challenge simply because it has more allies depending upon it and, therefore, defending it.

Seeing these relations between knowledge and power allows us to see that the inseparability of knowledge and power, the "/" of "knowledge/power," should not lead us toward skepticism.[6] Instead, knowledges and powers form circular relationships, building each other.

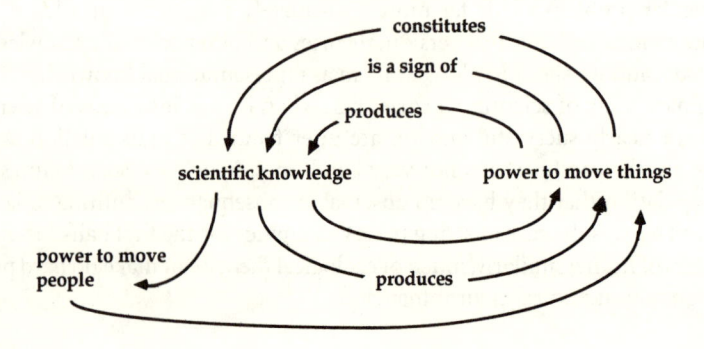

These knowledge/power relations show how communities can use power to produce knowledge and vice versa. Thus science does not require an overarching rationality—a singular scientific method—in order to create knowledge. What is required instead are:

a) *Common cultures* into which scientists have been initiated, in which they participate, and to which they contribute. Scientific cultures, like all cultures, include (or perhaps are made up of) norms of behavior, sanctions for noncompliance with these norms, definition of goals, and rewards for the attainment of those goals. These cultures also contain

b) *Effective domain-specific tools*, including both material tools for the shaping of raw ingredients, and conceptual tools for the shaping of data, information, and decisions. In both cases they are themselves the result of knowledge-production processes—some of them may be nothing more than facts.

c) *Pragmatic checks.* The tools and claims have to be subject to scrutiny, forced into contests among themselves. These checks can take the form of attempts to use others' results and resources.

d) *Communities* to participate in and judge these contests. Scientific knowledge is a community property, something that the appropriate community accepts and uses as true. Relatively high mutual dependence is probably a feature of the most fact-productive scientific communities.

e) *Incentives.* Again, these need not be uniform across the sciences. Whether the dominant interest in any particular case is a technical interest (in a wide sense), a cognitive interest (the attainment of true knowledge), or a political interest (such as the accumulation of resources), the multiple power/knowledge relations show that knowledge can be a step in the production of powerful networks that can satisfy these interests.

f) *Raw ingredients.* Nature contributes to the power of knowledge, providing one of the stable ingredients on which claims rest. In addition, science needs access to resources such as money and energy—usually external support.

Scientists *use* available resources in the production of their own results, and some of the most useful resources are pieces of knowledge for which others are given credit. This sets up a dynamic in which the continued construction of knowledge is likely. We can create an evolutionary picture of the development of scientific knowledge, in which the ideas that are most useful remain central and prominent. Those ideas that are unuseful are either forgotten or disputed. As we saw, truths are sometimes useful and, thus, truths will be among the ideas retained.

CONSTRUCTIVE REALISM

Recognizing that science is a set of practices indicates that there is some important relativism in science.[7] As long as there are different types of scientific practice, there will be different types of natural order; scientific ideas, theories, and representations will hook onto the material world in different ways. Any reasonably concrete notion of rationality that can be applied to the sciences will likely be applicable only locally: scientific methods are domain specific (see Shapere 1985). The universalistic or near-universalistic *principles* that come out of my account—such as the Baconian idea that knowledge production consists of the transformation of less useful objects (both material and social) into specific types of more useful ones—are insufficient to define any rational *procedures* or even rational *methodologies*. It is local criteria, accrued through the activities of past and present scientific communities and present as tools, cultural resources, or cultural boundaries, that determine local procedures. The picture that emerges is of science fragmented into a large number of interdependent—because they use each others' resources—but also somewhat autonomous communities.

With fragmentation and an evolutionary account of science we can have no Linnaean classification of the sciences—in Linnaeus's ideal world every organism had a place in the system, and to every place in the system corresponded an organism—because given this evolutionary picture there is no unique set of sciences and knowledges. Science is a historical entity. What is and has been scientific, or inside science and its disciplines, is not a matter of necessary and sufficient conditions but a combination of tradition, convention, historical accident, political boundary drawing, and subject matter. Disciplines like Plasma Physics, Molecular Biology, and Paleoanthropology need not occupy any preestablished space in a systematic division of knowledges; rather, they occupy niches jointly defined by the resources and restrictions of institutional, ideological, theoretical, and empirical environments, and created in part by themselves. Scientists and their disciplines participate in an ecology of knowledge.[8] With Nelson Goodman I would defend a "relativism" based partly on the "humanistic" grounds that there are different forms of scientific life:

> in what sense are there, as Cassirer and like-minded pluralists insist, many worlds? Just this, I think: that many different

world-versions are of independent interest and importance, without any requirement of reducibility to a single base. (Goodman 1978, 4)

Kuhn does not connect power and knowledge, yet there are a number of reasons for returning to a Kuhnian touchstone. Although scientific communities are in some ways continuous across time, there are also relative discontinuities. The partial structuring of science by sociological and artifact paradigms helps to explain these discontinuities, because exemplary achievements and new resources change the culture, by changing, perhaps only slightly, what counts as a good research program. As well, paradigms, defined by *exemplary* achievements or by tools that are *widely recognized* as productive of knowledge and power, are clearly one sort of entity that can bring the relative homogeneity that is often seen in research communities. An achievement that can serve as a model for others *will* so serve if the community recognizes it as a substantial achievement. Thus the idea of a paradigm can contribute to explanations of the social phenomena we see in science.

If an addition to a scientific culture and its repertoire of practices can be productive of knowledge and power through the research programs it enables, then the flip side of this coin is that it shuts out research programs; paradigms and other components of cultures have both positive and negative heuristics (Lakatos 1970). Kuhn is a constructivist, I argued, in the sense that he sees these heuristics as sufficiently important to shape what the scientist looks for and, hence, observes. They shape the world in which researchers work by defining what does and does not exist, what can and cannot be done. They provide, perhaps only implicitly, maps of the world that are invaluable in helping the scientist to make his or her way about. Scientific research is then tightly circumscribed by the tools available within scientific disciplines; these boundary conditions define routes and avenues, but also the entities that can be taken to be real. Even the tools with which the community works define what can be found out. Cultures construct social worlds. Yet such a constructivism is in no way antithetical to realism: to construct a social world—to construct what can be taken as real—is not to construct a material world.

We can imagine, then, a community of researchers exploring some little corner of the material world, equipped with a set of tools, some directions, a preliminary map, and other resources. The better maps that they eventually produce can genuinely represent the material reality the community is investigating, but the more complex that reality, the more partial the maps will appear. If Nature is the Coyote or Trickster as Donna Haraway contends, then what is right in neo-Kantian constructivism is that frameworks, practices, and resources can have a profound influence on what scientists find. And the necessary limitations imposed by the resources of a culture themselves create "partial perspectives" (Haraway 1991b). Observation *is* theory- and practice dependent, as Hanson, Kuhn, and Feyerabend have famously claimed. This is because practices and methods are theory dependent, as well as being dependent on other features of the environment or culture; the partial perspective adopted at any time will depend upon material, cognitive, and social resources and constraints.

Feminist and externalist studies of science show us that some of the resources of scientific cultures have origins outside the scientific community. Metaphors and other thought structures are produced, but also *reproduced*, in scientific cultures, imported from other cultures. As feminist critics of science have shown, these structures may have ideological valence, which becomes particularly important when they are re-exported for a wider market, with science's stamp of legitimacy. Metaphors used to represent nature become themselves naturalized.

The theory-, practice-, and culture dependence of research points to the relevance of standpoint theory: scientific communities have typically lacked some cognitive and social resources that would enable their partial perspective to overcome certain types of biases in scientific theorizing. The almost complete exclusion of women has meant the exclusion of feminist insights to correct for androcentric assumptions, thought patterns, and metaphors. The conclusions of standpoint theorists in conjunction with the recognition of the social character of knowledge indicates that to maximize objectivity in many areas scientific communities should be diverse, representative, and democratic. Though all maps will necessarily be partial, ones that are less ideologically partial require that scientific communities be genuinely representative of social groups—particularly oppressed groups—and that they be relatively open to the contributions of all of their members.

The many relations between power and knowledge suggest that if we are interested in knowledge we must pay more attention to power (and hence politics) in science, not less—because, among other things, power is productive of knowledge and truths. This conclusion will seem strange to rationalists interested in identifying aspects of the scientific process that insulate and free science from the distorting influences of power. But it should be uncontroversial to other members of the S&TS community, who insist that problems of natural order are always simultaneously problems of social order.

Nonetheless, this does not mean that we are forced into claiming that knowledge either is entirely unconnected from the material world or straightforwardly produces that material world. Rather, the material world, with its many natural orders, is a resource and constraint on scientific action and, hence, interpretation. This allows us to maintain the possibility of normative analysis and to maintain the possibility of claims that some past and present scientific results are simply wrong.

Paying attention to power/knowledge relations brings forward active aspects of science. An image of scientists as passive knowers gives way to one of scientists as active doers when they are seen to *use* knowledge and other tools in the production of more knowledge and power. Paying attention to power/knowledge relations allows us to see science as a social and political institution without forcing us to let go of the possibility of scientific truths and errors.

NOTES

CHAPTER ONE. INTRODUCTION

1. The best-known defender of this position is Ian Hacking (1983), but Hans Radder (1988) and others have very similar viewpoints.

2. Even an empiricist like Bas van Fraassen (1980) might assent to this part of my minimal realism, though for him the emphasis is misplaced, since there are more important goals.

3. Prominent among defenders of this position are Richard Miller (1987), Nancy Cartwright (1989b), and William Newton-Smith (1989). The deflationary position as a whole is quite similar to Arthur Fine's "Natural Ontological Attitude" (NOA) (Fine 1986a, 1986b; Rouse 1991b). Fine objects to global commitments to realism or any other philosophical picture. However, he is more firmly in the antirealist camp than I am: he finds empiricist arguments against realism, of the sort discussed in chapter 2, quite convincing (1986b), though not sufficient to motivate a generalized antirealism about science.

4. In popular usage rationalism is called "positivism," but I avoid using the latter term in this sense because in philosophical contexts "logical positivism" or "positivism" are the names given to positions articulated by the Vienna Circle in the 1920s and 1930s. Although logical positivism is a paradigmatic "positivist" position, it is importantly distinct; for example, logical positivism is an antirealist position, whereas positivism as commonly understood is realist in orientation.

5. Michael Friedman (1991, 1987) has recently argued that the early years of logical positivism were considerably less empiricist and considerably more Kantian than is commonly thought (even while positivists rejected central parts of the Kantian tradition). I think that Friedman is right in this, and right to reject the interpretation of this movement as naive empiricism. However, for my purposes logical positivism was an empiricist position because (a) it became one over its years of hegemony, partly through the appropriation of it by empiricists like A. J. Ayer, and (b) post-positivist realists and their critics, who shaped the varieties of realism in question, usually argued against an empiricist reading of positivism.

CHAPTER TWO. THE GROUNDS FOR TRUTH IN SCIENCE: AN EMPIRICIST/REALIST DIALOGUE

1. These are described in Conant (1972), and have been much discussed, for example by Farley and Geison (1974), Farley (1974), and Roll-Hansen (1979). This experiment is also described in Duclaux (1920, 98ff.).

2. The experiment is so elegant and simple because it was largely for demonstration purposes. By the time that it was performed Pasteur had already done others that made his case more thoroughly. This experiment was *performed* as a rhetorical gesture, important in the context of his very public debate with Felix Pouchet.

3. "Doing nothing original" is meant to avoid the possibility that the new computer will change the nature of the work. Even then it is not strong enough, because changing computational power can sometimes have a significant effect on scientific practice, for example by allowing modeling in ways that were understood but previously infeasible.

4. Michael Williams (1986) reformulates Boyd's argument in this fashion. He argues that nothing is lost with this reformulation, but clearly there is something lost beyond rhetorical power. Williams's discussion comes as part of a deflationist attempt to show that a theory of truth is not necessary to do epistemology and philosophy of science.

5. Lakatos (1970) points this out with respect to research programs. A research program in its early stages is unlikely to do well on any criteria, including empirical adequacy. Most original ideas, precisely because they are original, are viewed with suspicion by the established community of researchers until they have been articulated sufficiently to show that they are plausible.

6. Even if engineers do not apply scientific knowledge, engineering successes suggest a parallel to the abductive argument on scientific methodology: success must be parasitic on the approximate truth of the background beliefs, wherever they come from.

7. Even Arthur Fine, who makes some of these points and claims not to be an empiricist, faces this difficulty: it is difficult to reconcile his "trusting" attitude toward the sciences with his claim that successes are few and far between (Fine 1986b). He has to be talking about two different types of phenomena here, a group of results in which one should have confidence, and a group of results in which one shouldn't.

8. Hilary Putnam pointed this out in conversation.

9. Although not all philosophers would agree or would have agreed with either position, the recent trend among philosophers to pay more attention to scientific practice has created a corresponding trend toward the use of "theory" in the sense of a systematic treatment of a subject matter. (See for example Darden 1991.) Hacking, in explaining how he can be a realist about experimental entities without being a theory realist, says:

> Even people in a team, who work on different parts of the same large experiment, may hold different and mutually incompatible accounts of electrons. This is because different parts of the experiment will make different uses of electrons. Models good for calculations on one aspect of electrons will be poor for others.... But might there not be a common

core of theory, the intersection of everybody in the group, which is the theory of the electron to which all the experimenters are realistically committed? I would say common lore, *not* common core.... Even if there are a lot of shared beliefs, there is no reason to suppose that they form anything worth calling a theory. (Hacking 1984, 156–57)

10. In slightly different terms the claim that classical genetic theory is not true is a straightforward consequence of most versions of the semantic view of theories (e.g., Beatty 1981; Suppes 1967; Thompson 1988; van Fraassen 1972). The points here and following about the relation of classical to molecular genetics are made (in very different terms) in Kitcher (1984). Kitcher attempts to show the irreducibility of classical genetics to molecular genetics. Gasper (1992) provides interesting commentary on Kitcher's article, agreeing with the conclusions but disagreeing with the reasons given for those conclusions.

11. Theories that are approximations away from the truth about this messy world may be approximations of some other truths, truths about a world cleaned up and its capacities. A theory of gravitation, which posits a certain force between objects of specific masses isn't true about objects in *our* world because there are so many other forces in play. But it is true about objects in extremely pared-down worlds. And it is in a sense true about this world, since there are some situations in which the results of gravitational forces can be seen separated from other forces. In the laboratory experimenters can clean things up so that the theory, suitably added to, does describe reality. This position especially appealing regarding classical physics, with its neatly separable forces. But it may not be so easy for other examples. Margaret Morrison (1995) looks at cases in which the "structures" analysis of idealization does and does not work, in the context of modeling in physics.

CHAPTER THREE. EPISTEMOLOGY BY OTHER MEANS

1. By this account a discipline can shift cognitive style from Facts to Science-in-the-Making. Fuchs doesn't apply his model in this way, reserving Science-in-the-Making for fields that are in a more or less continuous state of innovation, but which nonetheless solidify facts and paradigms. Conflict and innovation enter the fact-producing style through "normal accidents" (Fuchs, 102ff.), and are only temporary events.

2. This chart and discussion is actually the jumping-off point for Fuchs's analysis; for example, each of the cognitive styles is also posited to have an associated epistemological attitude. In addition, Fuchs creates a more complex model of these and other variables, which I am not going to describe here (Fuchs, 180).

3. Examples include or are discussed in Anne Fausto-Sterling (1985), Ruth Bleier (1984, 1986a, 1986b), Lynda Birke (1986), Brighton Women in Science Group (1980), Hubbard, Henifen and Fried (1979), and Hubbard and Lowe (1979)

4. My own emphasis in this book on perspectives, truth, and realism similarly fails to engage these different aspects of science as much as I would like. This is in part

a reflection of the lack of philosophical tools for, and interest in, analyzing scientific activity in terms not directly connected to belief.

5. John Dewey (1938) also agrees with today's S&TS on this account, and with Longino and Popper he retains some normative force to his claim. But Dewey would have knowledge even a little more democratically based than they; he insists that knowledge is not obtained until it has been used in practice, in the public sphere where possible. He says, for example, that

> Until agreement upon consequences is reached by those who reinstate the conditions set forth, the conclusions that are announced by an individual inquirer have the status of an hypothesis, especially if the findings fail to agree with the general trend of already accepted results. While agreement among the activities and their consequences that are brought about in the wider (technically nonscientific) public stands upon a different plane, nevertheless such agreement is an integral part of a *complete* test of physical conclusions wherever their public bearings are relevant. (490)

6. Even the normative task of looking for the best procedures for the production of knowledge, which is an important part of Goldman's program, requires attention to the social context of science, because individual reasoners often perform very poorly. Faust (1984) surveys some problems with individuals' cognitive performance ("the 'news' about human cognitive capacity *is bad*" [xxvi]) and then recommends more reliance on machines and social checks to reasoning.

7. The large, so-called constructivist part of S&TS that I am concerned with here and in the next chapter is tightly connected with the sociology of scientific knowledge: it can be taken to include all work drawing on or exemplifying David Bloor's tenet of symmetry; in addition to Bloor 1991, see Barnes and Bloor 1982, Barnes 1974. Some important or representative texts include: Barnes and Shapin 1979, Brannigan 1981, Callon 1986, Collins 1992, Collins and Pinch 1985, Dear 1985, Farley and Geison 1974, Fleck 1979, Gilbert and Mulkay 1984, Knorr-Cetina 1981, Knorr-Cetina and Mulkay 1983, Laqueur 1990, Latour 1987, 1988, Latour and Woolgar 1986, Law 1986a, Le Grand 1990, Lynch 1986, Lynch and Woolgar 1990, MacKenzie 1978, 1981, Myers 1990, Pickering 1984, 1992a,b, Pinch 1985, Richards and Schuster 1989, Schaffer 1989, 1992, Shapin 1975, 1982, Shapin and Schaffer 1985, Smith and Wise 1989, Woolgar 1988.

8. This makes Bloor's recommendation one against "Whig history," or "whiggism" (Butterfield 1931). Symmetry and antiwhiggism both demand that history not be drawn toward the present, that historical actors not be allotted resources unavailable until later.

9. E.g., MacKenzie 1978, 1981, Jacob 1976, Jacob and Jacob 1980, Rudwick 1974, Farley 1974, Farley and Geison, Shapin and Schaffer 1985, Shapin 1975, Harwood 1976, 1977. Shapin 1982 contains further references.

10. My use of the concept of a 'resource,' in this abstract way, owes much to the work of Peter Taylor (e.g., 1995b).

11. Although Shapin and Schaffer connect the dispute to the religious and political upheavals in England in the middle of the seventeenth century, those events serve more to provide reasons for the search for social order than to provide reasons for the particular positions taken—both Boyle and Hobbes are reacting to disorder. *Leviathan and the Air-Pump* is more microsociological history than are strong program accounts, in that it attempts to explain the positions taken with reference to the politics within the community of natural philosophers; the experimental form of life is a way of ordering that community. In the process of establishing that form of life as a legitimate one, Boyle established a new set of self-evident principles, principles that regulate and legitimate experiment.

12. Though even what it means for a technology to work may be controversial, and may require negotiation. Donald MacKenzie shows that what counts as a measurement of "accuracy" for missiles had to be negotiated (MacKenzie 1990).

13. One might want to add a number of criteria to this list. For example, theoretical plausibility is something that Collins leaves out, though it is a prominent feature of debates about experimental results. The controversy over cold fusion experiments involved many of the items on Collins's list, but was also affected by judgments that physical theory couldn't account for the supposed results.

14. Any doubts about it should be resolved in chapter 9, where I argue, among other things, that knowledge of the material world produces power over it. Given the multifold relations of knowledge and power, the will to power can easily become a will to knowledge.

15. I explore the place of standpoint theory in science more fully in Sismondo (1995). There I argue that standpoint theory is correct, but also limited in scope: standpoints will be relevant only to areas of science in which social relations are at issue. Social relations may be at issue in any science, but occupy a very different place in physics and mathematics than they do in sociology or biology.

CHAPTER FOUR. EXPLORING METAPHORS OF "SOCIAL CONSTRUCTION"

1. In this chapter I discuss only a few texts that help to define uses of the construction metaphor. Thomas Nickles (1992) discusses aspects of this tradition in ways that complement my discussion here.

2. This insight about institution building is similar in some ways to points made in the sociological study of deviance (e.g., Lemert 1967). The article "Labelling Theory" in *The Social Science Encyclopedia* (Kuper and Kuper 1985) provides a concise overview.

3. See, for example, De Lauretis 1987 on film and literature, Roman et al. 1988 on popular culture, and Fausto-Sterling 1985 on biology. A number of positions on

the constructedness or "essentialism" of homosexuality are represented in Stein 1990.

4. See, for example, Judith Long Laws and Pepper Schwartz's *Sexual Scripts* (1977). This was one of the earlier books on gender roles to explitily acknowledge Berger and Luckmann, and they point out this addition of competition to the social constructivist model.

5. In addition to these examples, I argue in chapter 6 that one reason for a particularly persistent misreading of Kuhn's *Structure of Scientific Revolutions* has to do with a failure to appreciate the extent to which Kuhn is talking of social objects and the social world.

6. Harry Collins's study of closure of debates, described in chapter 3, provides some examples of the value of ad hominem arguments.

7. Van den Daele credits a 1974 talk by Mendelsohn with the idea of studying the social construction of science (48).

8. Her earlier articles are under the name Karin Knorr.

9. A typical example of this tenet occurs in Richard Boyd (1984), who includes among the four theses that he takes to embody realism: "(iv) The reality which scientific theories describe is largely independent of our thoughts or theoretical commitments" (42). This is intended to be read as asserting that reality is not mind-dependent, not that scientists don't choose what to study on the basis of their theoretical commitments. Realism is in this way distinguished from those readings of Kuhn that take him to be asserting the mind-dependence of the world in an idealist or perhaps a Kantian sense. But, as we've learned from Knorr-Cetina, the phenomena that science studies are extremely dependent on thoughts and theoretical commitments, for often they would not exist were it not for the experimental development of these theoretical commitments. Thus this realist thesis would have to be refined to allow for this type of mind dependence.

10. The second edition appeared in 1986, with the addition of a new postscript and the subtraction of the word *social* from the subtitle. This latter change reflects Latour and Woolgar's argument that attention to "social factors" creates an apparent dichotomy between the social and the technical, or between the social and the intellectual, dichotomies which they feel are unwarranted from the point of view of the observer. "The distinction between 'social' and 'technical' factors is a resource drawn upon routinely by working scientists"—thus something to be explored and explained. And in their case their "interest in the details of scientific activity cuts across the distinction" (Latour and Woolgar 1986, 27), giving them good reason to ignore it. They claim that the change in the subtitle does not reflect more of a change than their recognition by 1986 that they could do away with the "term" *social construction*.

11. I do not mean to claim that they are fully original in introducing this more radical sense of construction. Kant and Husserl are some obvious forerunners, and Bachelard and Kuhn sometimes seem to say very similar things about science.

12. Though to produce bacteria we may need other parts of the laboratory: Petri dishes, heating devices that keep reasonably constant temperatures, and nutrients are important in the production of bacteria for study under the microscope.

13. Harry Collins (1992) makes this argument. I discuss it and respond in chapter 7, where I claim that the constructivist heuristic is not clearly implicated in the successes of antirealist S&TS.

14. Actually, they could have told a richer story, with more social input. See, for example, Granzotto 1988.

CHAPTER FIVE. NEO-KANTIAN CONSTRUCTIONS

1. There are other sources of nominalism about science that appeal to fans of science rather than critics. A strong faith in the power of logic and mathematics to make sense of observations can lead to a belief in the irrelevance to our particular categorizations, and hence the possible irreality, of any real similarities between objects. For such a fan of logic the task of science is to organize our observations, rather than to achieve any understanding of the structure of the world. The problems that this version of nominalism faces do not significantly differ from those the more debunking version faces.

2. Nelson Goodman's "New Riddle of Induction" (the well-known "grue" problem) shows this in a particularly striking way (Goodman 1983). One can define a predicate in such a way as to create the grounds for some obvious inductive inferences which are nevertheless extremely counter-intuitive. Goodman defines *grue* as applying "to all things examined before *t* just in case they are green but to other things just in case they are blue," where *t* is some point of time in the future (1983, 74). All emeralds we have observed are grue, and hence this gives us good reason to believe that all emeralds are grue. Except, of course, that most people would vigorously deny that emeralds are grue, believing that emeralds first examined after *t* would be green, not blue, and hence not grue.

Although it is not agreed what Goodman's problem shows, it clearly shows the implausibility of the idea that one category is as good as the next when we are engaged in making predictions. It suggests then, that the value of a category will in part depend upon its fit with causally relevant features of the world.

3. The standard characterization of supervenience is largely due to Jaegwon Kim (e.g., 1984). For Kim, a property supervenes on a set of physical properties if it covaries with those properties, though he offers several different versions of covariance. In a recent discussion Kim points out that there is no unique definition of supervenience applicable to all of the subject matters in which we would want such a concept (1990), and hence that we should "let one hundred supervenience concepts bloom!" He argues that there are three central relations which philosophers want as part of supervenience: covariance, dependence, and nonreduction (though he claims that only covariance has been made precise). That is, if a linguistic message super-

venes on material signals, it should vary with those signals, be in some sense dependent upon them, and yet not be reducible to them. My use of 'supervene' also assumes that these three relations hold.

CHAPTER SIX. THE *STRUCTURE* THIRTY YEARS LATER

1. References will be to the 2d edition (1970a), which, aside from the postscript, differs from the first in no way that is pertinent to the argument of this chapter.

2. Gutting argues that metaphysical paradigms aren't useful in any philosophical thinking about science, though the other senses of 'paradigm' can be very valuable (1984).

3. His essay "Mathematical Versus Experimental Traditions in the Development of Physical Sciences"(1985) shows some of Kuhn's concern for the importance of manipulation in some sciences.

4. Arthur Fine (e.g., Fine 1986a) is a good example of a person who is skeptical about truth, but doesn't hold anything like idealist or constructivist views. He simply wants to abandon truth altogether as a well-defined concept, and accept that the word *truth* has different uses in different situations, uses that are not connected in any important way.

5. One reason for the similarity in the positions that Kuhn and Putnam take might be their characterization of their opponent. Like Kuhn, Putnam sees the realist position as demanding that there be a limiting truth: on the (metaphysical) realist "perspective, the world consists of some fixed totality of mind-independent objects. There is exactly one true and complete description of 'the way the world is'" (1981, 49).

6. There are exceptions. Truth may be a very convenient shorthand for congruent observations when discussing consensus. Consensus about a novel but highly repeatable observation might be explained in terms of the truth of the statements about it. We should note that this doesn't commit one to the global rather than the local notion of truth.

7. There is also the sense in which scientists physically construct the world, stemming from the fact that scientists' objects of study are usually many times purified versions of what occurs in nature, forced into situations that are distinctly unnatural.

8. The move to texts is a much-disputed one: "'Textualization' of everything in post-structuralist, post-modernist theory has been damned by Marxists and socialist feminists for its utopian disregard for lived relations of domination that ground the 'play' of arbitrary reading" (Haraway 1985, 69). But Haraway defends the textualizing move, by moderating it, and thereby denying its arbitrariness and reducing its scope, and by pointing out the importance of textualization and interpretation

to lived social relations: "Who cyborgs will be is a radical question; the answers are a matter of survival" (70).

9. In her more recent *Whose Science? Whose Knowledge?* (1991), Harding returns to standpoint theory, but a standpoint theory that can accomodate multiple perspectives.

10. Yet Haraway distances herself from realism, in at least its traditional characterizations: "The approach I am recommending is not a version of 'realism', which has proved a rather poor way of engaging with the world's active agency" (1991b, 199)

11. The logical positivists' protocols and protocol sentences were very different creatures (e.g., Neurath 1959; Schlick 1959).

CHAPTER SEVEN. CREEPING REALISM: BRUNO LATOUR'S HETEROGENEOUS CONSTRUCTIVISM

1. Rationality might not appear to belong on this list, because, it might be argued, what is rational and irrational can be judged in advance of the resolution of a controversy. Collins (1981a) argues that in fact, rationality is no more timeless than the other possible criteria, because there are no firmly accepted accounts of what is rational behavior in a given situation; in particular, he argues, scientists' decisions rest on much more complex grounds than any philosophical account of scientific rationality.

2. A number of the papers in Pickering (1992b) are alternative accounts. In addition, Latour's work is only the most visible part of a larger school, what could be called the "Parisian actor-network approach." Other prominent members of this school are Michel Callon (1986; Callon and Latour 1981) and John Law (1986a).

3. Latour drops the notions of actors and agents in favor of "actants." This is because he has a textualized account of agency: not doing, but making do. Although Latour's account of agency is an intriguing one there is no particular reason to explore it here. Thus I stick with the more familiar "actors" of "actor-network theory."

4. Collins and Yearley (1992) also make this point, though they see it as a negative feature of Latour's work. Callon and Latour's response (1992) to this point questions the framework of the debate.

CHAPTER EIGHT. METAPHORS AND REPRESENTATION

1. The classic source for thinking about metaphors and analogies in science is Hesse 1966. For some other theoretical treatments see Bloor 1991, Hoffman 1985, Hoffman et al. 1984, Coetzee 1982, Boswell 1981, Martin and Harré 1982, Leatherdale 1974. A few examples of explorations of particular metaphors are:

Cohn 1987, Easlea 1986, Haraway 1989, 1991a, Hoffmann and Leibowitz 1991, Keller 1992, Mirowski 1989, Mitman 1993, Stepan 1986.

2. For example, recent work by David Cummiskey (1992) shows how an appreciation of the role of scientific metaphors can add a necessary descriptive element to the causal theory of reference for the introduction of new scientific terms. This provides one way of refining the causal account so that we are not forced to accept that all reasonably successful scientific terms refer for trivial reasons. The descriptive component limits possible reference in an intuitive way.

3. These points are related to criticisms of the "received view" by proponents of the semantic approach to scientific theories (e.g., Beatty 1981; Suppes 1967, Thompson 1988; van Fraassen 1972), though in the semantic approach the key models are highly abstract mathematical structures.

4. Leszek Nowak is prominent among philosophers studying idealization. His "The Idealizational Approach to Science: A Survey" (1992) contains his central positions and references.

5. Conceptual approximations and idealizations are related, because in cases of large doses of idealization terms may appear to lose their referentiality: it is sometimes hard to identify the objects that an idealized term refers to. For example, when discrete objects are modeled as continuous the objects are idealized out of existence in the model.

6. Kittay actually uses *topic* rather than *tenor*, and she defines *topic* and *vehicle* to make them quite different from Richards's *tenor* and *vehicle*. I'm going to ignore those changes here, however, as they don't make a substantial difference to this short sketch.

7. Although these studies lend some support to this account of metaphor, they create problems for Kittay's account of metaphor recognition, at least for conversational situations. They show that, given the right context, there is little perceived incongruity to metaphors. What acceptable theory of metaphor recognition is compatible with this is unclear.

8. John Searle (1981) analyses metaphors in terms of indirect speech acts, though his goal is to develop some machinery for understanding the difference between speaker's utterance meaning (metaphorical meaning) and sentence meaning (literal meaning).

9. John E. Waggoner (1990) reviews some of the psychological literature on metaphor and questions this and other feature of the interactionist account. The studies he cites, though, explore only short-term changes in the effects of metaphors upon the associations of the vehicle.

CHAPTER NINE. POWER AND KNOWLEDGE

1. Thomas Kuhn claims that this was connected to the rise of corpuscularism, because previous (Aristotelian or Platonic) traditions could not justify the data taken

from nature in other than its most natural state: for these earlier traditions, "to experiment or to constrain nature was to do it violence, thus hiding the role of the 'natures' or forms which made things what they were" (Kuhn 1985, 184).

2. See Rachel Laudan (1984). In particular, Edward Constant's paper in that volume argues strongly that technology is relatively independent of basic scientific research (Constant 1984). The distinction between use and application is made by Thomas P. Hughes (1989).

3. Rachel Laudan (1995) argues that one problem with the appropriation of technology as an explanatory resource in the study of science, and as an explanatory metaphor for scientific techniques, is that how technologies are made to work is itself not well understood.

4. The introduction of the social sciences into this discussion confuses some of the multiple relations between power and knowledge, because the power produced by knowledge is the same power given to knowers: the power to reshape societies and people.

5. Antonio Pérez-Ramos puts this in a slightly different light, seeing this pragmatism as Bacon's participation in the "maker's knowledge" tradition, which "postulates an intimate relationship between objects of cognition and objects of construction, and regards knowing as a kind of making or as a capacity to make (*verum factum*)" (Pérez-Ramos 1988, 48).

6. Pauline Rosenau draws this conclusion when she paraphrases Foucault as saying that "it is impossible to separate truth from power, and so there is no real possibility of any absolute, uncorrupted truth" (Rosenau 1992, 78).

7. As I point out in chapter 1, there are a number of philosophical positions one could call "scientific realism." The phrase "constructive realism" is used by at least one other philosopher, Ronald Giere (1988); in using it I don't mean to claim that the perspective sketched here is the same as his, though there are a number of congruences, stemming from our naturalistic approaches to scientific epistemology. But my perspective here is more geared to understanding science as a social phenomenon.

8. For some interesting discussions of ecologies of scientific knowledge, see Peter Taylor (1990, 1992), and Charles Rosenberg (1988). Taylor in particular attempts to model the practice of science in the context of a heterogeneous environment of institutions, tools, and data. Douglas Allchin (1991) argues for an ecological model of knowledge focussed primarily on the place of theory in an environment of empirical data. Ian Hacking's notion of "styles of scientific reasoning" is another contribution to ecologies of knowledge (Hacking 1985).

WORKS CITED

Achenbach, Joel. 1988. "Creeping Surrealism." *The Utne Reader* 30: 112–16.

Ackermann, Robert. 1985. *Data, Instruments, and Theory: A Dialectical Approach to Understanding Science.* Princeton: Princeton University Press.

Allchin, Douglas. 1991. *Resolving Disagreement in Science: The Ox-Phos Controversy, 1961–1977.* Ph.D. Dissertation, University of Chicago.

Amann, K., and K. Knorr-Cetina. 1990. "The Fixation of (Visual) Evidence" in Michael Lynch and Steve Woolgar (eds.), *Representation in Scientific Practice.* Cambridge, MA: MIT Press, 85–121.

Ashmore, Malcolm. 1989. *The Reflexive Turn.* Chicago: University of Chicago Press.

Austin, J. L. 1962. *How to Do Things with Words: The William James Lectures Delivered at Harvard University in 1955.* Cambridge, MA: Harvard University Press.

Bachelard, Gaston. 1984. *The New Scientific Spirit.* Arthur Goldhammer (trans.). Boston: Beacon.

Bacon, Francis. 1864. *The Works of Francis Bacon,* vol. V. James Spedding, Robert Leslie Ellis, and Douglas Denon Heath (eds.). New York: Hurd and Houghton.

———. 1902a. *Novum Organum.* New York: P. F. Collier and Son.

———. 1902b. *Advancement of Learning.* New York: P. F. Collier and Son.

Barnes, Barry. 1974. *Scientific Knowledge and Sociological Theory.* London: Routledge and Kegan Paul.

———. 1988. *The Nature of Power.* Urbana: University of Illinois Press.

Barnes, Barry, and David Bloor. 1982. "Relativism, Rationality and the Sociology of Knowledge." In M. Hollis and S. Lukes (eds.), *Rationality and Relativism.* Cambridge, MA: MIT Press.

Barnes, Barry, and Steven Shapin (eds.). 1979. *Natural Order: Historical Studies of Scientific Culture.* London: Sage.

Baudrillard, Jean. 1983. *In the Shadow of the Silent Majorities . . . Or the End of the Social*, Paul Foss, Paul Patton, and John Johnston (trans.). New York: Semiotext(e).

Beatty, John. 1981. "What's Wrong with the Recieved View of Evolutionary Theory?" In P. D. Asquith and R. N. Giere (eds.), *PSA 1980*, vol. 2. East Lansing, MI: Philosophy of Science Association, 397–426.

Berger, Peter L., and Thomas Luckmann. 1966. *The Social Construction of Reality: A Treatise in the Sociology of Knowledge.* New York: Doubleday.

Berger, Peter, and Hansfried Kellner. 1964. "Marriage and the Construction of Reality." *Diogenes* 46: 1–24.

Bhaskar, Roy. 1986. *Scientific Realism and Human Emancipation.* London: Verso.

Bijker, Wiebe E., Thomas P. Hughes, and Trevor J. Pinch. 1987. *The Social Construction of Technological Systems: New Directions in the Sociology and History of Technology.* Cambridge, MA: MIT Press.

Binkley, Timothy. 1981. "On the Truth and Probity of Metaphor." In Johnson, *Philosophical Perspectives on Metaphor.* 136–53.

Birke, Lynda. 1986. *Women, Feminism and Biology: The Feminist Challenge.* New York: Methuen.

Black, Max. 1981 (1955). "Metaphor." In Johnson, *Philosophical Perspectives on Metaphor.* 63–82.

Bleier, Ruth. 1984. *Science and Gender: A Critique of Biology and Its Theories on Women.* New York: Pergamon.

———.1986a. "Lab Coat: Robe of Innocence or Klansman's Sheet?" In Teresa de Lauretis (ed.) *Feminist Studies/Critical Studies.* Bloomington: Indiana University Press, 55–66.

———. (ed.). 1986b. *Feminist Approaches to Science.* New York: Pergamon.

Bloor, David. 1991. *Knowledge and Social Imagery*, 2d ed. (1st ed. 1976) Chicago: University of Chicago Press.

Boswell, D. A. 1981. "Metaphor and Observation in Science." *Psychological Record* 31: 25–28.

Boyd, Richard N. 1979. "Metaphor and Theory Change: What is 'Metaphor' a Metaphor For?" In Andrew Ortony (ed.) *Metaphor and Thought.* Cambridge: Cambridge University Press, 356–408.

———. 1984. "The Current Status of Scientific Realism." In Jarrett Leplin (ed.) *Scientific Realism*. Berkeley: University of California Press, 41–82.

———. 1985. "Lex Orandi est Lex Credendi." In P. M. Churchland and C. A. Hooker (eds.), *Images of Science: Essays on Realism and Empiricism*. Chicago: University of Chicago Press, 3–34.

———. 1990. "Realism, Conventionality, and 'Realism About.'" In George Boolos (ed.), *Meaning and Method: Essays in Honor of Hilary Putnam*. Cambridge: Cambridge University Press, 171–95.

———. 1992. "Constructivism, Realism, and Philosophical Method." In J. Earman (ed.), *Inference, Explanation and other Frustrations*. Berkeley: University of California Press, 131–98.

Brannigan, Augustine. 1981. *The Social Basis of Scientific Discoveries*. Cambridge: Cambridge University Press.

Brighton Women in Science Group (ed.). 1980. *Alice Through the Microscope: The Power of Science over Women's Lives*. London: Virago.

Broad, William, and Nicholas Wade. 1982. *Betrayers of the Truth*. New York: Simon and Schuster.

Brown, James Robert. 1989. *The Rational and the Social*. New York: Routledge.

Butterfield, Herbert. 1931. *The Whig Interpretation of History*. London: Bell.

Callon, Michel. 1986. "Some Elements of a Sociology of Translation: Domestication of the Scallops and the Fishermen of St. Brieuc Bay." In *Law, Power, Action and Belief*, 196–233.

Callon, Michel, and Bruno Latour. 1981. "Unscrewing the Big Leviathan: How Actors Macro-Structure Reality and How Sociologists Help Them to Do So." In Knorr-Cetina and Cicourel, *Advances in Social Theory and Methodology*, 277–303.

———. 1992. "Don't Throw the Baby Out with the Bath School! A Reply to Collins and Yearley." In Pickering, *Science as Practice and Culture*, 343–68.

Cartwright, Nancy. 1983. *How the Laws of Physics Lie*. Oxford: Clarendon Press.

———. 1989a. "A Case Study in Realism: Why Econometrics is Committed to Capacities." In Arthur Fine and Jarrett Leplin (eds.), *PSA 1988*. East Lansing, MI: Philosophy of Science Association.

———. 1989b. *Nature's Capacities and Their Measurement*. Oxford: Clarendon Press.

Chance, M. R. A. 1948. "A Peculiar Form of Social Behaviour Induced in Mice by Amphetamine." *Behaviour* 1: 64–70.

Coetzee, J. M. 1982. "Newton and the Idea of a Transparent Scientific Language." *Journal of Literary Semantics* 11: 3–13.

Cohn, Carol. 1987. "Sex and Death in the Rational World of Defense Intellectuals." *Signs* 12: 687–718.

Collins, Harry M. 1981a. "What is TRASP? The Radical Programme as a Methodological Imperative." *Philosophy of the Social Sciences* 11: 215–24.

———. 1981b. "Stages in the Empirical Programme of Relativism." *Social Studies of Science* 11: 3–10.

———. 1990. *Artificial Experts: Social Knowledge and Intelligent Machines*. Cambridge, MA: MIT Press.

———. 1992 (1985). *Changing Order: Replication and Induction in Scientific Practice*, 2d ed. Chicago: University of Chicago Press.

Collins, Harry M. and Trevor J. Pinch. 1985. *Frames of Meaning: The Social Construction of Extraordinary Science*. London: Routledge and Kegan Paul.

Collins, Harry M., and Steven Yearly. 1992. "Epistemological Chicken." In Pickering, *Science as Practice and Culture*: 301–26.

Collins, Patricia Hill. 1986. "Learning from the Outsider Within: The Sociological Significance of Black Feminist Thought." *Social Problems* 33, no. 6: 14–32.

Conant, James Bryant (ed.). *Harvard Case Histories in Experimental Science*, vol. 2. Cambridge, MA: Harvard University Press.

Constant, Edward W., II. 1984. "Communities and Hierarchies: Structure in the Practice of Science and Technology." In Laudan, *The Nature of Technological Knowledge*: 27–46.

Cowan, Ruth Schwartz. 1983. *More Work for Mother: The Ironies of Household Technology from the Open Hearth to the Microwave*. New York: Basic Books.

Cummiskey, David. 1992. "Reference Failure and Scientific Realism: a Response to the Meta-induction." *British Journal for the Philosophy of Science* 43: 21–40.

Darden, Lindley. 1991. *Theory Change and Science: Strategies from Mendelian Genetics.* Oxford: Oxford University Press.

Davidson, Donald. 1974. "On the Very Idea of a Conceptual Scheme." *Proceedings and Addresses of the American Philosophical Association*, vol. 47: 5–20.

———. 1981. "What Metaphors Mean." In Johnson, *Philosophical Perspectives on Metaphor.* 200–20.

Dear, Peter. 1985. "*Totius in Verba*: Rhetoric and Authority in the Early Royal Society." *Isis* 76: 145–61.

De Lauretis, Teresa. 1987. *Technologies of Gender: Essays on Theory, Film, and Fiction.* Bloomington: Indiana University Press.

Derrida, Jacques. 1977. "Limited Inc a b c . . ." In *Limited Inc*, Samuel Weber (trans.). Evanston, IL: Northwestern University Press, 29–110.

Dewey, John. 1938. *Logic: The Theory of Inquiry.* London: George Allen and Unwin, Ltd.

Duclaux, Emile. 1920. *Pasteur: The History of a Mind.* Erwin F. Smith and Florence Hedges, (trans.). Philadelphia: W. B. Saunders.

Eagleton, Terry. 1992. *Ideology: An Introduction.* London: Verso.

Easlea, Brian. 1986. "The Masculine Image of Science with Special Reference to Physics: How Much does Gender Really Matter?" In Jan Harding, *Perspectives on Gender and Science.* 132–58.

Farley, John. 1974. *The Spontaneous Generation Controversy from Descartes to Oparin.* Baltimore: Johns Hopkins University Press.

Farley, John, and Gerald L. Geison. 1974. "Science, Politics and Spontaneous Generation in Nineteenth Century France: The Pasteur-Pouchet Debate." *Bulletin of the History of Medicine*, 48.

Faust, David. 1984. *The Limits of Scientific Reasoning.* Minneapolis: University of Minnesota Press.

Fausto-Sterling, Anne. 1985. *Myths of Gender: Biological Theories About Women and Men.* New York: Basic Books.

Feyerabend, Paul. 1989. "Realism and the Historicity of Knowledge." *The Journal of Philosophy* LXXXVI, 8: 393–406.

Fine, Arthur. 1986a. *The Shaky Game: Einstein, Realism and the Quantum Theory.* Chicago: University of Chicago Press.

———. 1986b. "Unnatural Attitudes: Realist and Instrumentalist Attachments to Science," *Mind* 95: 149–79.

———. 1991. "Piecemeal Realism." *Philosophical Studies* 61: 79–96.

Fleck, Ludwik. 1979. *Genesis and Development of a Scientific Fact.* Thaddeus J. Trenn and Robert K. Merton (eds.), Fred Bradley and Thaddeus J. Trenn (trans.). Chicago: University of Chicago Press.

Foucault, Michel. 1980. *Power/Knowledge: Selected Interviews and Other Writings 1972–1977.* New York: Pantheon.

———. 1990. *The History of Sexuality. Volume 1: An Introduction.* Robert Hurley (trans.). New York: Vintage.

Franklin, Allan. 1986. *The Neglect of Experiment.* Cambridge: Cambridge University Press.

———. 1990. *Experiment Right or Wrong.* Cambridge: Cambridge University Press.

Friedman, Michael. 1987. "Carnap's Aufbau Reconsidered." *Nous* 21: 521–45.

———. 1991. "The Re-evaluation of Logical Positivism." *The Journal of Philosophy* 88: 505–19.

Fuchs, Stephan. 1992. *The Professional Quest for Truth: A Social Theory of Science and Knowledge.* Albany: State University of New York Press.

Fuller, Steve. 1988. *Social Epistemology.* Bloomington: Indiana University Press.

Galison, Peter. 1987. *How Experiments End.* Chicago: University of Chicago Press.

Gasper, Philip. 1992. "Reduction and Instrumentalism in Genetics." *Philosophy of Science* 59: 655–70.

Gentner, Dedre. 1982. "Are Scientific Analogies Metaphors?" In David S. Miall (ed.), *Metaphor: Problems and Perspectives.* Sussex: Harvester, 106–32.

Gergen, Kenneth J. 1986. "Correspondence versus Autonomy in the Language of Understanding Human Action." In Donald W. Fiske and Richard A. Shweder (eds.) *Metatheory in Social Science: Pluralisms and Subjectivities.* Chicago: University of Chicago Press, 136–62.

Gibbs, R. W., Jr., and R. J. Gerrig. 1989. "How Context Makes Metaphor Comprehension Seem 'Special.'" *Metaphor and Symbolic Activity*, vol. 4: 145–58.

Giere, Ronald N. 1988. *Explaining Science: A Cognitive Approach.* Chicago: University of Chicago Press.

Gieryn, Thomas F. 1983. "Boundary-Work and the Demarcation of Science from Non-Science." *American Sociological Review* 50: 392–409.

Gilbert, Nigel and Michael Mulkay. 1984. *Opening Pandora's Box: A Sociological Analysis of Scientists' Discourse.* Cambridge: Cambridge University Press.

Glucksberg, S. 1989. "Metaphors in Conversation: How are they Understood? Why are they Used?" *Metaphor and Symbolic Activity*, vol. 4: 125–43.

Goldman, Alvin I. 1985. "Epistemics: The Regulative Theory of Cognition." In Kornblith, *Naturalizing Epistemology.* 217–30.

Goodman, Nelson. 1981. "Metaphor as Moonlighting." In Johnson, *Philosophical Perspectives on Metaphor.* 221–27.

———. 1983. *Fact, Fiction, and Forecast*, 4th ed. (1st ed. 1954). Cambridge, MA: Harvard University Press.

Gould, Stephen Jay. 1981. *The Mismeasure of Man.* New York: W. W. Norton.

Granzotto, Gianni. 1988. *Christopher Columbus: The Dream and the Obsession.* Stephen Sertarelli (trans.). London: Grafton.

Gross, Paul R., and Norman Levitt. 1994. *Higher Superstition: The Academic Left and Its Quarrels with Science.* Baltimore: Johns Hopkins University Press.

Gutting, Gary (ed.). 1980. *Paradigms and Revolutions: Applications and Appraisals of Thomas Kuhn's Philosophy of Science.* Notre Dame: University of Notre Dame Press.

Gutting, Gary. 1984. "The Strong Program: A Dialogue." In J. R. Brown (ed.), *Scientific Rationality: The Sociological Turn.* Dordrecht: Reidel, pp. 95–111.

Habermas, Jürgen. 1970. "The Scientization of Politics and Public Opinion." In *Toward a Rational Society: Student Protest, Science and Politics.* Jeremy J. Shapiro (trans.). Boston: Beacon.

Hacking, Ian. 1983. *Representing and Intervening: Introductory Topics in the Philosophy of Natural Science.* Cambridge: Cambridge University Press.

———. 1984. "Experimentation and Scientific Realism." In Jarrett Leplin (ed.), *Scientific Realism*: 154–72.

———. 1985. "Styles of Scientific Reasoning." In John Rajchman and Cornel West (eds.), *Post-Analytic Philosophy*. New York: Columbia University Press, 145–65.

Haraway, Donna. 1976. *Crystals, Fabrics, and Fields: Metaphors of Organicism in Twentieth-Century Developmental Biology*. New Haven: Yale University Press.

———. 1985. "A Manifesto for Cyborgs: Science, Technology and Socialist Feminism in the 1980s." *Socialist Review* 80: 65–107.

———. 1989. *Primate Visions: Gender, Race, and Nature in the World of Modern Science*. New York: Routledge, Chapman and Hall.

———. 1991a. *Simians, Cyborgs, and Women: The Reinvention of Nature*. New York: Routledge.

———. 1991b. "Situated Knowledges: The Science Question in Feminism and the Privilege of Partial Perspective." In *Simians, Cyborgs, and Women*, 183–201.

Harding, Sandra. 1986. *The Science Question in Feminism*. Ithaca, NY: Cornell University Press.

———. 1991. *Whose Science? Whose Knowledge? Thinking from Women's Lives*. Ithaca, NY: Cornell University Press.

Harré, Rom (ed.). 1986 *The Social Construction of Emotions*. Oxford: Basil Blackwell.

Hartsock, Nancy C. M. 1983. "The Feminist Standpoint: Developing a Ground for a Specifically Feminist Historical Materialism." In *Discovering Reality: Feminist Perspectives on Epistemology, Metaphysics, Methodology and Philosophy of Science*. S. Harding and M. Hintikka (eds.). Dordrecht: Reidel, 283–311.

Harwood, Jonathan. 1976. "The Race-Intelligence Controversy: A Sociological Approach, I—Professional Factors." *Social Studies of Science* 6: 369–94.

———. 1977. "The Race-Intelligence Controversy: A Sociological Approach, II—'External' Factors." *Social Studies of Science* 7: 1–30.

Hennessy, Rosemary. 1993. "Women's Lives/Feminist Knowledge: Feminist Standpoint as Ideology Critique." *Hypatia* 8: 14–34.

Hesse, Mary B. 1966. *Models and Analogies in Science.* Notre Dame: University of Notre Dame Press.

———. 1987. "Tropical Talk: The Myth of the Literal." *The Aristotelian Society,* Supplementary Volume LXI: 297–311.

Hirschauer, Stefan. 1991. "The Manufacture of Bodies in Surgery." *Social Studies of Science* 21: 279–319.

Hobbes, Thomas. 1968 (1651). *Leviathan.* C. B. Macpherson (ed.). New York: Penguin.

Hoffman, R. R. 1985. "Some Implications of Metaphor for Philosophy and Psychology of Science." In Wolf Paprotté and René Rirven (eds.), *The Ubiquity of Metaphor: Metaphor in Language and Thought.* Amsterdam: John Benjamin, 327–80.

Hoffman, R. R., E. L. Cochran, and J. M. Nead. 1984. "Metaphors in Experimental Psychology." In M. Bamberg, S. B. Heath, and R. R. Hoffman (eds.), *Metaphor, Knowledge and Culture.* The Hague: Mouton.

Hoffmann, Roald, and Shira Leibowitz. 1991. "Molecular Mimicry, Rachel and Leah, the Israeli Male, and the Inescapable Metaphor of Science." *Michigan Quarterly Review* 30: 383–97

Hoyningen-Huene, Paul. 1989a. *Die Wissenschaftsphilosophie Thomas S. Kuhns: Rekonstruktion und Grundlagenprobleme.* Braunschweig: Friedr. Vieweg and Sohn.

———. 1989b. "Idealist Elements in Thomas Kuhn's Philosophy of Science." *History of Philosophy Quarterly,* vol. 6, no. 4: 393–401.

———. 1993. *Reconstructing Scientific Revolutions: Thomas S. Kuhn's Philosophy of Science.* Alexander T. Levine (trans.). Chicago: University of Chicago Press.

Hubbard, Ruth. 1990. *The Politics of Women's Biology.* New Brunswick, NJ: Rutgers University Press.

Hubbard, Ruth, Mary Sue Henifen, and Barbara Fried (eds.). 1979. *Women Look at Biology Looking at Women: A Collection of Feminist Critiques.* Cambridge, MA: Schenkman.

Hubbard, Ruth, and Marian Lowe (eds.). 1979. *Genes and Gender II: Pitfalls in Research on Sex and Gender.* Betty Rosoff and Ethel Tobach (series eds.). New York: Gordian.

Hughes, Thomas P. 1989. *American Genesis: A Century of Invention and Technological Enthusiasm.* New York: Viking.

Hull, David L. 1988a. "A Mechanism and Its Metaphysics: An Evolutionary Account of the Social and Conceptual Development of Science." *Biology and Philosophy*, 3: 123–55.

———. 1988b. *Science as a Process: An Evolutionary Account of the Social and Conceptual Development of Science.* Chicago: University of Chicago Press.

———. 1990. "Conceptual Selection." *Philosophical Studies* 60: 77–87.

Jacob, Margaret C. 1976. *The Newtonians and the English Revolution, 1689–1720.* Ithaca, NY: Cornell University Press

Jacob, James R., and Margaret C. Jacob, 1980. "The Anglican Origins of Modern Science: The Metaphysical Foundations of the Whig Constitution." *Isis* 71: 251–67.

Johnson, Mark (ed.). 1981. *Philosophical Perspectives on Metaphor.* Minneapolis: University of Minnesota Press.

Jones, Roger S. 1982. *Physics as Metaphor.* Minneapolis: University of Minnesota Press.

Keller, Evelyn Fox. 1985. *Reflections on Gender and Science.* New Haven: Yale University Press.

———. 1992. *Secrets of Life, Secrets of Death: Essays on Language, Gender and Science.* New York: Routledge.

Kim, Jaegwon. 1984. "Supervenience and Supervenient Causation." *Southern Journal of Philosophy* 22, Supp.: 45–56.

———. 1990. "Supervenience as a Philosophical Concept." *Metaphilosophy* 21: 1–27.

Kitcher, Philip. 1984. "1953 and All That: A Tale of Two Sciences." *Philosophical Review* 93: 335–73.

Kittay, Eva Feder. 1987. *Metaphor: Its Cognitive Force and Linguistic Structure.* Oxford: Clarendon Press.

Klama, John. 1988. *Aggression: The Myth of the Beast Within.* New York: John Wiley and Sons.

Knorr, Karin D. 1977. "Producing and Reproducing Knowledge: Descriptive or Constructive?" *Social Science Information* 16: 669–96.

———. 1979. "Tinkering toward Success: Prelude to a Theory of Scientific Practice." *Theory and Society* 8: 347–76.

Knorr-Cetina, Karin D. 1981. *The Manufacture of Knowledge: An Essay on the Constructivist and Contextual Nature of Science.* Oxford: Pergamon.

———. 1982. "Scientific Communities or Transepistemic Arenas of Research? A Critique of Quasi-Economic Models of Science." *Social Studies of Science* 12: 101–30.

———. 1983. "The Ethnographic Study of Scientific Work: Towards a Constructivist Interpretation of Science." In Knorr-Cetina and Mulkay, *Science Observed*: 115–40.

———. 1993. "Strong Constructivism—From a Sociologist's Point of View." *Social Studies of Science* 23:

Knorr-Cetina, Karin D., and Michael Mulkay (eds.). 1983. *Science Observed: Perspectives on the Social Study of Science.* London: Sage.

Kordig, Carl R. 1971. *The Justification of Scientific Change.* Dordrecht: Reidel.

Kornblith, Hilary (ed.). 1985. *Naturalizing Epistemology.* Cambridge, MA: MIT Press.

Kuhn, Thomas S. 1970a. *The Structure of Scientific Revolutions*, 2d ed. Chicago: University of Chicago Press.

———. 1970b. "Reflections on My Critics." In Imre Lakatos and Alan Musgrave (eds.), *Criticism and the Growth of Knowledge.* Cambridge: Cambridge University Press: 231–78.

———. 1974. "Second Thoughts on Paradigms." In Frederick Suppe (ed.), *The Structure of Scientific Theories.* Urbana, IL: University of Illinois Press: 459–82.

———. 1979. "Metaphor in Science." In Andrew Ortony (ed.), *Metaphor and Thought.* Cambridge: Cambridge University Press: 409–19.

———. 1985. "Mathematical Versus Experimental Traditions in the Development of Physical Science." In John Rajchman and Cornel West (eds.), *Post-Analytic Philosophy.* New York: Columbia University Press, 166–97.

Kuper, Adam, and Jessica Kuper (eds.). 1985. *The Social Science Encyclopedia.* London: Routledge and Kegan Paul.

Lakatos, Imre. 1970. "Falsification and the Methodology of Scientific Research Programmes." In Imre Lakatos and Alan Musgrave (eds.),

Criticism and the Growth of Knowledge. Cambridge: Cambridge University Press, 91–196.

Lakoff, George, and Mark Johnson. 1980. *Metaphors We Live By.* Chicago: University of Chicago Press.

Laqueur, Thomas. 1990. *Making Sex: Body and Gender from the Greeks to Freud.* Cambridge, MA: Harvard University Press.

Latour, Bruno. 1980. "The Three Little Dinosaurs or a Sociologist's Nightmare." *Fundamenta Scientiae* 1: 79–85.

———. 1983. "Give Me a Laboratory and I Will Raise the World." In Knorr-Cetina and Mulkay, *Science Observed*: 141–70.

———. 1987. *Science in Action: How to Follow Scientists and Engineers through Society.* Cambridge, MA: Harvard University Press.

———. 1988. *The Pasteurization of France.* Alan Sheridon and John Law (trans.). Cambridge, MA: Harvard University Press.

———. 1989. "Clothing the Naked Truth." In Lawson and Appignanesi, *Dismantling Truth*: 101–26.

———. 1990a. "The Force and the Reason of Experiment." In H. E. Le Grand (ed.), *Experimental Inquiries.* Dordrecht: Kluwer, 49–80.

———. 1990b. "Postmodern? No, Simply Amodern! Steps Toward an Anthropology of Science." *Studies in History and Philosophy of Science* 21: 145–71.

———. 1992. "One More Turn after the Social Turn." In Ernan McMullin (ed.), *The Social Dimensions of Science*: 272–94.

Latour, Bruno, and Steve Woolgar. 1986. *Laboratory Life: The [Social] Construction of Scientific Facts.* Princeton: Princeton University Press.

Laudan, Rachel (ed.). 1984. *The Nature of Technological Knowledge: Are Models of Scientific Change Relevant?* Dordrecht: Reidel.

Laudan, Rachel. 1995. "Beyond Subsumption, Beyond Separate but Equal: Whither the Histories of Science and Technology?" *Technology and Culture*, forthcoming.

Law, John. 1986a. "On the Methods of Long-Distance Control: Vessels, Navigation, and the Portuguese Route to India." In *Law, Power, Action and Belief*: 234–63.

Law, John (ed.). 1986b. *Power, Action and Belief: A New Sociology of Knowledge?* London: Routledge and Kegan Paul.

Laws, Judith Long, and Pepper Schwartz. 1977. *Sexual Scripts: The Social Construction of Female Sexuality*. Hinsdale, IL: Dryden.

Lawson, Hilary, and Lisa Appignanesi (eds.) 1989. *Dismantling Truth: Reality in the Post-Modern World*. London: Weidenfeld and Nicolson.

Leatherdale, W. H. 1974. *The Role of Analogy, Model and Metaphor in Science*. Amsterdam: North Holland.

Le Grand, H. E. 1990. "Is a Picture Worth a Thousand Experiments?" In H. E. Le Grand (ed.), *Experimental Inquiries*. Dordrecht: Kluwer, 241–70.

Leiss, William. 1972. *The Domination of Nature*. Boston: Beacon.

Lemert, E. 1967. *Human Deviance, Social Problems and Social Control*. Englewood Cliffs, NJ: Prentice Hall.

Leplin, Jarrett (ed.). 1984. *Scientific Realism*. Berkeley: University of California Press.

Longino, Helen E. 1990. *Science as Social Knowledge: Values and Objectivity in Scientific Inquiry*. Princeton: Princeton University Press.

Longino, Helen E., and Evelynn Hammonds. 1990. "Conflicts in the Feminist Study of Gender and Science." In Marianne Hirsch and Evelyn Fox Keller (eds.), *Conflicts in Feminism*. New York: Routlege, 165–83.

Lorenz, Konrad. 1981. *The Foundations of Ethology*. New York: Simon and Schuster.

Lynch, Michael. 1986. *Art and Artifact in Laboratory Science*. London: Routledge and Kegan Paul.

Lynch, Michael, and Steve Woolgar. 1990. *Representation in Scientific Practice*. Cambridge, MA: MIT Press.

Lynch, William T. 1994. "Ideology and the Sociology of Scientific Knowledge." *Social Studies of Science* 24: 197–227.

MacKenzie, Donald A. 1978. "Statistical Theory and Social Interests: A Case Study." *Social Studies of Science* 8: 35–83.

———. 1981. *Statistics in Britain, 1865–1930: The Social Construction of Scientific Knowledge*. Edinburgh: Edinburgh University Press.

———. 1990. *Inventing Accuracy: A Historical Sociology of Nuclear Missile Guidance*. Cambridge, MA: MIT Press.

Martin, J., and R. Harré. 1982. "Metaphor in Science" In David S. Miall (ed.), *Metaphor: Problems and Perspectives*. Sussex: Harvester, 89–105.

Marx, Karl. 1964. *The Economic and Philosophic Manuscripts of 1844.* Dirk J. Struik (ed.), Martin Milligan (trans.). New York: International.

Masterman, Margaret. 1970. "The Nature of a Paradigm." In Imre Lakatos and Alan Musgrave (eds.), *Criticism and the Growth of Knowledge.* Cambridge: Cambridge University Press, 59–89.

Maynard Smith, John. 1982. *Evolution and the Theory of Games.* Cambridge: Cambridge University Press.

Maynard Smith, John, and G. R. Price. 1973. "The Logic of Animal Conflict." *Nature* 246: 15–18.

Mayr, Ernst. 1982. *The Growth of Biological Thought: Diversity, Evolution, and Inheritance.* Cambridge, MA: Belknap/Harvard.

McMullin, Ernan. 1984. "A Case for Scientific Realism." In J. Leplin (ed.), *Scientific Realism.* Berkeley: University of California Press.

———. (ed.). 1992. *The Social Dimensions of Science.* Notre Dame: University of Notre Dame Press.

Mendelsohn, Everett. 1977. "The Social Construction of Scientific Knowledge." In Mendelsohn et al., *The Social Production of Scientific Knowledge*: 3–26.

Mendelsohn, Everett, Peter Weingart, and Richard Whitley (eds.). 1977. *The Social Production of Scientific Knowledge.* Dordrecht: Reidel.

Merchant, Carolyn. 1980. *The Death of Nature: Women, Ecology and the Scientific Revolution.* San Francisco: Harper and Row.

Merton, Robert K. 1973. *The Sociology of Science: Theoretical and Empirical Investigations.* Norman W. Storer (ed.). Chicago: University of Chicago Press.

Miller, Richard. 1987. *Fact and Method: Explanation, Confirmation and Reality in the Natural and the Social Sciences.* Princeton: Princeton University Press.

Mirowski, Philip. 1989. *More Heat than Light: Economics as Social Physics: Physics as Nature's Economics.* Cambridge: Cambridge University Press.

Mitman, Gregg. 1993. "Defining the Organism in the Welfare State: The Politics of Individuality in American Culture, 1890–1950." Manuscript.

Mooij, J. J. A. 1976. *A Study of Metaphor: On the Nature of Metaphorical*

Expressions, with Special Reference to their Reference. Amsterdam: North-Holland.

Morrison, Margaret. (1995). "Approximating the Real: The Role of Idealisation in Physical Theory." In N. Cartwright and M. Jones (eds.), *Idealizations in Physics*, forthcoming.

Myers, Greg. 1990. *Writing Biology: Texts in the Social Construction of Scientific Knowledge.* Madison, WI: University of Wisconsin Press.

Nersession, Nancy. 1988. "Reasoning from Imagery and Analogy in Scientific Concept Formation." In *PSA 1988.* East Lansing, Michigan: Philosophy of Science Association, 41–47.

Neurath, Otto. 1959. "Protocol Sentences." In A. J. Ayer (ed.) *Logical Positivism.* New York: Free Press, 199–208.

Newton-Smith, W. H. 1989. "Rationality, Truth and the New Fuzzies," In Lawson and Appignanesi, *Dismantling Truth*: 23–42.

Nickles, Thomas. 1992. "Good Science as Bad History: From Order of Knowing to Order of Being." In Ernan McMullin (ed.), *The Social Dimensions of Science*, 85–129.

Nowak, Leszek. 1992. "The Idealizational Approach to Science: A Survey." In Jerzy Brzezinski and Leszek Nowak (eds.), *Idealization III: Approximation and Truth.* Posnan Studies in the Philosophy of the Sciences and the Humanities, 25. Amsterdam: Rodopi, 9–63.

Papin, Liliane. 1992. "This Is Not a Universe: Metaphor, Language, and Representation." *PMLA* 107: 1253–65.

Pérez-Ramos, Antonio. 1988. *Francis Bacon's Idea of Science and the Maker's Knowledge Tradition.* Oxford: Clarendon Press

Pickering, Andrew. 1984. *Constructing Quarks: A Sociological History of Particle Physics.* Chicago: University of Chicago Press.

———. 1992a. "From Science as Knowledge to Science as Practice." In Andrew Pickering (ed.), *Science as Practice and Culture*: 1–26.

Pickering, Andrew (ed.). 1992b. *Science as Practice and Culture.* Chicago: University of Chicago Press.

Pinch, Trevor J. 1985. "Toward an Analysis of Scientific Observation: The Externality and Evidential Significance of Observational Reports in Physics." *Social Studies of Science* 15: 3–36.

Pinch, Trevor J., and Wiebe E. Bijker. 1987. "The Social Construction of Facts and Artifacts: Or How the Sociology of Science and the Sociology of Technology Might Benefit Each Other." In Bijker et al., *The Social Construction of Technological Systems*: 17–50.

Popper, Sir Karl R. 1979. *Objective Knowledge: An Evolutionary Approach*, 2d ed. Oxford: Oxford University Press.

Price, Derek J. de Solla. 1984. "Notes Towards a Philosophy of the Science/Technology Interaction." In Rachel Laudan (ed.) *The Nature of Technological Knowledge*. Amsterdam: Reidel.

Putnam, Hilary. 1975. "The Meaning of 'Meaning.'" In *Mind, Language and Reality*. Cambridge: Cambridge University Press.

———. 1981. *Reason, Truth and History*. Cambridge: Cambridge University Press.

———. 1984. "What is Realism?" In Leplin, *Scientific Realism*: 140–53.

———. 1987. *The Many Faces of Realism: The Paul Carus Lectures*. LaSalle, IL: Open Court.

Radder, Hans. 1988. *The Material Realization of Science*. Assen/Maastricht: Van Gorcum.

Rescher, Nicholas. 1987. *Scientific Realism: A Critical Reappraisal*. Dordrecht: Reidel.

Richards, Evelleen, and John Schuster. 1989. "The Feminine Method as Myth and Accounting Resource: A Challenge to Gender Studies and Social Studies of Science." *Social Studies of Science* 19: 697–720.

Richards, I. A. 1936. *The Philosophy of Rhetoric*. Oxford: Oxford University Press.

Roll-Hansen, Nils. 1979. "Experimental Method and Spontaneous Generation: The Controversy between Pasteur and Pouchet, 1859–64." *Journal of the History of Medicine and Allied Sciences*, 34.

Roman, Leslie G, Linda K. Christian-Smith, and Elizabeth Ellsworth (eds.). 1988. *Becoming Feminine: The Politics of Popular Culture*. London: Falmer.

Rorty, Richard. 1987. "Unfamiliar Noises." *The Aristotelian Society*, Supplementary Volume LXI: 283–96.

Rosenau, Pauline Marie. 1992. *Post-Modernism and the Social Sciences: Insights, Inroads, and Intrusions*. Princeton: Princeton University Press.

Rose, Hilary. 1986. "Beyond Masculinist Realities: A Feminist Epistemology for the Sciences." In Ruth Bleier (ed.), *Feminist Approaches to Science*. New York: Pergamon.

Rosenberg, Charles E. 1988. "Woods or Trees: Ideas and Actors in the History of Science." *Isis* 79: 565–70.

Rouse, Joseph. 1987. *Knowledge and Power: Toward a Political Philosophy of Science*. Ithaca, NY: Cornell University Press.

———. 1991a. "Philosophy of Science and the Persistent Narratives of Modernity." *Studies in History and Philosophy of Science* 22: 141–62.

———. 1991b. "The Politics of Postmodern Philosophy of Science." *Philosophy of Science* 58: 607–27.

Ruben, David. 1989. "Realism in the Social Sciences." In Hilary Lawson and Lisa Appignanesi (eds.), *Dismantling Truth: Reality in the Post-Modern World*. London: Weidenfeld and Nicolson, 58–75.

Rudwick, Martin J. S. 1974. "Poulett Scrope on the Volcanoes of Auvergne: Lyellian Time and Political Economy." *The British Journal for the History of Science* 7: 205–42.

Schaffer, Simon. 1989. "Glass Works: Newton's Prisms and the Uses of Experiment." In D. Gooding, T. Pinch, and S. Schaffer (eds.), *The Uses of Experiment*. Cambridge: Cambridge University Press, pp. 67–104.

———. 1992. "Self Evidence." *Critical Inquiry* 18: 327–62.

Scheffler, I. 1967. *Science and Subjectivity*. Indianapolis: Hackett.

Schlick, Moritz. 1959. "The Foundation of Knowledge." In A. J. Ayer (ed.), *Logical Positivism*. New York: Free Press, 209–27.

Searle, J. R. 1979. "Metaphor." In *Expression and Meaning*. Cambridge: Cambridge University Press, 76–116.

Shapere, Dudley. 1985. "Objectivity, Rationality, and Scientific Change." In Peter D. Asquith and Philip Kitcher (eds.), *PSA 1984*, vol. 2. East Lansing, MI: Philosophy of Science Association, 637–63.

———. 1993. "Astronomy and Antirealism." *Philosophy of Science* 60: 134–50

Shapin, Steven. 1975. "Phrenological Knowledge and the Social Structure of Early Nineteenth-Century Edinburgh." *Annals of Science*, vol. 32.

———. 1982. "History of Science and its Sociological Reconstruction." *History of Science* 20: 157–211.

———. 1994. *A Social History of Truth: Civility and Science in Seventeenth-Century England*. Chicago: University of Chicago Press.

Shapin, Steven, and Simon Schaffer. 1985. *Leviathan and the Air-Pump: Hobbes, Boyle, and the Experimental Life*. Princeton: Princeton University Press.

Sismondo, Sergio. 1995. "The Scientific Domains of Feminist Standpoints." *Perspectives on Science* 3: 49–65.

Smith, Crosbie, and M. Norton Wise. 1989. *Energy and Empire: A Biographical Study of Lord Kelvin*. Cambridge: Cambridge University Press.

Smith-Rosenberg, Carroll. 1985. *Disorderly Conduct: Visions of Gender in Victorian America*. Oxford: Oxford University Press.

Stepan, Nancy Leys. 1986. "Race and Gender: The Role of Analogy in Science." *Isis* 77: 261–77.

Suppe, Frederick (ed.). 1974. *The Structure of Scientific Theories*. Urbana, IL: University of Illinois Press.

Suppes, Patrick. 1967. "What is a Scientific Theory?" In S. Morgenbesser (ed.), *Philosophy of Science Today*. New York: Basic, 55–67.

Taylor, Peter J. 1990. "Mapping Ecologists' Ecologies of Knowledge." In *PSA 1990*, vol. 2: 95–109.

———. 1992. "Re/constructing Socioecologies: System Dynamics Modeling of Nomadic Pastoralists in Sub-Saharan Africa." In Adele E. Clarke and Joan H. Fujimura (eds.), *The Right Tools for the Job: At Work in Twentieth-Century Life Sciences*. Princeton: Princeton University Press.

———. 1995a. "Construction as a Heterogeneous Process: Promoting Hybrids against the Distinctions Set Up by Sismondo and Knorr-Cetina." *Social Studies of Science* 3: 66–98.

———. 1995b. "Building on the Metaphor of Construction in Analytic Social Studies of Science." *Perspectives on Science*, forthcoming.

Thompson, Paul. 1988. *The Structure of Biological Theories*. Albany: State University of New York Press.

Tuana, Nancy. 1989. "The Weaker Seed: The Sexist Basis of Reproductive Theory." In Tuana (ed.), *Feminism and Science*. Bloomington: Indiana University Press, 147–71.

van den Daele, Wolfgang. 1977. "The Social Construction of Science: Institutionalisation and Definition of Positive Science in the Latter Half of the Seventeenth Century." In Mendelsohn et al., *The Social Production of Scientific Knowledge*: 27–54.

van Fraassen, Bas C. 1972. "A Formal Approach to Philosophy of Science." In R. E. Colodny (ed.), *Paradigms and Paradoxes*. Pittsburgh: University of Pittsburgh Press.

———. 1980. *The Scientific Image*. Oxford: Clarendon.

Visser, Marcel E., Jacques J. M. van Alphen, and Henk W. Nell. 1990. "Adaptive Superparasitism and Patch Time Allocation in Solitary Parasitoids: The Influence of the Number of Parasitoids Depleting a Patch." *Behaviour* 114 (1–4): 21–36.

Waggoner, John E. 1990. "Interaction Theories of Metaphor: Psychological Perspectives." *Metaphor and Symbolic Activity*, vol. 5: 91–108.

Whitney, Charles. 1986. *Francis Bacon and Modernity*. New Haven: Yale University Press.

Williams, Michael. 1986. "Do We (Epistemologists) Need a Theory of Truth?" *Philosophical Topics* 14: 223–42.

Woolgar, Steve. 1988. *Science: The Very Idea*. Chichester, Sussex: Ellis Horwood.

Wylie, Alison. 1989. "The Interpretive Dilemma." In Valerie Pinsky and Alison Wylie (eds.), *Critical Traditions in Contemporary Archaeology: Essays in the Philosophy, History, and Socio-Politics of Archaeology*. Cambridge: Cambridge University Press, 18–27.

Yoxen, Edward. 1987. "Seeing with Sound: A Study of the Development of Medical Images." In Bijker et al., *The Social Construction of Technological Systems*: 281–303.

INDEX

A

abductive argument for realism, 13–17, 152–53
 objections to, 18–21
 limitations of, 21–23
abductive argument for antirealism, 125–26
Achenbach, Joel, 115
Ackermann, Robert, 76, 128, 148
actor-network theory, 70, 72, 118–21, 171
 See also Latour, Bruno; constructivism, heterogeneous
Allchin, Douglas, 173
alliances, 32, 43, 118, 120, 124
Amann, K., 20
animal behavior
 changes in study of, 103–4
 energy metaphor, 131
 game theory, 129–30
Ayer, A. J., 163

B

Bachelard, Gaston, 65, 68
Bacon, Francis, 146–55
 abductive argument for realism, 152–53
 on domination over nature, 147–48
 his geographical metaphor for science, 146–47
 his picture of science in society, 151
 on vita activa and vita contemplativa, 146
Barnes, Barry, 54
Berger, Peter L., 50–54, 61, 63, 64
Bijker, Wiebe E., 49, 71–72
Binkley, Timothy, 138–39

Black, Max, 133
Bleier, Ruth, 3–5
Bloor, David, 36–37, 113–14, 116, 166
boundaries, scientific, 21, 40, 158
Boyd, Richard N.
 and realism, 14–15, 23, 153, 168
 on Thomas Kuhn, 90, 102
 on metaphor in science, 127–28
Boyle, Robert, 39–40, 167
Brannigan, Augustine, 73–74

C

Callon, Michel, 72
Cartwright, Nancy, 24–25, 67, 76, 130, 145, 163
cognitive styles, 28–29
Collins, Harry M.
 on experimenters' regress, 41–42, 115–16, 167, 168
 on methodological relativism, 44, 114–16, 125–26, 169, 171
 on science as social knowledge, 34–35, 117
Constant, Edward W., II, 173
construction
 of material reality, 64–66, 68–69
 mathematical, 54
 of social reality, 52–55, 63–64
 of solid banks, 84
constructivism
 central position, 6
 vs. essentialism, 9, 51–58
 heterogeneous, 8–9, 70–72, 114–15, 125
 multiple meanings of, 49–50
 neo-Kantian. *See* neo-Kantian constructivism
 weak, 58–61

contingency, 107–10
controversy studies, 37–38, 42
credit, 32, 43, 44, 46
Cummiskey, David, 172
Curie, Pierre and Marie, 120–21

D

Darwin, Charles, 95
data, 105
Davidson, Donald, 133, 136, 137–39
decontextualization, 33, 40–42, 60
  replication, 34–35, 117
Derrida, Jacques, 82
Dewey, John, 166
Diesel, Rudolf, 120–21
discovery of America, 73–75

E

empiricism, 13–14, 62–63
  central position, 6–7
enculturational model, 34–35, 117
epistemic fallacy, 84
evolutionary epistemology, 45–48, 157–58
experiment, 39–40, 56–57
experimenters' regress, 41
externalist accounts of science, 37–39, 59

F

Faust, David, 166
Fausto-Sterling, Anne, 47
feminist empiricism, 2, 29–32, 86, 107
feminist epistemology, 2, 29–32, 47–8, 105–8, 142–44
Feyerabend, Paul, 109–10
Fine, Arthur, 21, 163, 164, 170
Foucault, Michel, 147, 154
foundationalism, 12, 35–37
Friedman, Michael, 163
Fuchs, Stephan, 28–29, 165

G

Gasper, Philip, 165
gender, 47–48, 55, 142
genetics, 24, 142–43
Gentner, Dedre, 129, 137
Geschwind, Norman, 4
Giere, Ronald N., 56, 173
Gieryn, Thomas F., 37
Goldman, Alvin I., 166
Goodman, Nelson, 133, 139, 158–59, 169
Gross, Paul R. , ix
Gutting, Gary, 170

H

Habermas, Jürgen, 151–52
Hacking, Ian
  and ecologies of knowledge, 173
  on entity realism, 23–24, 163
  on experiment and theory, 65, 76, 148, 164–65
Hammonds, Evelynn, 3
Haraway, Donna, 106–9, 127, 170, 171
Harding, Sandra, 3, 107–8, 171
Herschel, William, 94
Hesse, Mary B., 127–28, 133
Hirschauer, Stefan, 65
Hitler, Adolf, as metaphor for Saddam Hussein, 135
Hobbes, Thomas, 39–40, 133, 167
Hoyningen-Huene, Paul, 173
Hull, David L., 45–46
Hume, David, 14

I

idealization, 24, 128–32, 165, 172
ideology, 22, 47–48, 141–44
institutions, 52–54, 59, 167
interdependence, 28–29, 32–35, 46
interests, 37–38, 120–21, 122
interpretive flexibility, 13, 70, 71, 106–7, 117
  constraints on, 19–20, 44–45

J

Johnson, Mark, 134–35

K

Keller, Evelyn Fox, 105–6, 142–43
Kim, Jaegwon, 169
Kitcher, Philip, 165
Kittay, Eva Feder, 134, 135–37, 139, 172
Knorr-Cetina, Karin D. (Karin Knorr), 20, 115, 148, 168
  on scientific constructions, 49, 61–67, 68
knowledge. *See* power and knowledge
Kordig, Carl R., 90
Koyré, Alexander, 101
Kuhn, Thomas S. 89–105, 168, 170, 172
  as constructive realist, 101–5, 110–12, 159
  on data, 97–98
  as historian, 96–97, 99, 101
  idealist readings of, 89–90, 91–92
  similarity relations, 92, 94–95
  on truth, 98–101

L

laboratories, 62, 64–65, 68, 118–19, 123, 124, 130, 148
Lakatos, Imre, 159, 164
Lakoff, George, 134–35
Laqueur, Thomas, 80, 140
Latour, Bruno, 42–44, 113–26, 145, 148, 149, 152, 168
  and heterogeneous constructivism, 70–72, 86, 114–15, 118–26
  realism in, 121–23
  on scientific constructions, 49, 58, 61, 67–70
Laudan, Rachel, 173
Laws, Judith Long, 168
legitimation, 52–53
Le Grand, H. E., 149

Levitt, Norman, ix
Longino, Helen E., 3, 29–32
Lorenz, Konrad, 131
Luckmann, Thomas, 50–54, 61, 63, 64

M

MacKenzie, Donald A., 117, 167
Marx, Karl, 34
Masterman, Margaret, 95
Maynard Smith, John, 129–30
McClintock, Barbara, 105
McMullin, Ernan, 132, 144
Mendelsohn, Everett, 58–59, 168
Merchant, Carolyn, 148
Merton, Robert K., 145
metaphor, 127–46
  Davidson and Rorty on, 136–39
  why important in science, 127–29
  Kittay on, 135–37
  as speech act, 143
  structure mapping account of, 133–41
methodological relativism (agnosticism), 37, 43, 51–52, 106–8, 114, 166
Miller, Richard, 163
Mooij, J. J. A., 137
Morrison, Margaret, 165
Myers, Greg, 59–61, 80

N

naturalistic epistemology, 35–36
neo-Kantian constructivism, 8, 69–70, 71, 73–75, 79–88, 132
  readings of, 80–82
  arguments against idealist readings of, 82–87
Newton-Smith, W. H., 163
Nickles, Thomas, 167
nominalism, 81–82
Nowak, Leszek, 172

O

objectivity, 30–31, 160

P

Pasteur, Louis, 15–16, 119, 152, 164
Pérez-Ramos, Antonio, 173
Pickering, Andrew, 20, 43–44, 115, 116
Pinch, Trevor J., 32–33, 49, 71–72
plausibility, 19–21
political criticism of science, 2–3, 30, 86–87, 105–8, 124, 141–44, 162
Popper, Sir Karl R., 33–34
positivism, 9, 80–81, 163
postmodernism, 12, 106–8
power and knowledge, 123
    connections between, 145–56
Price, Derek J. de Solla, 95
Price, G. R., 129
protocol, 111, 171
Putnam, Hilary, 13, 100, 131, 164, 170

R

Radder, Hans, 76, 163
rationality of science, 39, 44, 158, 171
rationalism, 8, 56, 59, 145, 163
realism
    central position, 5–6, 168
    entity vs. theory, 23–25
    one true theory, 8, 92, 98, 108, 111, 170
reductionism, 66
    sociological, 116–18, 124
reflexivity, 72
replication. *See* decontextualization
Rescher, Nicholas, 82
resources, 29, 32, 43, 157, 167
rhetoric, 42, 56, 60, 124
Richards, I. A., 133
Roentgen, W. K., 94–95
Rorty, Richard, 133, 138–9
Rosenau, Pauline Marie, 173
Rouse, Joseph, 145, 155–56
Royal Society, 58

S

Schaffer, Simon, 39–40, 167
Scheffler, Israel, 89
Schutz, Alfred, 52, 54
Schwartz, Pepper, 168
Searle, J. R., 172
sex differences research, 4
Shapin, Steven, 39–40, 167
Smith-Rosenberg, Carroll, 86
social knowledge, science as, 29–35, 36, 149, 157
social objects. *See* social worlds
social worlds, 55–6, 64, 152, 156
    Kuhnian, 97, 111–12
    vs. material worlds, 57–8, 67, 75, 76–77, 85
socialization, 34–35
spontaneous generation, 15–16
standpoint theory, 2, 47–48, 144, 160, 167, 171
Stepan, Nancy Leys, 142
S&TS (science and technology studies), definition, 2
strong program, 36–8, 113, 123
success of science, 21, 77, 116, 153, 164
symmetry in accounts of science, 36–37, 43

T

Taylor, Peter J., 115, 125, 173
TEA-laser, 34, 117
technology, and its relation to science, 21, 150, 164
theory
    meanings of the term, 23, 164–65
    as metaphor, 132, 141–44
    received view and semantic view, 128, 165
theory dependence of methods, 15, 160
tools, scientific 118–19, 148–49, 156, 157
TRF, 67, 68–69
truth
    approximate, 13, 129–32, 165

deflationary, 18–19, 164
Tuana, Nancy, 140

U

underdetermination of theory by data. *See* interpretive flexibility

V

values, 30–31
van den Daele, Wolfgang, 58, 168
van Fraassen, Bas C., 15, 62–63, 132, 163

W

Waggoner, John E., 172
Watson, James, 4
Williams, Michael, 164
Woolgar, Steve, 42–44, 49, 61, 67–70, 168
　as neo-Kantian, 72–75, 82, 115
World Three, 33–34, 166
Wylie, Alison, 20

Y

Yearly, Steven, 171
Yoxen, Edward, 116